The 12 O'Clock
Skiddoo

by L. Marie Baker

Author's Note

This book of memories drawn from early childhood is neither a complete nor accurate history of my hometown. Also, I had many playmates during those early years, but to give the stories some continuity, one or another named playmate took on the experiences of a playmate not mentioned. Those whose names have been omitted are, I am sure, grateful, and those named, with some exceptions, have been given an alias for the sake of continuing our friendship. To protect myself from scurrilous "dummkoph" remarks of family and others, I, too, took an alias. This is the official unedited, unexpurgated, unpasteurized edition of my Montana childhood adventures.

TWELVE O'CLOCK SKIDOO

Copyright © 1998 TX 4-704-341 L. Marie Baker

Published by: Wheels Within Wheels, LLC
Printed by: Ingram Spark, Inc. in the USA
Book design by: DesignWise Art

ISBN 979-8-9870914-0-1

To my three daughters.

Introduction

This book of memories is a cheerful, lighthearted story about family and playmates during the early 1940's. The story takes place in a small farming town in the upper plains of Montana.

The "12 O'Clock Skiddoo" was a milk train that rolled into town at noon hour. Our first encounter with this train was when we kids were walking along the railroad tracks and heard the whistle of a train about to come around a bend. As it barreled towards us we stood to watch as it passed. When the engineer saw us he gave us a great wave, and while returning the wave the whistle of the train blew a loud "whoooowhooooah." From that day to many more the "12 O'Clock Skiddoo" became our lovable train to meet at noon hour.

Taught, as kids, to be respectable of adults, one big rule heard often was set down by parents, "Children should be seen and not heard." The "should be" was not to be, as kids we needed to be free to shout our, "whoopees!" So it was, we were sort of "wild 'n' woolly" kids while in play. If a parent became concerned for us not being "seen" there was someone to call, to ask, "Have you seen my kid?" "Sure did, saw the gang headed for" . . . wherever it was on a particular day.

As a usual "gang" we pre-kindergarten ones had older ones to lead the fun. We grew strong and sure-footed while enjoying our freedom so as not to be "heard."

Now in my twilight years, echoes of the past fade with few left to share with, until, hearing a far off whistle of a train. It is a soothing sound that carries my thoughts to the days of fun with playmates, so long ago. I love to hear the whistle blow.

I, L. Marie Baker, owe great gratitude to Amy of DesignWise Art for being extremely helpful and easy to work with in preparing another book for publication. Thank you Amy, it has been fun working with you.

The 12 O'Clock
Skiddoo

by L. Marie Baker

Chapter 1

I, Marie, soon to be four years old, wanted to see what real dead bones of a cat looked like. I tippee-toed into the kitchen and snuck a spoon from a kitchen drawer to dig up a grave.

Last winter, our kitty cat got killed by a car. I was sad and my mother consoled me with words of kindness, "When God is ready to do so, He will take the sweet little animal up to heaven to live with all the angels."

When watching my brother Bobby bury the stiff ball of fur under the eave of the porch, where the soil was not frozen from the winters cold, my sister Patty sensing I needed comforting, wrapped an arm around my shoulders.

When the job of burying was done, Bobby said to me, "Come springtime all that will be left will be its bones."

Tucking my hair behind my ears and making a frowning face, when knowing, it was springtime! And I did not find any bones in that grave!

I then knew, dumb Bobby had been teasing me! And knew too! I should have remembered and believed what my mother had told me, about God taking the animal with Him to Heaven. Gee whiz, that meant the bones too!

That year of my archeology dig for bones, my sister Patty was eight years older than I, and Bobby being four years older could dig a hole, a whole lot deeper than I could with a spoon!

The cat was from a litter of kittens that came to our house the previous summer during a heavy rain. A sopping wet mama cat appeared on our back step with a tiny-itty-bitty kitty dangling from her mouth. My mother had a soft, tender feeling for the poor, pathetic looking mama cat and opened the door.

The stranger came in with her kitty and went straight down to the basement. Mother made a bed for the two from a box and an old rug. Mama cat hopped in, set her kitten down and licked it dry. Then, she hopped out of the box, climbed the stairs and went to the back door. After Mother let the cat out, we watched it disappear into the pouring rain.

Mother seemed to sense what was happening, for she waited. It wasn't long before the mama cat returned with another itty-bitty kitty dangling from her mouth. She made two more trips and then, with four babies safe and warm in our basement, settled down to washing and loving them. She then stretched out in the box with her belly up and all the babies with their tiny heads bobbing back and forth found a little, pink nipple.

Mother then said, "It's time to leave so mama cat and her kittens can rest."

Our dad, when he was a boy, lived on a farm where there was a warm, dry barn for all the animals. He didn't consider our home a barn and had made it perfectly clear to Mother that if we had any animals they would have to live outside.

This meant that Dad could not know that our poor, drenched mama cat with her four precious itty-bitty, cute babies had found our home to be the best barn she could find.

Whenever Patty, Bobby and I tripped down the stairs to visit the warm balls of fur, I had to cross my heart, each time promising to keep our new family a secret from Dad. I found keeping a secret was fun. Bobby played a game, making me mimic his motion to zipper my lips shut just as he was doing.

Then Patty told a story that made me feel very, very sad when imagining our kitties out in the cold rain dying. I promised, again, I would not tell Dad.

After Dad came home from work, supper and the evening slipped by just fine as my fellow conspirators made sure my thoughts focused on all else, but the kittens. When we went to bed with our secret still kept, I heard Patty end her prayer very loud, "Please, dear God, don't let Dad find out about the sweet, dear little kitties in our basement."

Early in the morning I was awakened by bright sunlight in my eyes coming from a crack in the window shade.

Like the sun, I felt bright and full of excitement remembering what was below and plum forgot that Dad should not know. I ran from my bed to my parents bedroom shouting, "Daddy, Daddy, we have lots of baby kitties in ah basement!"

My dear mother, and Patty and Bobby waited in fear over what Dad was going to say, but to their surprise, the thunder expected was not heard.

My older sister and brother, through the years, had mellowed my parents, and I was young enough to be still full of innocence as well as being Dad's little "Tootse." So, if Dad had to find out about the kitties, I was the best one to tell him.

Mama kitty and tiny Inky, Dinky, Polly and Vu now had a secure home in our basement and much attention was devoted to all.

My birthplace was a small community on the northern plains of Montana. The town was supported by farmers who raised grain, sheep and cattle. During the struggle to recover from the Great Depression the population did not change much; when someone died, someone was born. Few people moved in and few moved away.

The railroad, with its many sets of iron rails, divided our town. On the south side of the tracks, across from the train depot, was the First Avenue business area, but this part of town was called Front Street.

On Front Street for three blocks was a gas station, a liquor store, a drug store, a clothing store, a grocery and bakery, a hardware store, a barbershop, a bank, and a whole lot of taverns.

On Second Avenue were more businesses and the movie theater. There were houses at both ends of First and Second Avenues.

On Third Avenue was the courthouse and beyond it, the grade school. There was the hospital, lots of houses, a church or two, and a civic center that had a big swimming pool. Skirting the south side of town was a dike in the murky river built to protect our town from the river's mean waters.

On the north side of the tracks were more churches, a lot more houses and another school. The fairgrounds were at the far western end which was where the circus would set up when one came to town.

A main highway passed by a few more businesses and at the far eastern end of town, the highway went right by the house where I lived.

Out my front door and across the paved highway was a dirt road that went up to the cemetery on the hill. From there you could see far and wide over the town. Beyond the cemetery was prairie country.

Out the back door and down the driveway, past an empty lot and a huge billboard sign, a dirt road veered to the left for a stretch and connected to a larger dirt road that paralleled the railroad tracks.

The train was so important to farmers and business people. A fascination to the children, though not to their mothers! I can remember my mother becoming very upset over the black soot that drifted into the house from the engines smoke stack.

I can remember, too, at nighttime, all snuggled down in my bed, the comfort felt when hearing the faraway lonesome whistle of a train coming into town, whooooooo, then its soft chug choo, chug choo, chug choo, chug choo, then another whooooooo as it passed on through.

The winters, with heaps of snow, created a
wonderland of gleeful fun for all children.

The springs were an awakening of new life to see and smell.

The summers hot, dry weather was a stimulation
for adventure to happen from the time the sun
came up until long after it went down.

The autumn's pacifying colors from dying leaves
and the sometimes dreary days, renewed an
appreciation of the warmth of a home.

The tomorrows were of no concern, only the very day
the children played, whatever the season.

My best friends lived nearby on the north side. Kathleen, Sonny, Bubber and Betsy. Another good playmate was Julia. She lived on the south side of town and like the rest of us, could only cross the tracks when a parent was along. Other playmates sometimes were Laura, Maxine and Donnie.

Sonny and Kathleen were sister and brother. Sonny was two years older than I and Kathleen was one year younger, with short, blond, curly locks all over her head. Her glasses were always slipping down her nose and she had this peculiar way of wiggling her nose to move them back up.

Bubber and Betsy were also sister and brother. Bubber was the same age as Sonny, and Betsy was one year older than I. She had lots of freckles and was tall and very skinny, and had long brown braids, so long she could sit on them.

Bubber and Sonny were, ah, just boys!

My special best friend was Kathleen because we were the youngest. I couldn't pronounce the R's in words and Kathleen couldn't say L's at all.

Sometimes the three older ones would play a game, asking us to take turns saying words like, "caa, piwwow, woad, bankit, wock, fower, twee, miwk, wabbit, sweeve." They laughed and we laughed, too! It was fun!

My friends and I had a lot of respect for grownups. We knew if we did not behave we could expect to be punished by any adult whose path we might have crossed wrong.

It was an early summer day when we learned about an extra crabby grownup in our neck of the woods. While playing a game outdoors, we did not notice the sky becoming dark with rain clouds. Only when heavy drops of rain began pelting our skin did we realize we needed to find shelter. We raced to take refuge in an old abandoned cabin.

The cabin had two empty rooms, a kitchen with no table or chairs and a larger room with only one thing in it, a black, pot bellied stove.

With no electricity, the black clouds outside made the big room very, very dark. Suddenly a flash of light from a mean streak of a lightning lit up the room, making great big, ghostly gray shadows appear on the wall behind the pot bellied stove.

Having been overwhelmed by this ominous sight, a moment of silence passed until Sonny shouted, "Hey! Let's tell ghost stories—me first!"

Ghost stories told during daylight hours were always fun and we all flopped down on the floor in a big circle to listen to Sonny's ghost story.

Expecting a scary tale, we listened intently until he started in on his mumbo jumbo about a boogeyman coming after our livers. We jiggled with laughter!

Sonny was not amused and tried harder to spook, whispering his words and wiggling his fingers like a magician, but what he came up with sounded like a bunch of baloney. Our response was more laughter which really made him mad! He called us "poopey drawers" and "nitwits" and more names until we all made ourselves serious to make him happy.

Sonny lowered his voice to talk even more like a boogeyman and we burst into hysterical laughter so bad we had to roll on the floor to ease the pain in our sides.

We could not help ourselves. Sonny scowled at us and puckered his lips like he'd just taken a bite from a sour lemon, refusing to speak again.

An ear splitting crack of a lightning bolt preceded an earthshaking, wall rattling rumble of thunder over the cabin, terrifying us! With a fearful look on her face, Betsy whispered, "My turn."

Betsy's tall tale of ishy, long legged, crawling things gave me goosebumps and made me tremble. I did not like creepy, crawling things with long legs and I wanted her to stop the story! She did, after another frightening lightning bolt ripped open the sky, creating a dance of phantom-like shadows behind the black, pot bellied mass of evil! We had to slap our hands over our mouths to stop screaming and screeching! The creepiness put us in the mood to huddle closer, and we closed our circle until our elbows touched.

After another rumble of thunder, Bubber lowered his voice, his words coming out like a frog's as he croaked out, "I ~~ have ~~ a ~~ scary ~~ story ~~ to ~~ tell. Listen ~~ to ~~ the ~~ creaking ~~ door. Creeeeeeeak."

Bubber's story, taking us beyond that door, made me feel like I, too, was "stepping down, down, deeper and deeper into a scary, ghoulish, ancient crypt filled with the dead coming to life. Mummies! All wrapped from head to toe in dirty, puss dripping, tattered bandages."

The terror I felt made goosebumps pop up again! Bubber's mummy was near and coming after me! It was in the room with us, its stiff leg hitching, its foot dragging, getting closer and closer, making my screaming meemies feel the heebie jeebies as the mummy's slimy hand was about to grab me on my shoulder!

Suddenly, a loud RAP! hit the cabin's door and we screamed! Then, the old door blew open, like a super strong mummy had hit it, and in burst a policeman! The frightening jolt made us bolt to our feet.

The policeman demanded in an angry tone, "What are you kids doing in here?"

Too stunned and scared, we could not answer until his harsh stare made Sonny utter with a stutter, "Nnnnothing, officer, jjjjust tellin' some ghost stories is all."

The policeman towered over us, rainwater streaming from the brim of his hat, his raincoat drenched and dripping. He frowned, making that grownup face that says, "Don't you lie to me, youngster." His eyes fixed on us, awaiting a better answer. Bubber added, "Honest, we weren't doin' anything wrong."

"I will see!" snapped the policeman as he walked into the kitchen, searched it and came back, his eyes scanning us and the room. We hadn't drawn on the walls or tracked dirt in but he still gave us an awful finger shaking and bawling out. "Next time Mrs. Beaner calls to tell me you kids are in here I will put each and every one of you in jail! Do you hear me?" The five of us were so terrified we could only bob our heads that we'd heard.

As we left the cabin, the beady eyes of the policeman shot holes in our backs making us feel like notorious criminals. Our hearts pounding hard, we sauntered away at a snail's pace trying to act respectful of the law to prevent another scolding. A distance away, Sonny stole a look over his shoulder and seeing the policeman getting into his patrol car, yelled to the rest of us, "Git going!" We ran pell-mell and ran and ran until we were forced to stop to hang our heads while panting for air to ease our burning lungs.

After our rest, we ambled out from the side of a shed that had concealed us. Realizing we were on the dirt road headed in the direction of the railroad tracks, we knew we were safe. It'd stopped raining and as the thunder clouds drifted away, out came the sun high over our heads.

While strolling along, a discussion began over the event that had just happened with the policeman. Bubber, acting so angry, kicked a rock as he uttered in a grumpy tone, "Old Lady Beans!" The rest of us perked up hearing this new name for Mrs. Beaner and we had a hearty good laugh.

Mrs. Beaner was a strong looking lady with hefty arms and a husky, stern sounding voice. She lived in a house at the top of a hill in our neighborhood, and now we knew she could see everything going on below her.

All thought now was focused on Mrs. Beaner instead of the policeman and Betsy was the first to declare her opinion as she said smartly, "She is a spy! It's true, she is!"

Sonny, in defense of our innocence, asked, "How come she thought we were doin' something wrong?"

Kathleen, with her hands on her hips, answered with a snooty comment that sounded funny. "Cuz she's mean and foe of beans, ots and ots of them, huh, Bubber?"

Just then Bubber stopped dead in his tracks, spun around to face the direction she lived, cupped his hands about his mouth and shouted, "Mean Old Lady Beans!" The rest of us imitated him which cleared our thoughts of an awful experience.

The road ahead took a slight dip. To avoid the mud caused by the rain, we marched catty corner through a weedy lot to reach the dirt road that paralleled the railroad tracks. We scared a chicken hidden in the weeds and it scared us as it cackled and fluttered away.

Lots of old looking buildings were along the dirt road, one was a beer warehouse. The clinking of beer bottles drew our attention to watch the beer man unload empty bottles from his beer truck. In the wide expanse of the dirt road were many potholes, all filled with black water with pretty rainbow colors floating on top. I jumped to leap over the smaller potholes all the way until reaching the railroad tracks.

We knew we dared not cross the many sets of silver tracks. We went the long way along an iron rail that guided us to the outskirts of town. We came to a tall wooden grain elevator that stretched up to the bright blue sky. I had to lean back on my heels to see all the way up to its top. The train collected the grain, as did a number of homeless vagabond chickens, eagerly scratching in the dirt road to uncover old kernels that spilled over. Sonny and Bubber ran, zigging and zagging to stir up a ruckus amongst the chickens. They scattered and cackled, beating their wings and squawking, loose feathers and yellow feet flashing in every direction. When Sonny and Bubber caught up to us girls, the chickens returned like the tide, never the wiser.

The ding-a-ling of a bell drew our attention to a cream colored cow in a fenced in backyard. Her neck was stretched to greet us with a "moo" as we walked by; she was a gentle, nice cow.

Birds all around were chirping loudly as they do after a rain and from the morning's drenching, the wet smell was a mixture of earthy gumbo, manure, chickens, oil from the tracks, and old wet grain.

A vibration buzzed through the bottoms of our shoes alerting us to a train coming. Then, far ahead , coming round a bend was a black engine pulling two passenger cars, two boxcars, and a red caboose. I had been taught to stay away from trains and with such power chugging towards us, I wanted to run from the tracks, but Sonny and Bubber moved closer to watch as it passed. Betsy, then, Kathleen did the same and I squeezed between the two. In a row, we five stood watching the mighty, powerful train bearing down the tracks.

Betsy yelled, "Here it comes!"

The stimulating thrill had the three of us girls jumping when feeling the strength of the iron dynamo dead ahead. In the mighty, engine, we could clearly see Mr. Engineer in stripes of gray and white with a red scarf about his neck.

Upon seeing us, he gave a big wave out the window, swooping his arm through the air. His other hand pulled a long cord to make the train's whistle blow, "Whoooooowhooo-oooah!"

The boys, like us, were now jumping and waving, returning a lively greeting to the nice engineer, then to the people in the two passenger cars, to a hobo sitting on the floor of the second boxcar, and to the man dressed in all blue standing on the step of the red caboose.

After the train zoomed by we watched as it rolled its way into town. I sighed and whispered my thoughts, "I like that twain."

Betsy, as though awakening from a trance, asked, "What did you say?" I simply shrugged my shoulders, feeling a bit silly to like a train as I did, for I did not know at that moment the others liked it as I did.

An exciting friendship began on that day. Whenever we'd be playing together and the sun would be high over our heads and we'd hear that far away whistle blow "Whooooooah! Whooooooah!", we'd run with a burst of energy to make it to the tracks in time to wave to our new friend, Mr. Engineer. He'd return our greeting with a wave and a pull of the cord for the whistle to sound "Whoooooowhooooooah!" We then waved to the many passengers to the very last person on the red caboose, all riding on the train called the 12 O'Clock Skiddoo.

I sat alone at the kitchen table toying with my plate. I did not like a sandwich made with awful peanut butter! When Mother passed by on her way to the bathroom, she gave me a nasty look and I knew what that meant; I had to eat before going out to play!

When hearing the sound of the toilet flushing, I tore away a little bite and I made a loud smacking noise when Mother came out of the bathroom. She said, "Good girl!" then disappeared into the other room.

The peanut butter and bread, as it sometimes did, stuck to the roof of my mouth like plaster to a wall! A sigh over lost hope of ever leaving the table made me sulk in my chair. Using my pointing finger, I jammed it inside my mouth and dug around the glob until it dropped! I choked it down and sat staring at what was left of my sandwich, knowing I could not bear another bite! Then the idea came to me. I never eat the crust so I tore it away and very carefully scooted back my chair. I tippytoed to the garbage can, dumped the offending item in, and pushed it way, way down. At the table again

I eased the plate down, picked up the half-moon shaped crusts I had saved and placed them on the plate as proof I had eaten my sandwich. Then, I was ready for play.

I heard a rap at the back door and ran to let Kathleen in. There'd been a very early morning rain, but the sun had broken through the disappearing gray clouds and it had become hot and sultry outside. Kathleen was wearing her swimming suit and I wanted to wear mine, so she followed me to my bedroom and waited while I wiggled into mine.

We left by the back door and waddled barefoot down the driveway jumping into the puddles in our way. When reaching the dirt road, and seeing the drainage ditch full of water, the urge was great to get down into it.

Once in, we realized, hiding beneath the water was clay-like mud and we had to push our way through the thick, slick sludge. It was a fun challenge causing us to giggle and giggle until we became so weakened we had to pull ourselves out.

We sat on the rim to rest, dangling our feet in the cool mud. If I lifted my foot coated with thick mud and squeezed my toes under real fast, the mud would erupt like coffee perking in Mother's coffee pot. Kathleen did it, too, and we did it again and again until our legs began to itch real bad. The hot sun had dried the mud that covered our legs and we had to peel off the chunks that made us itch.

The sound of a croaking frog was casting a sleepy spell on us and we sat dreamy eyed. Suddenly cool water was running down our hot backs and we shrieked with shock! Sonny had snuck up from behind and jumped into a puddle, purposely splashing us.

We were mad! Kathleen scooped up a handful of mud and slapped it on Sonny's arm as she cried, "I'm going to teww mother on you!"

Sonny oozed spit between the split in his front teeth and snapped, "Go ahead, cry baby!" He scooped up a mud ball and we quickly jumped back thinking he was going to slap it on one of us. Instead, he threw it at the billboard on the other side of the ditch, but missed. We teased him. With much confidence, he said, "Neither one of you could do any better!"

We had to prove we could, and tried, but our heavy mud balls fell even shorter than Sonny's, making him laugh and call us, "Weaklings!"

The sultry heat was too much for Sonny. He headed for the huge billboard and we followed. Crickets hopped at each step with our bare feet and we hopped, too, to avoid stepping on them. The monstrous structure had two sides that came together like a big "V" and once in between the two sides, we were out of the hot sun and in the cool shade.

On the ground was a spot worn smooth from older kids sneaking to smoke their cigarettes; butts were everywhere. Sonny said he knew who smoked, but he wouldn't tell us.

Keeping his secret made him act tough and he kicked at a crushed cracker can, uncovering a snake that slithered in my path and made me almost do the splits to keep from stepping on it!

That scared me so bad I had to let Sonny know. "I'm going to tell ya motha on you!" He simply strutted away, ignoring my anger.

In the distance were Bubber and Betsy. "Com'on, let's catch up to them!" said Sonny.

We ran to meet them and running in such heat made us down right hot! Kathleen huffed and puffed an exhausted plea, "Et's find a sprinker somepace."

After a little thought, I piped up with, "I know who has a spwinkla!"

Bubber, with a disgusted sigh blubbered, "No, that's baby stuff. I know of somethin' better; let's go to the dairy farm!"

"Great idea!" shouted Sonny.

The dairy farm up the road had a long metal tank filled with cool water for the cows to drink. We all liked Bubber's idea and the five of us headed for the dairy farm for a dip in the tank.

To avoid the highway's hot pavement with our bare feet, we walked in the ditch. Once at the farm, the last of the milk cow herd was seen heading for the other side of the barn where there was shade.

While racing to the tank with Sonny in the lead, we were stopped by him yelling, "Whoa!" We saw then, too, the moist ground around the tank was peppered with fresh, golden-brown and grass green cow pies. It was a mess! Yet, wherever a hoof print had been the hot sun was already drying the higher ridges.

Sonny and Bubber, enjoying the challenge, hopped from one dry ridge of a hoof print to another until reaching the plank jutting out from under the tank.

Kathleen and I, on our tippytoes, did the same. We made it to the tank but heard a "screech!" We turned to see Betsy kicking one foot in the air. She'd stepped in a squishy cow pie and the mess was flying everywhere!

When she reached the plank, Bubber made her feel better by splashing water out of the tank to wash away what was left between her toes.

Kathleen and I already had our swimming suits on, waited for the other three to strip to their underpants. Before getting into the tank, we had to scoop up the green scum floating on the surface and toss it to the ground. With this chore done, Sonny and Bubber interlocked their hands with each other to make a step and lifted us girls up and over the rim.

The water felt cool and refreshing. After the boys slipped over the rim, we splashed and bobbed up and down. There was little else we five could do in the long, narrow tank until Bubber suggested we play leapfrog. We didn't understand how the game could work until Bubber explained how to leapfrog in water. Instead of hopping, we had to dive under and swim between another person's legs.

After forming a line, I was last behind Bubber and Kathleen was to go first. Kathleen tipped, dove down, and disappeared. The rest of us had our stance wide to allow her to frog swim between, but she must not have understood how to do it because Kathleen immediately shot up out of the water gasping for air! Then, while pulling herself along the edge of the tank to the back of the line she angrily cried, "I don't ike paying weap frog!"

The line then worked its way up until Bubber became the last in line and it was my turn! I sucked in a deep breath, closed my eyes and mouth real tight, tipped down and grabbed for the first set of legs, but could not hold my breath!

After bobbing up gasping for air, I, like Kathleen, thought playing leap frog was a dumb idea! I splashed lots of water into Bubber's face! The others joined in the new game of splashing water, causing much water to slop over the tank's edge.

The cows moon eyed us from the shade. Realizing we had an audience, we made ugly faces at them. They still just stared, looking so dumb, which made us feel it was time to get out.

The boys pulled themselves up and over the side of the tank and when the three had their clothes on, we girls hopped back to dry ground. The cows moon-eyed us all the way out of the gate, then sauntered up to the tank. They were nice cows.

We headed for Kathleen and Sonny's house. Once there, we sat in the shade of the house sipping cool glasses of good tasting cherry kool-aid. The rest of that day, and the many more days that followed, were filled with play and adventure in the great outdoors.

A place of interest to my friends and me was the cemetery on the hill during any season of the year. Our carefree, youthful minds enabled us to accept God's part in death's sleep. I knew, with refreshing simplicity, when animals and people died, they went to heaven to live with God. I knew, because Mother told me so.

It was the end of a hot summer and all around was parched ground as my friends and I headed up the dirt road for the cemetery. Betsy, Kathleen and I, our hands interlocked, trailed behind Sonny and Bubber. To our right, we passed the old gray shack where the scary old gray-haired hermit lived.

Further up, we came upon the weathered barn that was partly falling down. Behind it was a house painted white with two big trees in front. On our left was a hillside and when we neared the end of the road, we passed by the empty house that had lots of junk scattered about the yard.

We reached the cemetery, and walked along the outside of its fence line looking over it at all on the other side, knowing it was a place we had to be respectful of.

There were lots and lots of different kinds of monuments all over. In front of some were pretty, colorful flowers. The green grass was neatly trimmed, and there were trees and small shrubs about to give it a cheerful parklike look; a place made especially for children like us to want to be, to play, and to explore.

When we reached two tall brick pillars, we knew we were at the entrance to the cemetery. Once within, we raced to the middle to reach our goal, the great stone cross called a monument.

Our playful imaginations made the stone cross look like a caring person, large and strong, with arms stretched out. Near the top, carved in the stone, were the letters "R.I.P." giving this very caring person a name; we called him "Mr. Rip."

Our heads tipped back to look up at its letters, we cried in unison, "Hi ya, Mr. Rip!"

I added, "Betcha Mista Wip is weally happy we say 'Hi' to him evewy time we come hewe."

Kathleen, agreeing, piped up with, "Yah!"

Bubber, Sonny and Betsy giggled, making the two of us wonder what was so funny.

Bubber saw our puzzled expressions and he explained, "This is a game! We call this cross Mr. Rip cuz there is no one really dead here. Mr. Rip is telling all to 'Rest In Peace,' R.I.P. You see?"

I liked our game and I liked what our Mr. Rip was telling all of us, but most of all, I learned that no one had to be dead and living in heaven first to have a monument; anyone could have one any time they wanted one, like Mr. Rip. Bubber said so.

Bubber bolted away from us at the cross and Sonny let out a loud "whinny" when riding his imaginary horse to catch up to Bubber. Betsy, Kathleen and I, knowing we did not have to go far to catch up, simply strolled along. My memory flashed to another time when we'd played in the cemetery with Julia along. She'd told us if we stepped on a grave that would make someone in the family die. I did not want my mother, father, sister or brother to die—no one must've stepped on a grave because no one I knew died, except our cat, but that did not count. Julia told me so.

As we snaked around the plots called graves, Bubber, in the lead, shouted made up names to the tombstones and the rest of us echoed the same, all shouting, "Hi, Mr. Fiddledeedee; hi, Mr. Stinky cheese; hi, Mr. Rumpelstiltskin; hi, Mr. Stub'your-toe; hi, Mr. Puddin'pie; hi, Mr. Sassafras; hi, Mr. Mud-in-your-eye; hi, Mr. Pick'your-nose."

Sonny belted out a loud, "Whoa!" We did as commanded. Sonny trotted a few steps to a patch of sunken fresh earth.

Bubber must have known what Sonny was thinking because when we were all looking down at the sod, Bubber asked, "Hey, Sonny, who were them robbers, the ones who stolt lots of gold and hid it in a grave?"

Sonny oozed spit between his teeth before answering with a question. "Jesse James?"

Bubber was about to reply when Betsy murmured in a quivering voice, "I think grave robbers were here."

Kathleen was wiggling her nose to move her glasses up when I looked at her to see if she understood. I kept thinking, What would wobbas wanna gwave fa? Musta been cuz they wanted the gold down thewe.

Bubber was a bit upset at Betsy for interrupting. Looking smart, he spit to the ground before he told her, "Doncha know, dumb sister, it was not grave robbers, but bad cowboys who dug up this dirt to hide their stolen loot!" To stamp it in her head, he whacked the seat of Betsy's pants with his hand and that made her fiery mad!

She screamed, "You're so stupid, Bubber! There are no bad cowboys in this cemetery! It was grave robbers, don't you see, see, see?"

Bubber snapped back, "I don'wanna see, see, see cuz you don't know whatcha talkin' about!" He beckoned with his arm for Sonny to follow. "Let's git away from these dumb, dumb blockheads!"

Betsy wiggled her hips as she shouted at the two who were trotting away like cowboys on horses. "Sticks 'n' stones may break my bones, but names will never hurt me! And a rooty-toot-toot!"

Kathleen and I chimed in with, rooty-toot-toots, too. The boys acted unconcerned as they trotted on their way.

Betsy, Kathleen, and I were glad to be alone to do just as we pleased! We zigzagged around many tombstones until we were where we'd never explored before, at a far corner of the cemetery. The grass and weeds were dry and stiff, giving us the feeling we'd discovered a long, long ago part of the cemetery.

A baby's wooden crib was the first to catch our interest; it looked very old. The great number of small wooden, splintery crosses were easy to spot; most were set at graves smaller than I was. It was figured the markers told when the babies all died and went to heaven.

As we scouted about the area, we found a baby lamb nestled down on a flat stone bed; it was cute. A small concrete block had become a reddish yellow color and a bird like a pigeon was carved in it; we also found another.

I began to sense a mood of great sadness when discovering so many small graves until Kathleen perked up Betsy and me when she looked up, pointed to a far off grave and said, "Mr. What's His Name has ots and ots of pretty fowers."

I knew perfectly well what Kathleen was thinking; it was that Mr. What's His Name would like to share some of the flowers from his big, lovely bouquet that was on a bed of lush green grass.

Fear of getting caught stealing flowers caused us to hunker down close to the ground and waddle like ducks to the grave. For Mister What's His Name, we left behind two flowers in the canning jar that was half buried in the ground. When running back to the little markers, we placed a pretty colorful flower on the ground at each one, making the dry, parched ground look a whole lot prettier.

Betsy shouted, "Hey!" to get our attention. When Kathleen and I saw what she was pointing to we saw the boys about to leave the cemetery.

We ran to beat sixty to catch up! When reaching the brick pillars and passing through, we sang out, "Bye, Mr. Rip!" and we left all to "rest in peace."

As we three girls walked down the cemetery road on the heels of Bubber and Sonny, we watched them practice their strong arm, throwing rocks to see who could throw the furthest. A tinkling of glass bottles drew our attention to the old gray shack where the old gray hermit lived.

We saw the old gray hermit, with his gray beard and gray hair. He was wearing gray coveralls, placing empty, brown, beer bottles along the foundation of his old gray shack.

Sonny whispered an explanation, "Doncha see, he's doin' that to probably keep the mice out." I was afraid of the old gray hermit and was glad when all of my friends wanted to hurry past his place.

A loud pop came from the highway. It was a farm truck revved to a roar causing the noisy backfire. It headed up the road for out of town.

Sonny knew the two people in the truck. "That's Mr. and Mrs. Bloomer. I've been to their farm."

Kathleen whined, "I haven't. But Mrs. Boomer brings us her eggs."

The two in the truck did not see us, but we waved, just the same.

Betsy and Kathleen lingered at the door of my house as the boys went on. Betsy, so happy, said, "I git to go to kideegarden tomorrow." Betsy had reminded me that the next day was the first day of school and kindergarten for those who get to go!

I felt left out though I did ask, "Can we still play afta you git out of kid-ki-a-gaden?"

She raised both her eyebrows and her shoulders when answering, "Guess so."

I thought of a plan. "We can meet you up the stweet when you come home, huh, Kathleen?"

"We can!" said Kathleen, then my two friends left me to go home.

The next morning when I awoke I saw that Patty's bed was empty. I remembered that it was the first day of school. Voices were coming from the kitchen and I hopped out of bed to join them. The kitchen was warm and cheery with Patty, Bobby and Dad still home.

Bobby had a mouthful of cereal when he mumbled a good morning greeting of, "Hi, ugly."

Mother gave him a clear signal to stop teasing me, drawing out his name, "Bobbeeeee."

Dad grabbed for a toothpick, getting ready to leave for work. He told Patty and Bobby, "Learn something new in school today."

Patty disappeared into the bathroom. Bobby was still eating. Dad rested his hand on my head. "And you, Tootse, help your mother around the house all you can."

I knew what Mother's response might be and quickly glanced to see her raise one half of her upper lip in a mean sneer. I did not know what that meant, except maybe that Mother did not need my help that day.

While waiting for Patty to come out of the bathroom, I watched Dad get ready to go out the door. It was the usual every morning. The toothpick in his mouth moved from side to side then disappeared inside. After he kissed Mother goodbye, out popped the toothpick.

It seemed I had waited at the bathroom door forever before Patty came out, and before I could scoot in she stopped me, planting the weight of her hand on my shoulder. She looked me in my eyes and said, "You stay out of my things while I'm in school, okay?"

I tried to pull away, but her hand held until I replied, "Okay!"

"Promise?" she asked.

I gave an anxious answer, "I pwomise! I pwomise!" She squeezed me with a hug as though to seal the promise I had made. I bolted away to get inside the bathroom!

I was sitting on the toilet when I heard the expected reminder from Mother, "Only four squares!"

I had to respect my mother's wishes and do as she'd taught me, counting tissues, "One, two, thwee, fa," I tore number four from the roll.

When Patty and Bobby were ready to leave for school, they scrambled for the door at the same time, vying to be the first out. Bobby lost and he snapped back at me, "Lucky, ugly you, you git to stay home!" I was fast at sticking my tongue out before he disappeared out the door.

I watched as Mother placed one crisp biscuit of shredded wheat in a bowl for my breakfast then tipped the tea kettle to let a flow of steaming water cover it. She then held the biscuit in place with a spoon and the hot water flowed out into the sink.

I quickly grabbed for the bottle of milk to keep Mother from shaking it. I wanted the rich taste of cream off the top of the milk to cover my hot biscuit.

I was thinking while eating as Mother did her kitchen chores when a thought puzzled me. "Motha, why did Bobby say to me, "Lucky me," when he likes going ta school?"

Mother smiled. "It just seems the thing to do, to not like school when all kids really do. It is confusing, I know."

"Is that why Patty calls Bobby a peabwain?" Mother laughed, but did not answer. I carried my empty bowl to the sink and saw that she was preparing water to wash dishes. I saw lots of bubbles! I asked, "Can I help? I can help like Daddy told me ta do."

Mother sneered, then pulled a stool to the sink as she said, "You can wash and I'll wipe them dry."

I hopped up onto the stool and pushed my pajama sleeves up while Mother tied the apron strings around my neck. Below all the bubbles, the water was very hot! I pinched a finger and thumb to a glass and yanked it out!

I handed it to Mother to rinse and dry. The many bubbles I noticed were very beautiful. I cupped my hand to scoop up two big bubbles on my palm that were joined to make one giant bubble.

With a wisp of my breath, I blew and the double bubble was off in flight. "Look Mama!" I screamed, "Looky!" The two that were one floated upwards towards the kitchen cupboard where it hit, but popped only one, the other floated free.

We watched the fragile, glass-like bubble as it became airborne. The moment of splendor was captivating when the light from the window created a glistening rainbow of colors in the bubble as it floated away and away. Then it floated down, down, down and went poof!

It had hit the table and all that was left was a drop of water. I had spun around on my stool to scoop up another when Mother said, "Tell you what, how about you getting dressed, then come back." I ripped the apron off over my head and hopped down from the stool.

While in my bedroom hurriedly dressing, a warm ray of sunlight from the window made thoughts turn over in my head. I wondered about Betsy, Bubber and Sonny. *What awe they doing now? Awe they having fun? What is school like and especially this kid-kid-a-gaden?*

Once dressed, I ran back to the kitchen and up on the stool. Looking down, I saw the dishes had all been washed and not a bubble was left in the muggy water.

I began to pout until Mother said, "If you swish your hand real fast in the water, you can make bubbles." I did and like magic some bubbles appeared.

I cupped my hand, scooped up a few, and blew with a wisp of my breath. I squealed, "Look, Mama, looky!"

Later in the day, Kathleen and I were stretched out on the floor coloring in the same coloring book. I was doing good coloring my clown, a lot better than Kathleen was coloring her elephant. I wanted to teach her how to stay inside the line with her purple coloring crayon, but did not know how.

Once again I looked to see where the hands were at on the clock. Mother had shown me where they would be when it was time for Betsy to come home from kindergarten and they were there! I screamed, "It's time!" so Kathleen would know too and we leaped to our feet, ran out of the house, and up the street to the corner to wait for Betsy.

We did not have to wait long; it was Betsy coming way up ahead. Kathleen and I skipped along to meet her. Kathleen grabbed one hand of Betsy's and I took the other.

Excited, I asked, "Was it fun? What is this kid-a-gaden like?"

Betsy dropped our hands as she let out a disgusted sounding sigh, then, in a grown up way, said, "Please! It is not kid-a-gaden! It is kin-der-gar-ten!" I was very confused; the day before I remembered her calling it kid-a-gaden, too! Betsy started acting like a teacher, making Kathleen and me pronounce the word correctly until she appeared satisfied.

Holding hands again, Betsy told us all about it. "We colored, played with clay, and in two giant boxes there are lots and lots, so, so many toys! And you know what? There is this big dollhouse, it's so cute, and it has all this tiny furniture inside it, real looking furniture!

"And you know what? There's a store in the corner and it has real boxes of food like our mothers buy, but the boxes are empty. I got to be a store lady. Tomorrow my teacher is going to teach us how to speak on the telephone, properly. Teacher read us two stories, and remember one day when Junior came to play with Bubber? He's in my kindergarten, too! And we have to take these . . . naps."

"Naps?!" I screamed in surprise as I dropped Betsy's hand and pulled away.

Betsy knew I thought naps were for babies and tried to explain, "You see, it's like this, we have our very own rug and we have to rest on it for not very long. Not really sleep, doncha see?"

I was thinking and I thought I understood, and said to Betsy, "Guess it's okay with ya eyes opened to just west on a wug."

Kathleen and I walked Betsy to her house and waited for her to change into her play clothes. A bit later the boys came home from school. After they told us what first grade was all about, we still had lots of time left in the day to play.

Yet, as the days slipped by, and with the sun going down earlier and earlier, it made our play after kindergarten and school shorter and shorter.

A day too wet to go play at Kathleen's made me feel very dreary. I sat in the overstuffed chair with my dolly tucked in by my side. Resting my chin on my hand, I looked out the window to watch the heavy rain coming down. A faint honking sound became louder until the honking was heard above the house, yet I saw nothing through the gray outside.

The honking faded away. I sighed and looked down. The water dripping from the ledge above was forming a pool on the windowsill and it grew until it got so big it was forced to run off to the ground.

I watched another pool form, then run off, and another, then my thoughts drifted to the Saturday before.

I patted my dolly to get her attention to listen to what I wanted to tell her about that day with my friends. "Mista Jaspa was waking leaves and waked lots until he had a big, big pile. Misses Jaspa came out of ha house cawwying a bag of potatoes, one fa me, one fa Kathleen, and Bubba and Sonny, too, but not fa Betsy, she couldn't play that day. And one fa Maxine and Donny, too.

"I few my potato weal high on that big, big pile like Mista Jaspa told us to do. Then Mista Jaspa told us to git back, then he stwuck a match on his pant leg to make little fias all awound. The fia gwew so big and hot we had to git back mo'e cuz the puffs of smoke made us cough!

"We wan to the otha side and the smoke followed us, and the fia cwackled so vewy, vewy loud! When the fia was all out, Mista Jaspa took his wake and pushed the ashes awound and awound to find all awe bunt potatoes.

They wa so hot! We had to keep thowing them up and up lots of times to git them cool.

"The peeling was cwusty and we had to chip it away befa eating them. It was kind of waw inside but vewy, vewy good."

Not thinking of more I sighed, looking away from my dolly in time to see a pool of water run off the sill and another one form to run off again.

While watching the rain, I sat patting my dolly on her head letting her know she was my best friend. She had lots of hair and an idea for something fun that would be "real" to do perked me up. I picked up my dolly, left the chair, and checked where Mother was.

What I was about to do had to be done in secret. I eased the bathroom door closed behind me and when trying to be quiet I heard, "Only four squares." That so startled me, I let the toilet lid drop with a loud bang!

I was afraid Mother would want to check on the noise so I waited, but she never came. I sat my dolly on the lid of the toilet, then opened a drawer and lifted the scissors out. I snipped off each tight curl that wrapped around my finger until there was a big mess of stiff curls on the floor. I moved my dolly to the sink, put up the toilet lid and dumped the curls in. With a flick of the handle the evidence flushed away.

I looked at the bristly stubble on my dolly's head, then I hugged her stiff body, thanking her for letting me play a "real" beauty shop lady. I had to somehow get past Mother without her seeing what I did to my dolly. I feared she'd get mad at me. To keep from drawing her attention, I was very quiet going from the bathroom to my bedroom. Once there,

I rummaged through my dolly's box of clothes. With her bonnet on, Mother could not see that she was bald.

The days of autumn passed one by one and one day late in the season I left the house with my dolly to go to Kathleen's. I felt the bite of the cold through my coat and I cuddled my dolly real close so her blanket would help protect my face and hands from the cold air. When I entered Kathleen's house I felt warmly welcomed from a good, toasty smell of bread baking. Julia, from across the tracks, arrived with her mother; her mother then left leaving Julia to play with Kathleen and me.

We went into Kathleen's bedroom she shared with Sonny. Sonny was not home; he was in school. We played with our dollies until a bad mood made me tired of playing house! I had to always play the daddy because my dolly had the shortest hair.

Under Sonny's bed I had spotted his box of tinker-toys and I asked Kathleen, "Can we play with the tinka toys?"

Although Kathleen's glasses had not slipped down her nose, her nose wiggled as she frowned with a worried look as she explained. "Those are Sonny's!"

Julia, who did not have a brother, said, "But he's not here."

That meant Julia wanted to play with them as I did so Kathleen made an order, "You guys! We wiww have to put them back before Sonny comes home!"

When I grabbed for the box, Julia plucked the lid off, making the box fall from our grip and tinker toys rolled all over the bedroom floor. On the box were colorful pictures of ideas to build and we liked the windmill the best. We scooted about the bedroom floor for the pieces needed to fit and refit until our windmill grew and grew, then it was done. And it really worked! With a blow of our breath, the green cardboard blades would spin around.

We lost track of time. Suddenly, from far away, we heard Sonny say to Bubber, "See you later." We panicked! There wasn't time to put Sonny's tinker-toys away—we hid ourselves under the bed, the three of us laid in the cramped space, cheek to cheek to cheek. Dust got up my nose and made my nose tickle.

The door to Sonny's room opened and a long shadow stretched across the floor. Instantly, angry words barked, "Who's been playing with my tinker toys?"

We muffled our mouths with our hands to prevent him from hearing us breathing, hoping he would leave, but the shadow stayed. Julia did not know what it was like to be in trouble with a brother so when fuzz tickled *her* nose she snorted to blow it away! Now the shadow knew and we watched it shrink.

Sonny's knees landed on the floor in front of us. The corner of the bedspread lifted up and we were eyeball to eyeball with his mad face! A shower of spit sprayed my face as he commanded, "You shifty pie faces! Put my tinker toys away!" We scrambled out from under the bed and went to work. He was so fussy, making us drop each piece just right in the box, and as for the grandly built windmill that we'd so cleverly built? He made us take that all apart.

Kathleen's mother must've been listening from the kitchen because she gave us a great relief from our trouble, welcoming us to join her for a tea party.

There was no place set for Sonny at the table; his mother knew he would not want to be a part of our sissy tea party. It was for just us girls. The table was set to look fancy with pretty little plates, a lovely big ladies tea pot filled with milk, fancy cups, a plate with warm bread stacked high, a dish heaped with butter, and a bowl full of chokecherry jelly.

My slice of warm bread melted the butter and with the chokecherry jelly running like syrup, I had to be quick with my tongue to catch the drips.

I told Julia, "It makes me wememba the time I picked choke chewwies with my dad, he cawwyed me on his shouldas so I could weach the high bwanches. I had to wap my legs awound his neck weal tight and when my heavy lawd bucket got too heavy fa me, I set it on my dad's head and he laughed!"

The time came when I had to go home. Although it wasn't nighttime, it almost seemed that late when leaving the toasty warm house to go out into the cold air. The ground was hard and as I walked, tiny snowflakes commenced chasing each other making me feel gay and silly. I sang a song over and over to my dolly all the way home, "It's snowing, it's snowing, the old man is snahing." And it snowed and snowed.

After supper, and later when I went to bed, it was still snowing. I lay snuggled between my warm flannel sheets remembering that the next day would be a day with no school because, "It will be Saturday!" I glowed because all my friends would be home to play in the snow with me. I sat up to draw back the window shade and saw the night made bright by great big, fluffy, white flakes swirling so very gracefully up, down and around.

In early morning, from my bed, I yanked open the window shade causing Patty to shout from her bed, "Put back that shade!" I obeyed after she jerked her covers over her head because of the blinding light from the heaps and heaps of bright snow. I hopped out of bed.

Passing Mother in the kitchen, she sneered. She does not like snow. Being so alert made me feel so smart, when entering the bathroom I was first to say, "I know, Mama – fa squahs."

After breakfast, I put my snowsuit and boots on before entering the cold, back porch. I unhooked my sled from the nail on the wall, tugged the back door open, and a gush of crisp, fresh winter air rushed in.

The steps were buried under lots of snow and I gave a good tug on the rope to my sled and let it sail down the slope. Then I leaped in the air for the fun of sinking into the deepest heap against the house and rolled to get out.

A cheerful glow from the rising sun caused a vision of glittering diamonds on the widespread, covering of snow. A hush of silence was broken only by my boots breaking through the crust of snow and the runners on my sled; crunch, crunch, crunch, shhhh-hhhhhhhhhhhhhhhhhhhh.

Mrs. Try opened her door and her hand flew out, throwing bread crumbs in the air. Many hungry birds flitted about, their tiny feet making crisscross prints in the snow when scurrying after every tidbit thrown.

As I neared the corner of our street, the echoes of happy voices were heard from Laura, Maxine and Donnie who were already playing on a vacant lot. I hurried along to meet, too, Bubber, Betsy, Sonny and Kathleen at the vacant lot.

We had a jolly good time throwing snowballs at each other until it was suggested by the boys, to build forts! Boys against the girls.

With walls of snow for our forts, and a pile of ammunition stacked high, on the command of "Charge!" the battle began and snowballs flew through the air with a few hitting the mark. Not a soldier died, but our throwing arms weakened and we left a scarred battlefield behind as we headed along the highway, pulling our sleds to Beaner Hill.

During the winter months, Beaner Hill was a road too steep to be anything but a good sled run. Old Lady Beans lived at the very top. Her face and white bushy hair could be seen easily.

When we reached the top of the steep hill, we checked to see if Mrs. Beaner was at her kitchen window, and all we saw was the reflection of sunlight. That made it easy to convince ourselves she wasn't there.

To begin our fun, I pulled my sled in place, then plopped on my belly to be ready for my first descent when the run was clear of anyone else sledding. My turn came and I pushed with my toes to get started, "Weeeeeeeeeeeeeeeee," sailing so fast I had to be quick to guide my sled to the left when close to the end to keep from sledding up and onto the highway. The view was blocked and we could not see a car that might be motoring along.

It was so very stimulating feeling the exhilarating lickety split of sailing down the slick slope again, and again, and again until I felt too tired to climb the steep hill. The whistle of the noon Skiddoo was a telling of the time of day it was, and I was glad when Sonny yelled out, "I'm hungry! Com'on guys, let's quit and meet back after lunch."

In the weeks that passed, inexhaustible merriment was abundant for all of us who were young enough to enjoy the snow. Then one day, a sudden freezing north wind blew in that went right through our heavy clothing, ending our fun for the day. I pulled my scarf high over my face as I walked into the icy storm on my way home.

In the back porch with my boots and mittens off, my fingers and toes burned and tingled from being so cold. When opening the door and entering the kitchen, I took in a deep breath of what I figured was a good smell; it was of something fresh and green.

Except for the tree causing a wee flicker of a memory of a Christmas past, this would be my first Christmas that would be forever remembered.

Strewn about the floor were boxes filled with pretty balls, silver strings, and a little doll dressed in all white. When I saw her wings, I knew she was an angel.

Mother's warning, "Don't touch her!" came too late for I had already touched her pretty white hair and it cut my finger! Mother explained, "Her hair is made from glass and as you know now, glass can cut!"

I soothed my cut finger in my mouth as I watched Mother struggling to stretch out a rope of bright, colorful lights. Some were missing. When I tried to help, she ordered me to sit in the chair!

Mother then explained, "The lights are plugged in and you could get shocked by touching an empty socket! I will let you know when I need your help."

Sitting in the chair soothing my hurt finger, I looked down at that angel and started thinking. *How can'ha be glass? A dwinking glass is glass and a, a, a window is glass, but thewe was no glass to see in her pwetty white haiw.*

36

Mother unplugged the lights and began wrapping their long cord around the tree. When she was satisfied that they were where she wanted them to be, she looked down at me, and said, "Now you can help."

Mother took charge of putting the angel at the top of the tree while I plucked a shiny red ball with a frosted picture on it from the box and handed it to her. Then I handed her a shiny green ball, a blue ball, one of gold, and another red one.

"Hand me a silver one," said Mother. Those seemed not as pretty until I held one up and noticed its teardrop shape and what was so unusual in that shape. Mother grabbed it from me. I plucked another from the box. I was peeking in at what I had found to be so unusual when Mother snatched that one from me as well!

I took another and saw, at the end of the crinkly thumb-like print in the teardrop shape, a tiny reflection of all in the room, discovering even tiny me! And Mother, too! It was so funny, making me laugh, then Mother said, "Please, hand me a blue ball."

The ornaments from the box were all on the tree when Mother very carefully picked up what she called, "icicles." The shiny, thin, fragile silver strands draped across her hand did not look like the kind of icicles I knew about.

I giggled over Mother's fun of naming them icicles before I corrected her, "Huh-ah! Icicles hang fwom ah woof and we have sawd fights with them."

Mother was laughing as she said, "Well, you certainly could not have a sword fight with these! Would you like to help?" I held my hand up and Mother carefully laid the silver strands across my palm. I was very good at first, laying one strand at a time over a branch as Mother said I had to do, but became impatient and threw what was left on one big branch where it became a glob of silver.

Mother expressed her disapproval. It was fine with me that she finished the job without my help. Mother stood back to admire her work then looked at me with a pleasing smile. "Ready?" I shrugged my shoulders not knowing what more to be ready for.

After the light cord was plugged in, my glowing response was, "Ohhh, ahhh." I was looking at the most beautiful Christmas tree I had ever, ever seen. The sight created a spellbinding mood as the dazzling lights of reds, greens, blues and yellows reflected in the many colorful ornaments and danced in the fluttering shiny silver strands, called icicles.

All the glimmer and shimmer made the angel at the top glow, too, as though truly alive! She had a smile on her face. She smiled, looking down at her pretty tree, and at me!

The next day a box of nuts came from an aunt who lived somewhere. I knew what a peanut was, but Mother had to tell me what the others were. She cracked what she called a walnut; I liked it.

One called a pecan made her frown when she tried digging the nut out; it was good. The Brazil nut had a funny taste. The hazel nut was okay, but I giggled because I had an aunt named Hazel and I giggled more when I asked Mother, "Is she nutty?"

The almonds I could open all by myself; I liked them. After Patty and Bobby had a good share, Mother said the rest had to be saved for Christmas Day.

I had my first lesson from Patty about being good at Christmas time. She let me know I had to be good, stay out of her things, and be nice or Santa Claus would not come! I was very good; I did not touch one thing of hers, and this nice Santa snuck into our house when we were all sleeping and left presents under the tree.

What I liked best was the toy sewing machine Patty got; it really worked! But Patty told me I had to play with my own present.

I got a cradle for my dolly. Bobby got a BB gun. My dad's wool stocking that I had pinned to the arm of one chair, like Patty and Bobby had, bulged with stuff. I dumped it all out and I got an apple, an orange, a box of Cracker Jack, a candy cane, peanuts, and a marshmallow man!

Later on Christmas day, food and fun was shared by relatives who came to our house. That was when Mother pulled the box of nuts from under the tree to parcel out. A big surprise that I learned was that my aunt who sent the nuts was my cousins aunt too! Though Christmas day ended, Christmas stayed until Mother took the tree down.

I awakened with my ear hurting real bad and cried out for Mother to come!

She came, sat on my bed, felt of my forehead and calmly asked, "Would you like to sleep in my bed?" It did make me feel so much better crawling into the unmade bed of my parents.

Mother rubbed her cool soothing hand across my cheek, then left the room as Patty and Bobby were leaving for school.

I clutched Mother's pillow against my aching ear and laid motionless, afraid if I moved it would hurt more. Dinky, our cat, hopped up with me and curled into a ball at my feet. We both slept until I felt Mother's presence in the room.

I saw her lift up the sleeping ball of fur to carry him away. Soon after, I heard Dad home for lunch. He came and sat on the edge of the bed. "Tootse, I hear you have an earache." Although Dad comforted me, his caring made me feel more sorry for myself.

He then took a big puff of his smoking cigar and seeming to know what to do with it, he gently blew his warm breath of smoke in my aching ear and made it better. After Dad left I fell asleep again.

I always awaken during daylight time, so when I awoke to darkness all about in the bedroom, I felt hazy and confused. The smell of potatoes and sounds of cooking and voices in the kitchen made me crawl out of my parents warm bed.

In the cheerful light of the kitchen, Mother was busy cooking and Patty was setting the table with Bobby watching while waiting to eat. He was the first to see me and announced, "Hi, ugly."

Mother saw me wag my tongue out at him and commented, "I see you feel better."

Then Dad came out of the bathroom and asked, "How's my Tootse feeling?"

I answered, "Betta." Not long after supper I went back to bed. I felt in need of more sleep.

The next morning my ear did not hurt. Feeling much, much better, I got dressed to play outdoors until Mother explained, her finger pointing at me, "If you go out in the cold air too soon, your earache could come back!" She suggested I give my dolly a bath.

I set my dolly in the bathroom sink to give her a nice bath. There'd been a fire in the bathroom and the smell from the charred wall prompted me to tell my dolly what happened.

"Bobby did it; he filled the tub with wata to put his put-put boat in and to make it go putt-putt awound in the wata he had to light the candle with a match. When he stwuck the match on the wall the cutain caught fia. Befa Motha put the fia out the wall got bunt. Bobby got into twouble; he's not 'pose to play with matches; he knows that!"

Before drying my dolly with a towel, I powdered her with Mother's pretty smelling stuff. The other day Mother accidentally saw my dolly's bald head and all she said was, "Her hair will not grow back, you know."

I squatted on the front room floor next to the box of my dolly's clothes I had left there. When I was ready to slip her coat on over her dress, an idea came to mind that would be more fun to do. Instead of dressing a stiff cold body, I could dress a live warm one: Dinky!

Dinky, our cat, was sleeping by the warm stove. I crawled to it, picked up the warm ball of fur and set the sleepy, limp cat on my lap.

I shoved Dinky's left leg into an armhole of the coat, but he squirmed when I shoved the other leg in the other armhole and I had to scold, "Sit still!

I grabbed my dolly's bonnet and put it on his head and it pinned his ears down making him look very mad.

I could not make a bow and the strings in the bonnet ended up in a knot.

My live baby needed a nap. I put him in my dolly's box of clothes and covered him all up with my dolly's blanket to hide his mean look. His head popped out, but I pushed it down. Then, I patted him like a mother would to calm him as I sang, "Wock a bye baby in the twee top. When the bough bweaks the cwadle will fall," and he hopped out!

Dinky tried so hard to walk out of that coat, forewords and backwards, then stretched, rolled and pawed the air, acting so silly, making me giggle and giggle.

Mother walked into the room and upon seeing the plight of my live fur baby, shrieked, "Take those clothes off that poor cat!"

I got the coat off, but could not undo the knot in the bonnet; Dinky himself squirmed out of that. Restored to a cat again, he sped for the door that Mother had open and he disappeared outside. My dolly seemed, then, much too lifeless to want to play with so I followed Mother into the kitchen.

I sat at the kitchen table to visit with Mother as she did her kitchen chores.

She wasn't listening to me as I talked so I concentrated on an out of the ordinary thing to do. I twisted my elbow and tried to stretch it to meet my lips so I could kiss it. Mother noticed and asked, "What in the world are you doing?"

I let go of my elbow to try to explain, "Sonny toll me if I could kiss my elbow I'd tun into a boy! But I can't weach it!"

Mother groused, "That's ridiculous! Why would you want to be a boy?"

I frowned as I mumbled an answer, "Cuz boys, doncha know, git to do lots of things."

Mother was deep in thought before telling me, "Girls get to do a lot of things like boys do and when girls tire of doing boys things they can be girls again. Boys, on the other hand, have to be boys all the time."

The words were too much for me to understand so when Mother wasn't looking I stretched the skin of my elbow again to try to touch my puckered lips.

When Mother asked if I wanted to make ice cream, I unpuckered my lips and my answer was a big happy smile.

She dug in the cupboard for a small jar, poured cream from the top of the milk bottle into it and then added sugar and that nice smelling stuff called vanilla. She then screwed the lid on tight and shook the jar good. It was beginning to thicken when Mother handed the jar to me and instructed me to shake it more. I shook and shook that jar, looked and shook and shook again until Mother said it was ready. She then carried the jar through the back porch, opened the outside door and shoved it into a heap of snow next to the house.

I knew from when Patty made ice cream that it took a long time for it to freeze, but being overly eager made me ask too often, "Is my ice cweam weady yet?"

Mother seemed irritated when giving me an order, "Be patient! It won't be ready until after lunch!"

To be patient, I had to be busy. When Mother set up the ironing board, I knew that was how I could keep busy. I said to Mother, "I wanna iwon. Can I?" Mother told me to get my play iron. I wanted to do the real thing and whined, "I do not want to play with my toy iwon."

Mother sighed and gave me a mean sneer when pulling the stool to the ironing board. She then took a roll of dampened hankies of Dad's out of the basket and plopped them on the board.

I ironed the first hanky pretty good, the second one too; Mother seemed very pleased. The third hanky I ironed in a few wrinkles, that was because the iron was getting heavy. After the heavy iron did the same with the fourth hanky. Mother suggested she take over, but I answered, "No!" Then it happened; the heavy iron wouldn't stay propped up; it fell on my arm and my screaming alerted Mother to a terrible tragedy!

She set the iron up, yanked the plug out of the wall while snarling angrily, "I knew it! I knew this was going to happen!" She got a jar of salve and dabbed it on the red burn that helped to ease my hurt, but not my tears until Mother said, "By golly, look!"

I blinked to clear my eyes and saw what excited Mother. My burn was the shape of the bottom of the big iron, but was teenier than my toy iron.

Mother, acting astonished, said, "How remarkable."

The rest of the morning, feeling concerned over my "remarkable" burn, I held my hurt arm to my waist so I could keep looking at it. I knew Dad was home for lunch when hearing boots stomping off snow on the back porch. I ran to greet him at the kitchen door to show off my burn.

He took hold of my arm to get a closer look. "That is certainly a burn to be proud of; how did you get it?"

Mother broke in, "She was helping her mother!" Dad understood what Mother meant because he laughed, but Mother sneered.

I then explained, "I got bund weal bad by Motha's iwon, it was so hot."

Dad took a better, more serious look at my burn and stated with great knowledge, "Tootse, it looks like that hot iron branded you, yup! I would say so."

When sitting at the table eating lunch with Mom and Dad, Dad started a discussion about a house somewhere. I wasn't interested, for I had to take care of my burned arm and not brush it against something; that happened once and made it sting so bad.

After taking the last bite of my sandwich, I was ready for my ice cream. Yet I dared not ask for it and interrupt my parents who were still talking about a house. I knew that!

Dad did his toothpick trick, kissing Mother goodbye. Then, as he was heading for the door, he said to me, "Now Tootse, keep your mother busy, help her all you can!" Mother growled an awful growling sound as Dad laughed. Then Mother followed him to pluck the jar out from the heap of snow.

The jar was so cold Mother had a difficult time getting the cold, cold lid off. She struggled with the lid and when it finally popped off, her mood became very, very cheery because of the nice smell of vanilla. Vanilla made it smell like real store bought ice cream, but when looking in the jar it looked like frozen snow with bird tracks crisscrossing everywhere. Those were ice crystals that made it crunchy as I ate the flavorful taste of the ice cream I had made.

About midday, Kathleen came with her mother and I was quick to show them my "remarkable" burn. I told all about what happened when helping Mother and when the burn could be seen as the same shape as the bottom of the big iron, but was smaller than even my toy iron, it created a remarkable mystery, even for Kathleen and her mother. Kathleen said, "That is magic!" which made my very bad, "remarkable" burn even more special.

Kathleen and I scurried to the other room to play with our dollies while our mothers sat sipping coffee. I overheard my mother sigh, and in a tired voice, she said to Kathleen's mother, "I sure had a busy morning."

A sadness was felt inside me for my mother who had to work so hard. I was glad I could help her with her ironing.

It was the very dead of winter, though a day not stone-cold, and the ground was fleecy white and the sun glowed. It was Saturday; no school and a rallying cry from the boys was, "Let's hike to the cemetery!"

All six of us headed for the high country with sack lunches in our hands. Bubber and Sonny made a dash for a slide on the slick tire tracks on the road going up and ended up slipping back into Julia and me and the two of us back into Betsy and Kathleen. It was fun! We did it again and ended up slipping down on our hands and knees. Not getting ahead by sliding up because of slipping back and sometimes falling, we gave up, and took to the side of the road where our boots could dig into the snow.

Passing the old, gray hermit's shack, I saw, through a smoky window, a gray shadow move. Though it was daylight and I was with my friends, I felt a spooky chill. The old barn had lost part of its roof from the weight of too much snow and all that could be seen in the yard of the empty house were big white mounds covering the junk buried underneath. Then we reached the fence line to where we wanted to be.

The cemetery was under a thick, pristine blanket of new snow that had fallen during the night. We were the first to enter that day. After our greeting to Mr. Rip, our aim for a game was to get to the unused section to play Fox and Geese. Drifts of snow partly covered some tombstones, but enough were visible for us to call out made up names when frolicking around them.

Reaching the sea of perfect, untrodden snow, we played follow-the-leader, shuffling our boots along to form a gigantic circle. Then we created spokes to the middle to form a safety zone from the fox for one goose at a time.

The game began and we ran and ran to keep out of reach of the fox's hand. All but Betsy got to be a fox; her long legs kept her from getting caught. Julia, the fox again, picked me to chase and as her hand was about to touch me I collapsed in the snow from too much running and laughing. One by one the others gave up to join me.

After a short rest, Sonny suggested we eat and we dumped our sandwiches from their sacks to our laps. I was not happy with what Mother made for me, and asked, "Anybody wanna twade? I have a peanut butta sanmich."

Trading is fun and everyone joined in. I traded one half for a honey and butter, the other for a butter and catsup, and they both tasted so very good.

Sonny was smacking his lips on purpose to make someone notice what he was eating, half a peanut butter half on top of his jelly half. Bubber had the other halves and they chanted their "yum-yums," making us girls feel sick over mixing peanut butter and jelly!

Sonny let us know the taste was good, explaining, "The jelly helps the peanut butter go down, and no butts!" We let him know we did not care for butts and reached for clean snow to wash the last bites of our sandwiches down.

When Betsy stood up she winced in pain; she said her mother called it "growing pains." She stretched her long legs to make the ache go away. I did not feel pain when I stood up, but it felt so good to stretch; it did for the others, too, and that was when we noticed our town from the hill. The smoke from the chimneys of the houses was going straight up and up, except in the out of town direction there was a billowy cloud trailing from a moving train.

Sonny shouted, "The Skiddoo!" We cupped our hands about our mouths and we belted out a greeting, "Hellooo, Skiddoo!" Although Mr. Engineer could not hear us, we sure believed he did!

I toppled over backwards on the snow to make an angel. The others did the same to see who could make the biggest angel. We stretched our arms up and down to make the wings and we stretched our legs to and fro to make the gown.

Once on our feet we judged who won; between two, we did not know which to choose. Betsy's? Her angel was the tallest. Or, Bubber's? His angel was the funny, fattest one. It won! Our teasing laughter made Bubber mad!

To vent his anger, Bubber stomped his heavy boots in the snow, leaving good prints behind as he directed a course to lead us out of the cemetery. The rest of us made a game out of stepping in the prints made by our leader and by the time we got to the brick pillars, Bubber forgot he was mad. In a zippery fun voice he let go a, "Bye, Rip!" Sonny said it too.

We girls pivoted, then cried out with respect, "Bye, Mr. Rip!" That was when I noticed the many boot prints leading into the cemetery and only one big smudged set of boot prints leading out.

We sailed down the slick tire tracks all the way to the highway. Gleeful screeching was coming from Beaner Hill, making us anxious to get there! When closer, we saw Laura, Maxine and Donnie spinning wildly down the steep slope, but not on sleds.

Sonny knew what they were using. "They're using linoleum!"

Laura was the first to spot us and hollered, "Hurry up! I've got more!"

When we got there we grabbed a chunk of linoleum. Mean Old Lady Beans was at her window! I positioned a chunk of linoleum under my rump and tucked my feet under. Being cautious, I checked the window, found she was no longer there, and pushed to go down.

The linoleum, with its slick surface of built up wax, was like ice on ice, making me sail and spin so fast I could not control my drooling—it was whipped away by the wind. A bank of snow slowed me, then I plowed into three at the end.

Bubber was wiping his wet face with a sleeve and bursting with excitement, "Gee whiz! Let's do that again!"

Donnie suggested all nine of us go down together. Once situated we grasped each other's mittened hands and were off on the count of "three!" The uneven slope made us spin and lose control of our grip, and all became a blur, we were going so fast!

The first toppled over, creating a pig pile and that was fun, too! Shoving and pushing to get up on our feet, we saw that Kathleen, who'd been last, had blood oozing from a scratch on her cheek. A pat of snow by Sonny helped to deaden the sting.

We climbed the hill and there, at the top, was Old Lady Beans! My heart was beating out of control thinking we were in deep trouble. Her lips were drawn to a frown as she waddled towards us, then she dug into her apron pocket for a hanky. She dabbed at Kathleen's scratch with it, then covered it with a Band-Aid from her pocket.

She said to Kathleen, "You will be just fine." Then she waddled back into her kitchen without scolding us.

Bubber murmured, "Didja see what Old Lady Beans jus' did?"

We did! And at that moment we had a much kinder feeling for the old lady we had thought was so mean.

A warm house, food, and a night of rest restored our energy to begin anew the next day, and the next, and the next until the winter of '41 slipped by underneath my friends and me.

Spring brought the red breasted robins back from their winter homes and wild, blue crocuses dotted the prairie hills. Green was sprouting, kites were flying, and marbles rattled in pockets. Spring was the time for Easter colors.

It was Good Friday before Easter as I sat with my dolly beside me. I suddenly remembered a wooden ducky story, and she listened as I told it to her. "It must'a been fa Easta time cuz it had gwass and candy eggs in it; I we-memba. I wonda whewe my wooden ducky went? It had a vewy long wope and sometimes when I pulled on the wope it would woll too fast and bite the backs of my feets. It quacked and quacked! My ducky had a box in the back fa the gwass and my candy eggs wa on that gwass, colid ones. I wonda whewe it went? That's all I can wememba now."

Patty called out, "Ready!" She'd been preparing the kitchen table for coloring eggs. Mother had bought lots of eggs and the one carton for me had two missing. Mother said they broke in the pot when boiling.

I watched what Patty and Bobby were doing and I placed my eggs into the colored water. I liked the colors yellow and pink the best. When we were done, Bobby had lots of blue and green eggs, Patty had lots of purple eggs and I had what I wanted, mostly yellow and pink eggs.

We had to put our colored eggs back into our own carton. Doing so I counted each of mine, "One, two, thwee, fa, five, six, um, seven! eight, nine and a, a, whewe's my ten?" I spied it amongst Bobby's eggs and exclaimed, "You dodo! You stole my egg!"

Bobby made a sick expression as he plucked *my* egg from *his* carton. "Who would want to steal such an ugly egg as this?" he asked.

We heard from Mother, "Bobbeeeee."

Then I stuck my tongue out; he deserved it! My eggs were pretty, not ugly!

When I was in bed with my dolly beside me and all was quiet, I whispered to her, "This is a Good Fwiday day, Motha told me so, cuz baby Jesus died on a cwoss cuz he is all gwown up now, Motha said so. Then baby Jesus went up to heaven. Baby Jesus, wememba, was bawn in a manga and he had this gweat big stah and pwesents, and see, that's what Easta is all about."

The morning of Easter Sunday, very early, I saw a pretty basket on the floor next to Patty's bed. I rolled over, looked down to the floor at my bed, and there was my wooden ducky! I was so surprised! I lifted it up and onto the bed with me while thinking, the magical bunny must have had my ducky all along.

In the nest of green were candied eggs and two pairs of anklets, a white pair and a pink pair. A bite from a purple candy egg made my throat tickle. I put the other half back to eat later.

In the afternoon, Kathleen came with her colored eggs to have an egg hunt with me in the house. I was first, hiding my eyes so Kathleen could hide her eggs, and I found every one. Before Kathleen found all mine our hunt indoors was interrupted by her parents who'd come to visit my parents.

When they sat down in the living room, I pulled Kathleen into my room and declared, "Ya daddy sat on that gween chaw!" She looked around the door jamb at her daddy in that chair, then wrinkled her nose, not understanding. I whisper-shouted, "Unda that cushion on that chaw awe my thwee eggs–the ones you could not find!"

Kathleen giggled! I did not like my friend laughing over her daddy crushing my pretty eggs. It was not funny!

Kathleen's parents did not stay long and took Kathleen with them when they left. After they went out the door, I ran to that green chair and threw off the cushion, expecting to see an awful mess, but my three pretty eggs were laying in a well in the seat of that old chair, not broken!

My mother, curious, looked at what I was looking at, and cried, "Uff da! Uff da! That could have been an awful mess!"

Dad looked, too, and laughed heartily, so we all laughed and joked at how a big, big daddy had been "setting" on chicken eggs, keeping them warm.

After Easter, as the days passed, my colored eggs became stinky and Mother threw them away. I had no more candy left and my wooden ducky couldn' be found.

I was all alone with not a friend to play with so I waited at the corner for Betsy to come home from kindergarten. When she came into sight she had a paper basket dangling from her hand. When meeting her, I asked, "What's that faa?"

In a snooty way, she explained, "Doncha know? Honestly, how dumb. It's a basket for May Day!" That made me feel real bad.

When we reached my house I told her, "I can't play now."

I told my dolly what Betsy said to me and then my dolly did not like Betsy either! I had Mother explain to my dolly and me what May Day was about and found out it was to be the very next day!

After school, Patty showed me how to make a paper basket like the one Betsy carried. During the fun of making more, Patty and Bobby got into a fight over the paste Patty made. Bobby couldn't get the handles to stay glued to his baskets and he told Patty she did not make it right from the flour and water! Mother told Bobby he had to be more patient and wait some to let the paste dry.

I learned from Patty that giving May Day baskets away was more than just sharing candy. When I had pondered it over, I had to ask, "Why do I hafta chase my fwiends when they give me a basket?"

Bobby piped up first, "Geeze, ugly, doncha know?"

Patty, accidentally, shoved a basket of his from the table to the floor, then explained exactly what I had have to do. "When you hear a knock at the door and find a basket, you have to chase that friend who left it and give that friend a kiss."

"Oh!" I replied, letting Patty know I understood. Then I remembered, and said, "I kissed Kathleen once," then declared, "But I won't kiss any dumb boy! No siwee, I won't do that!"

Bobby, smart like, said, "Who'd wanna kiss your ugly mug?"

I frowned about him calling me "ugly," then answered back, "What boy would wanna kiss ya ugly lips?"

Bobby shook his head, "Geeze!"

When my baskets were done, I lined up all three and counted, "A gween one fa Kathleen and Sonny, a puple one fa Bubba and Betsy, and a pink one fa me!"

Bobby called out, "Mom!" then snapped at me, "You can't give youself one, gopher teeth!"

Mother had to remind Bobby, "I remember someone else who once hid all the baskets he made, just for himself."

I then expressed a "Ha! Ha!" along with a smug look and kept one for myself!

Early in the morning on May Day, Mother sent on the table whole peanuts, a sack of suckers and a bowl of gumdrops. In the baskets I was giving away I put in lots of gumdrops, and a few peanuts and suckers. In the basket for me, I put in lots of peanuts and lots of suckers, that's all. I did not like "gumdwops!"

To begin our fun of delivering May Day baskets, we scooted out the back door, then we scattered! Patty told me I had to be sneaky and when a sound alerted me someone was coming, I ran to hide in a bush and surprised Bobby who was hiding there.

He yelped, "Geeze!" then ran to beat sixty to get away from Mary Patricia chasing him to give him a kiss!

I delivered my two baskets without getting caught and from baskets I received, got some good candy, and gumdrops which I dumped into a sack and hid in my bedroom. Suddenly I heard a loud shriek from Mother, "Uff da! Uff da!"

I ran to the back door where Mother was and she was laughing while looking down at the brown lumps in a yellow May Day basket. It was barnyard horse manure!

We heard a giggling from around the corner of the house and Mother tiptoed towards it with me right behind her. Right before we got there, out jumped Kathleen and her mother!

"Surprise! Surprise!" her mother screamed, "Happy May Day!" Our mothers wrapped their arms about each other and did a silly jig. They then went into the house and Kathleen and I ran off to play.

After a week, the gumdrops in the sack had become a pasty glob. I carried the sack to the kitchen garbage can and was dumping it in when I heard Patty cry out to Mom and Dad, "A move to where?"

Dad's curt reply was, "To another house!" Nothing more was said as I headed back to my bedroom.

Patty had given in to my begging to let me play with her toy sewing machine.

The subject of the "house" came up once again. It was on a Sunday afternoon when our family walked across the tracks to the south side of town to look at an empty house. To learn we were going to live in it was exciting! I was anxious to tell someone, like Kathleen!

When Kathleen came to meet me the next day to play, I jumped leapedy leap in the air shouting, "Guess what? Guess what? We awe moving!"

Kathleen stood silent, wiggling her glasses up her nose, her voice sad. "Rewwy, are you rewwy moving? Far away?"

I wanted her to be happy and threw my arms about as I exclaimed, "It's okay! We awe jus movin' acwoss the twacks, ova not fa fwom Julia." I grabbed her hand. "Com'on I'll show you!" Hand in hand we hurried on our way to reach the road leading to the railroad tracks.

At the tracks, standing near the first of many sets of iron rails, I pointed to the other side between two warehouses, and said, "That house, the yellow stucco one."

Kathleen murmured, "Et's go see it. Can we?" I was high as a kite with excitement to want to show her, but I knew the rule "never cross the tracks without a parent along." Kathleen knew the rule just as I did, but with me really wanting to show her the house, I figured we could do it! I checked all around first to make sure no one would see us.

Even though there was no train in sight, I did as my mother would do, I yelled, "Coast is cleh! Wun!" And we ran lickety split hurdling the many iron rails until safe on the other side of the tracks.

The slight slope between the two warehouses was strewn with cinders and we took each step carefully, knowing if we slipped the cinders could make the skin sting real bad.

At the street, we looked up and down and with no cars motoring along we crossed to the boulevard, then onto the sidewalk in front of the fence to the yellow stucco house.

Before I could reach for the iron gate to push it open, Kathleen pulled back because gates were meant to keep dogs and kids out! I convinced her it was okay, and the gate squeaked as it closed behind us.

Standing under a big tree in the front yard, I told Kathleen what I remembered the house looked like inside.

She pointed to the upper windows and asked, "You going to seep up there?"

I answered, "Nope! Patty and Bobby, and my gwand-motha who is coming someday will sleep up thewe." I pointed to the lower floor and I told her, "My bedwoom is wight acwoss fwom Mom and Dad's bedwoom."

Kathleen wanted to go inside so bad and I explained to her, "We can't cuz my dad said new li-li-noem is 'pose to be put on the kitchen fla and we could cawwy wocks in on awe shoes, my dad said that."

I had an idea to show my best friend where my bedroom was at. "Com'on!" I pulled her along and at the back of the house we squeezed between two shrubs until reaching the window of my bedroom.

Kathleen pulled away to look down and said, "Is that a reo grave?"

On the ground, between us and where the kitchen jutted out, was a long plot of sod with the dirt sunken a bit. It took a spin of my imagination to put it together that the sunken area could be that grave from which Betsy said those robbers stole. Such a far-fetched thought could not be reasoned out so I answered, "I don't weally think so!"

With our noses pressed to my bedroom window Kathleen saw what my room looked like. Then I showed her the back yard all the way to the alleyway where an old, broken down wire chicken coop was. After showing Kathleen the garden area, clothesline, trees and shrubs, we were in the front yard again.

It was then Kathleen whined, "I have to go potty reo bad." I told her to squat under the lilac bushes, but she was too shy to do that! Then, when she crossed her legs trying to hold back her tremendous urge, I knew we had to go into the house, and fast!

It was very important no one see us going in as I pulled Kathleen to the back door. We entered the back porch and standing at the kitchen door, I made a quick decision to go to the bathroom upstairs. We kicked our shoes off and ran across the black tar paper on the kitchen floor to the stairs. We ran up and down the hall to the little bathroom and closed the door for privacy.

Kathleen was first, then after I went potty, I twisted the knob, but the door was stuck. I tried again and still the door wouldn't open. A key stuck out from the keyhole so I gave the key a twist and I yanked hard when turning the knob, still nothing happened!

I jumped into the bathtub to look out the window hoping to see someone. There was no one up the alley, nor down around junky cars or the red icehouse. I needed a rest to think and Kathleen and I sat quietly, not sharing our fears over being locked in.

As time slipped by, new energy surged within me and I knew the door would open, but it did not! Our fear became real. We were locked inside an empty house and no one knew where we were.

The feeling of great despair caused Kathleen to cry.

I sat on the rim of the tub next to her and wrapped my arm about her shoulders. With our warm cheeks together, I begged, "Don't cwy, don't cwy."

Out of fear of upsetting my friend more, I could not cry and was left with no way to express my fear. Balancing on the rim of the tub became uncomfortable and we slipped down to sit on the floor.

I had been bad and felt so sad. I had disobeyed my dad and this was my punishment to be locked in our prison. With such cruel thoughts and grieving hearts, we suffered all afternoon and when I began to feel hungry, I knew my family had eaten, and without me.

A "ping" was heard, it was a pebble that had hit the bathroom window above the tub! What followed was my dad's voice calling out, "You kids up there?" I jumped up! Then stepped into the tub, looked out the window and down to the ground. We'd been found!

I saw my dad, my mother and Kathleen's mother cradling our shoes in their arms, all looking up with worried expressions.

Dad disappeared and we heard the clomp, clomp of his shoes coming up the stairs, then down the hall. Dad turned the knob and pushed. "I should have fixed this door yesterday!" The door did not open for Dad either! He asked, "Is there a key?" I pulled the key out and shoved it under the door.

A click was heard, the knob turned, but nothing happened. Dad called out, "Hang in there kids." The clopping of his shoes faded away.

The next we heard was a thump, thump at the bathroom window, it was a ladder! Dad climbed it and peered in at us. He tapped at the middle part of the window at a lock signaling for me to unlock it.

I jumped into the tub, stretched, then flipped the lock. The fresh air that rushed in when Dad shoved the window up did not help to make me feel better; I was scared.

Dad climbed in and set a very comforting hand on Kathleen's head, and mine. When he spoke in soft words, "Been here all day?" I cried.

Dad took the key from his pocket and worked and worked it in the keyhole until he heard a click, with a very strong tug the door opened!

We ran past Dad, down the hallway, down the stairs, across the tar paper on the floor, through the back porch, and out to our angry mothers.

One was shaking a finger while screaming, "Do you know what you put us through?" The other, "What were you doing over here? You took ten years off my life!" Again the first, "Just wait! Just wait until I get you home!"

When heading across the tracks for home, Kathleen and I stayed a stretch ahead of what scared us more than anger, a great hush.

Dad spoke in a calm voice, "Well, it seems to me if one had to get locked in, what better place than a bathroom? You have all the water you need and a pot to pee in." The silence was then broken by the goodness of laughter, and Kathleen and I, no longer frightened, put a getup step in our walk when heading for home.

Chapter 2

I stood at the gate in front of the yellow stucco house waiting for Kathleen and Julia. I was anxious to show them a fun place, the long narrow crawl space in the upstairs in my house.

Kathleen came into view across the tracks with her mother who let go of her hand so Kathleen could cross the tracks alone. Up the street, I saw long, fluffy, black curls bouncing about and knew it was Julia. When my friends were in reach, I grabbed their hands. "I hafta show you guys a weal scawy place, it is so dawk; Bobby showed it to me yestaday."

I led the two into the vestibule of the house, then into the front room, dining room, and the kitchen where the stairs were. Kathleen knew about my bedroom downstairs, and said, "I wanna see your bedroom first!"

I led the two back through the dining room to the long hallway and at the first door, I pulled them into my bedroom. I showed them my bed, my dresser, and my closet.

Kathleen pulled away from me and went to the window. She looked down. "It stiww ooks wike a grave, reawwy it does."

I remembered what I had forgotten about and beat Julia to the window to see it again. Julia said, "That's no grave!

If it was a real one under your bedroom window you'd have bad luck, probably die." I stared at Julia pondering the bad luck stories she was always telling, like the one she'd told us about once before, "If a doggy howls outside a window at night, it means someone in that house will die that very night."

I tugged at their hands to remind the two I had a scary place to show them and pulled them back into the kitchen.

We climbed the stairs two steps at a time and at the top of the stairs took my friends into Patty's bedroom. On the sides of the room the ceiling came down to touch our heads, and on one side was a short dresser that fit there.

With the help of my friends, we pushed the dresser aside to expose an elf sized door. I yanked it open and light from the bedroom flooded the opening making it look not dark and scary, at all.

I winced when I dropped to my knees; they were still sore from a crawl through the day before with Bobby. To fool Kathleen and Julia, I giggled on purpose to let them think it would be fun, not scary. That was how Bobby fooled me. I was the first in, Kathleen was behind me, and Julia was last.

As we inched along, the odor of mothballs and dust gave the narrow cramped space a strong, stuffy smell. Then it became so dark I could not see the cobweb that brushed across my face, startling me. At the same time, the two behind me screamed! I thought they must've imagined seeing a spooky ghost, so I assured them, "Don't be afwaid, ghosts don't come out daing daytime."

Kathleen whined, "But you butted me hard on my forehead and it hurt!"

And Julia screamed, "You butted me, Kathleen!"

Hidden behind a box was a thin bead of light and I knew that was the door to Bobby's bedroom. We had one more door to crawl to and the space became pitch dark, and suffocating!

Our creeping along on hands and knees was going slower than it had with Bobby and me the day before and it wasn't as much fun either! I got mad and had to yell, "Stop pushing!"

Kathleen screamed, "I can't hewp it! I can't see!"

Julia cried, "It's so hot we will all die in here!" When I thought we'd gone far enough, I felt the wall for the up and down crack of the last elf sized door and finding it, gave the door a good whack to open it.

The rush of fresh air coming in was a great relief! When I crawled out I announced to the other two, "This will be my gwandmotha's bedwoom when she comes."

When Julia was crawling out, her shoe caught something that exposed two black, rubber tips and Kathleen asked, "What's that?"

I did not know and was curious, too. We yanked and tugged until we pulled out a pair of long crutches with a faded green, heavy belt wrapped around them.

The belt had a long metal case dangling from it. Julia knew what it was as she explained, "This is a sword like what my granddaddy wore in a war. He died."

When we pulled the sword used in a war out of its case, Kathleen was quick to spot something. She wiggled her glasses up her nose to get a closer look; then said, "This ooks ike bud." The sword had red, blood like spots on it and that meant the sword had killed someone.

I suddenly grew concerned about the crutches, blood on the knife, someone dead, and the "grave" under my window threatening me with bad luck. I screamed!

The others screamed and we ran from the bedroom, down the hall, down the stairs, through the kitchen, through the wash porch and outdoors to daylight and safety!

While playing in the yard I saw a girl my size on the other side of the fence. When she saw me looking at her, she ran back to her house. I had never known a stranger before and I did not know what to do to know this girl who lived next door.

When Julia had to go home, Kathleen and I got to walk in the out-of-town direction with her. Neither Kathleen nor I had ever been to her house and it was new territory to us, except for what was familiar on the other side of the road, the railroad tracks. The city sidewalk ended at the end of my street and we walked along the road for another block until coming to a vacant lot full of tall weeds. There, Kathleen and I stood to watch Julia head for her house that was back by the dike.

We hollered, "Bye!"

"Bye!" responded Julia, "watch out for Frankie!"

I did not know a Frankie nor did Kathleen and shouted, "Who's Fwankie?"

She shouted back, "He's a mean kid!"

I looked at Kathleen and she at me, neither one of us knew what a mean kid looked like. Fearfully, we looked among the tall weeds but a mean, big kid was not hiding there, nor was a mean big, big kid waiting for us around the corner of a house, nor the next.

When we reached Osterberg's junky car garage on my block, we feared this extra mean, big, big kid had to be waiting inside the garage door. He was not there, nor at the stairwell going up to the apartments above Osterberg's garage.

We were safe, then, with just one small house to pass before reaching my house; that was the house where the strange girl lived.

I waved to Kathleen as she crossed the tracks to meet her mother, then ran back to my house to ask Mother a question. I found her in the kitchen. "Do I have a gwave unda my bedwoom window?"

Mother gave me a strange look, then she lifted up, looked out the window above the sink to down to the ground. "By golly, that does look like a grave, but it's a long barrel in the ground that once held oil for the old cookstove."

I was satisfied with that, yet had another question. "Motha, if a doggy howls at night unda my window, will I die?"

Frowning, Mother snapped, "Hogwash!"

That meant it wasn't true and I was pleased to learn Julia was full of that "hog wash!" About the other, a sneaky thought came to mind. *I won't tell my fwiends what the gwave weally is; a gwave wobba's gwave with gold in it is mo fun to have than a dumb, old oil bawwel.*

At dinner time as we sat at the round dining room table, I could not remember not to talk at the table, and asked, "Guess what?" No one asked which was what I had expected so I told my family, "We found a soljas sawd and cwutches in Gwandmotha's bedwoom. The sawd killed someone dead cuz we found blood."

This sparked life in Bobby. "Show me!"

Mother explained, "The crutches and sword belonged to Mr. Moe, the elderly gentleman who once lived in this house."

I asked, "Did he git dead?"

"No," she replied, "He moved away."

After dinner Bobby made me show him the blood on the sword. It had all been put back in the crawl space and I had to pull it all out again; then pointed to the three red spots. "See? See! See!"

Bobby took the sword in his hands to get a closer look, then let it drop to the floor and said in a gruff tone, "Geeze! Don't you know rust when you see rust!?" Bobby stomped away and left me alone with that old sword. Not totally convinced it was not blood, I ran to get out of there!

When downstairs, I happened to look out the dining room window and saw that strange girl, my size, at the fence. I ran outside, stopped, and looked at her. She did not run back to her house, instead she stared back at me. I took one step toward her and she still did not run away. She tucked her chin in like a bird when I said, "Hi," then I asked, "Whatcha name?"

The shy girl murmured, "Lila."

"Can I come ova to play?" I asked.

Lila perked up, and said with much enthusiasm, "Yes!"

I ran into my house to tell Mother where I was going. Then, in two shakes of a leg, I was back out the gate running to her yard. Together, we were still shy, walking in silence until Lila took me into her house where there were others to meet.

I met my new friend's older sister, her baby brother, and her nice mother. Then Lila and I, with her brother, played in the bedroom that all the kids shared. When Lila's dad came home, he was carrying a huge tub of vanilla ice cream. I felt so welcomed by Lila's friendly family. They shared lots of ice cream with me because otherwise it would melt in their icebox. Then I had to go home.

That night, once I was settled in my bed I saw that I had forgotten to pull down my window shade. A feeling in my bones made the black window pane at the foot of my bed give the illusion it could be hiding someone looking in. I crawled to the edge of my bed, reached the pull and I pulled the shade down. I then pulled my covers over my head to hide, just in case someone spooky might be lurking in my bedroom's shadows.

The next day, while playing with Lila, she suggested we play 'knock on doors and run.' I had never played this game and it sounded like a lot of fun.

I followed Lila up the stairs to apartments above a garage on the other side of her house. There were lots of doors on both sides of a long, long hall and a doorway, way back. I knew what to do and when Lila said, "Go!" we ran with speed, thumping a good knock on every door we passed. We flew out the back door and scurried down the steps to the alleyway.

Lila led me to the other side of a junky car where she pulled me down to hide, just in time! We heard, then, loud and clear, "You kids stop that!" I was curious. I peeked, and at the top of the stairs I saw one who looked somewhat like Old Lady Beans!

Lila whispered, "That's Mrs. Oister, she's a battle-axe." After she shuffled back in, we sneaked away to go home; it was lunch time.

As I was entering the back porch, I heard a train's whistle coming from a great distance away. It was the noon Skiddoo, way out of town and just coming around the bend. I shouted to Mother, "I'll be back!"

I ran out the front door and across the street to the railroad tracks. As I waited for our train, I had the time to learn more about what was along the tracks where I now lived.

Towards town, there were lots of warehouses on both sides of the tracks. Near the red brick depot was the railroad crossing for people, cars, and trains. Beyond that was the underpass. In the out of town direction, there were more warehouses, a grain elevator, and the Skiddoo, coming!

I was so excited I jumped and yelled as though my friends were with me, "Hewe it comes! Hewe it comes!" Instead of zooming by, as it did when my friends and I greeted our train when further out of town, it was chugging very slowly towards me. I waved my arms about and when Mr. Engineer saw me he had such a surprised look! Quickly, he pulled the cord to whistle a greeting to me, "Whooooowhooooooah!"

As the powerful engine eased slowly by, I saw, clear as a bell, the smiling faces of the people waving back from the two passenger cars. The first boxcar had several milk cans lined up at the door; the door of the other was closed. On the step of the red caboose the man in blue smiled, and said, "Hello, young lassie."

As the squealing brakes brought our train to a stop at the depot, a feeling surged within me. The Skiddoo on that day, without my friends with me, became my train. My train greeted only me! I then made a big wish to someday take a ride on my train. I repeated while running back to my house, "I will; I will; I will."

While I was eating my sandwich, Mother warned, "Be very careful of trains!"

That made me ponder about the puzzle of telling one train from another. "How come the Skiddoo is a nice twain and all otha twains awe so scawy?"

Mother looked out into space, then said, "I don't quite know what you mean. All trains should be scary to you. The Skiddoo is simply a train that makes short runs carrying passengers, and milk from the farmers."

I began to think, and exclaimed, "Shah! Cuz it cawwies milk it has to be a nice twain, wight Motha?"

Her big smile reached me, and she said, "You bet, that is right!"

With Lila away for a while, Julia and I were alone and left Julia's house, heading for the river. That was when Julia pointed to where Frankie lived with his grandmother, next door. I hadn't seen this mean kid yet and I began to think he was another "hogwash" story! Behind the outhouse, we slipped down the steep slope where there were trees, weeds, and bushes near the river.

We strolled along until we saw an old green bench tipped over next to the path. Empty jars and lids were strewn about giving Julia the idea to make mudpies! We set the bench upright and with dirt and water in a jar, made a thick mixture of mud.

We filled several lids, then tapped them upside down so the mud pies would fall out. With the mud pies lined up on the bench, we looked for ideas to decorate with.

Julia startled me by grabbing my arm tightly while declaring, "Oh, oh, here comes mean Frankie!"

I looked up the path at a boy about the size of Bubber and Sonny walking with a kind of "I'll-beat-you-up" strut.

We jumped back off the path to allow him plenty of room to pass. Then, what we feared he'd do, he did. He stopped right smack in front of us!

His mean expression made me want to run, but I dared not for fear of being chased. Then, unexpectedly, he turned around. We heard the sound of splashing. When it stopped, he let out a crazy laugh, hopped, turned and was on his way up the path.

Julia and I stepped forward to inspect and saw what we'd suspected. He did! He'd peed all over our mud pies! I gave the bench a kick with my foot to make it topple over and all our dirtied mud pies hit the ground!

I found out that day that mean Frankie was not "hog wash." Julia was right; he was very real!

From that day forward, the terror began: looking for him hiding around a tree, or maybe a garbage can, a shed, or whatever could hide him where he could jump out and scare us! We had to always run very fast to keep two paces ahead of him.

A big afternoon had been planned to go to town with Kathleen, Sonny and Julia. I waited on the sidewalk watching the railroad tracks for Kathleen and Sonny until they came into view. Then I saw, too, Julia coming. I felt like a big girl getting to go to town without a parent along, only with just friends.

Exploring was learning, but I already knew on our walk up First Avenue the letters on the rubber stopper in the street that read: STOP, means to stop! My mother taught me that. On the empty corner of the next block, the yard was used for farm equipment; it belonged to Gruder's Garage. When passing the window of the garage I caught sight inside of what was very red and shiny, a pop machine!

We waved to the workers inside as we sniffed the heavy smell of grease when passing the big doors that were opened. We walked by a row of small houses before reaching, on the corner, a small, red brick shop with a boot shaped sign hanging over the door.

Sonny read what it said on the sign: SHOE REPAIR SHOP. A man inside was wearing a smudged apron while hammering on a shoe that was upside down.

On the shelves were old cowboy boots with their toes curled up and other shoes like what my daddy wears. The nice smell of leather was coming from the door of the shop, then we crossed the street. On the other side of First Avenue, blocking our view of the tracks, were warehouses. Above them were two tall silver tanks with the words FARMER'S UNION at the top, the same, I noticed, as the gas station we were walking by.

The block we were on became Front Street because of the businesses starting there, such as the tavern with its strong, sickening smell of cigar smoke and whiskey coming out its doorway. Then came a weedy lot and a hotel on the corner.

The day, being a Saturday, was farmer's day in town. Cars and small farm trucks lined the curbs and along the track side of the street, all the way to the depot the bigger farm trucks were parked. We stopped to wait for a vehicle to pass before crossing the street to reach the corner drug store.

We pressed our noses to the glass door and saw inside mostly kids with some sitting on a lower shelf of the magazine rack reading funny books. There were wooden booths further back and around the room were show cases filled with mostly pretty things for ladies.

A whirling sound of a milk shake maker drew our attention to the marble counter with kids sitting on stools buying ice cream. We had no money so we pushed away from the door and sauntered on.

We passed a farm stuff store full of farmers standing about talking. From the door of another tavern, the smell of whiskey and cigar smoke permeated the air again. Then there was a ladies store that sold unmentionables, like girdles and things. From another opened tavern door, along with the bad smell, we noticed, too, a boisterous ladies voice above the noisy talk from men that caused us to be curious.

With our noses pressed to the mesh screen door, we observed through a cloud of smoke what was going on in the tavern. The boisterous laughter was coming from a lady at the far end of the bar who was sitting between two gentlemen.

I heard the shuffling of cards and the clicking of poker chips and searched to see where it was coming from, but no one I could see was playing cards.

As the rolling smoke cleared a little, I saw at the same time what Kathleen saw as she screamed, "Ooky! ooky!"

Sonny said, "That's a buffalo's head on the wall."

What I saw was a massive, brown head with dark shiny eyes that burned a great sense of fear in me. We found more stuffed animals and birds, including what looked like a big lion with teeth that could tear us apart! Suddenly, a husky voice from behind startled us as it snapped, Scat, kids!"

TWO LOCAL COWBOYS, BILL MILLER & FRANK POWELL, FURNISHED THIS BUFFALO FOR A BARBECUE WHEN PRES. FRANKLIN D. ROOSEVELT VISITED THE FT. PECK PROJECT ON OCT. 3, 1937

OTTER

We jumped aside to let a tall, very important looking man go in. On our noses and chins were dirty mesh marks from the screen door and we made such fun of each other's dirty face.

Many grownups blocked the next store front and from another tavern door waddled a man who staggered our way. He made a snorting, throat clearing noise to spit, and a glob flew out of his mouth.

I shrieked when the slimy, tobacco colored glob landed on the tip of my shoe! When shaking my shoe it stuck like glue, and I ran to the curb where I scraped off the glob. The flow of saliva in my mouth suddenly had the taste of a cigar and swallowing would not make the icky taste wash away!

I caught up to my friends at Yondell's Grocery and Bakery store. The smell of sweet, fresh doughnuts helped to make the icky cigar taste go away.

Inside the store, ladies were shopping, visiting, or resting on upturned boxes. Sonny recognized one lady trading eggs for groceries. "That one is Mrs. Gouge."

When I saw the barber pole with its spiral colors of red and white hanging by the door of a barbershop, I told my friends, "That bawba pole is just like my uncle bawba pole at his bawba shop awound the canna. He is the daddy to my cousins."

A large hardware store was the last on the block. In the window of the store were such things as pots and pans, big and small tools, and all else that moms and dads use, and toys, too! Sonny was first to spot what he wanted, "That's my bike!" Then he said smart-like to Kathleen, "And you can't ride on it, ha, ha!"

Kathleen let him know, "If you don't et me, I wiww teww Mother on you!" I spotted the roller skates and let everyone know they were mine. Julia wanted the scooter. When not a toy was left to wish for, we crossed the street.

The big bank building was on the corner of that block and in turning there to head for Second Avenue we had to hug the wall of the bank building to avoid bumping into people. In doing so, we stepped on and across iron grates that covered the wells in the sidewalk. Before each grate Sonny would hesitate and look down.

At the third iron grate, I, too, looked down. I saw crumpled cigarette packs, candy wrappers, butts, bottle caps, rocks and dirt. Sonny scurried to the last grate and once there, beckoned for us to hurry over and look. Way down was one shiny dime. "Buried treasure!" screamed Julia.

Sonny hushed her, then made us huddle together to talk in secret as he whispered, "Tomorrow when no one is around we'll come back and git it out."

I asked, too loud, "How?"

Sonny grabbed my shoulder, "Be quiet about it or someone else will steal it. I'll show you how tomorrow."

Stacking hand on hand and giving a good shake, our secret was sealed. We nonchalantly continued our stroll as though we knew nothing.

We passed a jewelry store and hangout for coke drinks, then crossed an alleyway. From there, we passed a drug store, an eat shop, and a tall office building. When we rounded the corner of Second Avenue, the good aroma of popcorn made us run to the movie theater in the middle of the block.

The colorful pictures behind glass of the "Coming Attractions" poster got our attention. It was my favorite cowboy, Roy Rogers! And my favorite horse that did tricks, Trigger! I wanted to know when it was coming and I made Sonny ask the ticket lady.

She told us, "Next Saturday."

As I jumped with excitement, I said much too loud, "If we gits lots of money tomowwow, we can see Woy Wogas and Twigga next Satuday!"

Sonny curtly scolded, "Hush your trap!" I covered my mouth, then looked around and was relieved no one else had heard me enough to make them interested in knowing about our buried treasure.

We were satisfied to have been to town, but it was time to head back for our homes. Having to dodge so many people on the sidewalk, Sonny suggested we take the deserted looking alleys the rest of the way.

In the middle of the block Cory was on, we crossed the street to reach the first alley. Nothing but trash bins and weeds lined this quiet stretch of dirt road. Our attention was soon drawn to Mr. Yondell coming out the back door of his grocery and bakery store carrying a lumpy paper bag.

He was about to drop the bag into the trash bin when he saw us, then asked, "Would you kids like some doughnuts?"

We answered with a hearty, "Yes!" When he handed the bag to Sonny, we thanked him, then after he disappeared we looked inside the bag. There was a doughnut for each of us with two left over. My doughnut was a bit hard, but it was good as I ate around the hole while we strolled along.

We came to the back of one business we soon learned was a tavern judging by the sounds of shuffling cards and men's voices. Sonny was intrigued and climbed a stack of railroad ties for steps, and with us following he made the motion with a finger to his lips to be quiet.

Cigar smoke was drifting out the screen door. I popped the last of my doughnut in my mouth to sweeten the bitter taste again of a cigar.

"Oh, shit!" roared a deep voice from inside, shocking Julia into making a gasping noise. Afraid of being found, we scrambled to get down the steps. Sonny landed near an empty whiskey bottle, making it roll.

When the bottle stopped rolling we could see what'd stopped it—a dead man lying in the shade. We moved in closer for a better look at a "real dead body" and at that moment its leg moved! We did too! When we stopped running Sonny said, "Ah, he was just a drunk conked out."

Crossing the street to reach the other alley, I pointed to a garage on the block to show and tell where my dad worked on cars. Halfway down the next alley we reached my back yard gate, then crossed through the yard to the front gate.

Before everyone parted, plans were made for the next day, Sunday. Sonny believed more money could be found, maybe lots, under the iron grates at the bank building. Sonny's plan to get the money out had to be done with sticks and gum. He'd get the sticks and Julia volunteered to get the gum.

Sunday, at one o'clock on the button, my friends met me at my front yard gate. Sonny had the long sticks and Julia had the bubble gum. As instructed by Sonny, we bit off half the wad to chew to have ready to use. Saliva flowing juicy sweet in our mouths and sticks dragging behind, we were on our way to dig for buried treasure.

People stayed home Sundays; it seemed so with the streets so quiet. The rustle of leaves on the cottonwood trees could be heard and, too, the chirping of birds. Sonny, observing how lonely the streets were compared to the day before, said, "You can see a bird poop on someone's head five blocks away!" We looked before realizing that Sonny was telling another poppycock tale.

The only business doors opened on Sundays were the tavern doors. We did not have an interest to snoop, nor were we in the mood to wish for toys; we had a job to do. Sonny darted for the grate with the dime showing. I took a grate and Julia and Kathleen grabbed theirs.

I dropped to my knees and bent way over to look between the hefty bars of the grate to see far below. There was not a coin visible so I did as Sonny instructed us to do;

I used my stick to push wrappers and stuff around hoping to uncover lost coins.

Turning over a pop bottle cap, I proclaimed my excitement to all, "I found a nickel!"

Sonny cursed, "Oh, claptrap! You made me hit the dirt!" He'd told us if that happened the gum could lose its stickum.

I felt bad and bad for Kathleen, too, who whined, "I can't find any money."

Julia said to her, "I found two pennies and you can have one to try and get out." I stuck my wet wad of gum on one end of the stick and steadied my aim for that nickel, down, down, down; then gently touched that nickel with my wad of gum. I slurped up a drool as I pulled my stick up and the nickel stuck! But I held back my antsy excitement until I had accomplished getting my nickel out. Once in my hand, I screamed, "I got mine!"

Sonny yelled, "Oh, shi-shiminy!" I had shaken his concentration again, so I gave him my lucky stick and my extra bubble gum. He got his dime out.

Our dug up treasure was not enough for each of us to see a Roy Rogers movie. One dime, two pennies, and one nickel could only buy enough candy to share. We shrugged our shoulders, pondering aloud as to where on Sunday we could buy candy.

Sonny said, "I remember seeing candy on a shelf in the tavern yesterday." Again we shrugged our shoulders in answer. *Do we kids dare go in a tavern?*

Julia was determined to buy candy. "Let's go see!"

With our noses to the tavern's screen door, we saw boxes of candy sitting on the shelf inside. The tavern was empty except for two men sitting at the far end of the highly polished bar. Mr. Barman was talking to them. I seemed drawn by an unexplained disturbance within me to look at the buffalo head on the wall; its eyes in the massive, brown, furry head were frightening with it looking at me! I felt Sonny's hand on my shoulder and figured he wanted to pull me away. I saw Mr. Barman coming.

Instead of telling us kids to scat, Mr. Barman asked, "What can I do for you kids today?" Sonny acting big, oozing spit between his teeth as he declared, "We have come to buy some candy!" Mr. Barman pushed the screen door open and welcomed us in.

We followed Mr. Barman to the bar and wiggled up onto stools that could spin around. On the floor near our feet were several spittoons still full of icky spittle from a busy night before.

To look away from them, I gave myself a good spin on the stool then rubbed my hands across the smooth, slick shine on the counter as I looked at the boxes of candy on the shelf. Next to the candy was a punch board, and on down boxes of cigars and packs of cigarettes and way down were lots of mugs stacked high in front of a big mirror.

In that great mirror was the same buffalo head, its eyes still on me! I wrestled with an emotion I did not understand, not even when looking at the nickel in my hand which pictured a buffalo peacefully grazing. With the one on the wall disturbing me, I gave my bar stool another good spin.

Mr. Barman had noticed our interest in the stuffed animals and birds about the room and we learned from him that the lion was a cougar and the eagle was a bald one.

When Mr. Barman asked if we had any questions, Kathleen expressed her sorrow when asking, "Is that Santa C'aus's reindeer?"

As Mr. Barman hesitated to answer her, one man at the bar hollered, "She's got you there!"

Mr. Barman answered, "No, my dear, I would not have any reindeer of Santa's on my walls. That's an antelope."

All the animals and birds were dead and stuffed, a fact I accepted, yet the buffalo was different. I had been frightened by its gaze upon me and I, too, struggled with the disturbing feeling. I took one more look in the mirror at the massive, brown, furry head and it was then I sensed a new emotion of sorrow tugging at me. The expression in its eyes was now speaking of a wish for it to be free, like the buffalo on my nickel. There was nothing I could do but give my bar stool another spin.

From the great assortment of candy and nuts on the shelf, it was decided to buy a bag of corn candy. After plunking our coins down on the counter, Mr. Barman counted them and said, "You have two pennies too many." The two pennies could not be divided between four of us so it was decided to give them to Julia for the bubble gum she'd shared.

On our way out the door, Mr. Barman hollered, "Hey, kids!" Once he had our attention, he said, "If you want to earn money you can collect bottles and bring them in. I'll give you two cents for each one. Just ask for Stan." The thought of earning money had us so excited we shouted our "thanks" to our new friend, Stan, the barman.

Our sweet reward for a job well done was truly enjoyed as we walked home with thoughts of a new adventure, hunting for bottles, for money!

When getting close to Gruder's Garage I spotted an empty orange crush bottle by the door and ran ahead to snatch it up. As I dribbled the last drops out, I held the bottle up, and I said, "I'll save it!" Sonny knew we had to start sometime so he said, "How about collecting bottles tomorrow?"

After the rest of us agreed with Sonny's suggestion, plans had to be made for a time and place to meet. When we reached my front yard gate, my friends left me to go home.

I skipped around to the back of the house to leave my bottle in the wash porch. When entering the kitchen, I noticed a stillness in the house, usual on Sundays. I first searched downstairs and finding no one, I went upstairs hoping to find someone there.

A murmur of voices was coming from the far bedroom. As I walked into the room, there was a stranger with Mom and Dad. A trunk and a suitcase sat on the floor by the bed. I snuggled next to my mother as I studied the face of this older lady with hair as white as snow. Although I had never seen her before, I did have a clue as to who she was: my grandmother.

When Mother introduced her to me this grandmother spoke as though she'd known me before. She knew Patty and Bobby when they joined us, and they knew her! After warm greetings had been exchanged, we went downstairs as Mother had to prepare our supper. Patty got to help set the table, fancy like, for this new lady in our house.

Taking our usual places at the table we sat closer than before to make room for Grandmother. She sat between Dad and Patty where I could keep my eyes on her. The way she picked up her spoon and her fork, I did the same, and picking up my glass I, too, stuck out my pinky finger. My cloth napkin I was not used to slipped again from my lap to the floor. Picking it up, I dabbed at the corners of my mouth with it like she did.

I had been so busy observing that I hadn't noticed how quiet it was at the table until Dad broke the quiet spell when he asked Mother, "Did they tell you when the chickens will be in?"

I was surprised and the first to speak up, "Chickens! Awe we getting chickens?"

Mother said, "Yes," then told Dad, "John at the post office said to expect them in at the end of the week."

We'd never before had chickens and to get it straight I had to ask, "Weally? Will we have weal chickens in that old chicken coop, weally?"

Dad looked at me, then his eyes rolled to look at Patty, then to Bobby, then Dad said to Patty and Bobby, "That reminds me, you two get that pen ready, clean the coop and mend the wire."

Mean Bobby glared at me for reminding Dad of work that needed to be done. Then Bobby nudged Patty in her ribs as he said in a calm salesman-like talk, "You get the fun of cleaning the coop while I have to mend that old chicken wire."

Patty was not about to buy his sell and she did the sensible thing, she shook her head to say no. I realized how upset Dad could get over nonsense talk at the table, so when Bobby glared at me, *again!* I ignored him.

To change the subject I announced to all, "I have a pet snake! It is gween and he lives in the fwont yawd."

Bobby murmured, "He's just a dumb, old grass snake."

I puffed up my chest, and said, "He's not dumb; he talks to me!" I then saw Patty's eyes roll toward Dad reminding me of trouble if I did not shut up. I glanced at Dad, then to Grandmother, forgetting she would be listening, too, to our "nonsense" talk. I did not say one more word until

I swallowed my last bite of food, then I asked Mother, "Can I go to the coyote fawm with my fwiends next day afta tomowwow? Tomowwow we awe going to collect bottles fa money!"

I heard a sigh that came from Grandmother and saw a smile on her face as she said, "I sure wish I had such energy."

I wondered what she meant while I waited for an answer from Mother and when one did not come, I figured that meant I could go, probably.

Patty, acting like a helpful sister, said in a very grownup tone, "Remember, please, if you should stick a finger in a coyotes pen, one might bite your finger off." Patty had been to the coyote farm before and I figured she knew what she was talking about. Then when she saw I was through eating said, in highfalutin talk, "You may excuse yourself."

I did not know what she meant and puzzled, I asked, "Scuse myself fa what?" Dad snorted, I thought a laugh, but when he did not share what was funny I knew his snort wasn't a laugh.

Monday morning I awoke very early, and still in my bed, I heard footsteps from upstairs, then not, then again, then not. I knew it had to be Grandmother and I became very curious to know what she was doing.

I rolled out of bed and I tippee toed up the stairs and when I was quietly ambling past Bobby's bedroom, I saw him fast asleep. I had a gutsy urge to want to grab his dirty sock from the floor to stuff it into his gaping mouth, but I dared not for fear Grandmother would think bad of me.

Grandmother's door was ajar enough so I could see as she carried clothes from her trunk to the dresser. Without her seeing me, I wondered how she knew I was there when she said, "Good morning, my dear. Won't you come in?"

I then took two steps in. She sat down on her bed and beckoned for me to join her. As I sat beside her she wrapped a warm arm about my waist and I then noticed how nice she smelled of sweet lilacs. When she asked about my friends I played with, I told her all about them. Then, she put a strange question to me. "If you had a dime, what would you buy with it?"

I was puzzled; I had to think hard. Then a vision of a red shiny pop machine became the focus of my thought, and I blurted out, "I could buy a bottle of pop!"

Grandmother replied, "Well, I say, why not?" Then she uttered, "Oh, what the young can eat and drink." Her wrinkled hand slipped into the pocket of her dress and when she pulled it out, she had a dime she let drop onto my hand. "Now you can buy that bottle of pop."

I hesitated, wondering why she was being so kind and when we exchanged smiles, I thanked her very much for my shiny dime. When she said she better get back to her unpacking, I slipped off the bed so I could get back to my bedroom to get dressed.

I saw Mother coming out of the bathroom and told her, "I will be back!" I ran out the door and headed up the street for Gruder's garage.

The birds were awake, too, and chirping merrily. As I stood in front of the window at Gruder's garage, I could see it was dark inside. While deciding to wait or come back, light flowed in from a back door that had opened.

It was Mr. Gruder. He was whistling a merry tune as he moved about flipping on the lights. Then, searching for the right key from his keychain to unlock the door, he saw me looking in. When the door was unlocked, he greeted me in a lively tone, "Good morning, young lady, how can I help you?"

To act like a lady, I strutted up to the door and I said, "I have come to buy a bottle of pop."

He gave a slight bow as he beckoned me in with a swoop of his arm and a cheery voice, "Young lady, come in and help yourself."

As I stood looking at the red shiny pop machine, Mr. Gruder realized I did not know how to work it. He showed me where the slot was to slip my dime in, then he stood by and once he heard my dime go plink when hitting other dimes, he lifted the heavy door on top. I rolled up on my toes, looked in at the selection and made my request, "I will take a gwape soda, please." After Mr. Gruder removed the bottle from the icy water, he gave it a shake causing cold droplets to fly into my face! My response to the shock shocked Mr. Gruder, too, and we laughed! He then pointed to the cap removal gadget. When I snapped the cap off it dropped into a box that was so full it rolled off and across the floor.

After I got it back, Mr. Gruder asked, "Would you like that box of caps?" I was so surprised over his kindness I lit up with a smile as Mr. Gruder actually picked the box up and handed it to me. Mr. Gruder then said, "It has been a pleasure to have had your business, come back again someday, young lady." I gave a nod that I would, then strutted out the door.

With my box of caps secured by one arm, I had my other hand free to sip the good taste of grape soda while strolling slowly along. Once I was in my yard I noticed a hobo sitting on the front step. I was not supposed to talk to hobos. In taking the sidewalk to the back porch, I could avoid him, but

I spun too fast causing my box of caps to tip and many flew out of the box! The hobo hopped off the step to help me pick them up, even those that had rolled under the peony bush that was loaded with ants. He had been kind and I smiled, and he smiled at me.

I set my second bottle beside the first bottle in the wash porch, then I hightailed it to my bedroom with my box of caps. On the floor of my closet, I took three out of the box and sealed them on my T-shirt with the corks I had peeled away from the caps. Then I shoved the box way back in my closet to hide them from Bobby.

After breakfast, I grabbed my two bottles and took off for Julia's house. As we were leaving to go to Kathleen's, Julia grabbed my arm to pull me back, startling me! She had seen mean Frankie coming out of his grandmother's house headed for the outhouse. Once he was inside, we ran fast to the tracks to be safe from him.

At Kathleen and Sonny's, with also Bubber and Betsy, we were all set for our new money making adventure. With my two bottles and six from the others, we had to collect a lot more. Sonny pulled the red wagon and after knocking on doors, we'd collected a total of fifteen bottles.

When Bubber said that was not enough for us to go to the movie, he had to explain what his mother told him, "For all six of us to go to the movie that costs twelve cents each, we have to collect thirty-six bottles."

To find out how many more bottles we needed, Betsy found a stick and made thirty-six lines in the dirt like they were bottles. Recounting the same lines to fifteen, she wiped them away. Starting with number one, we counted the lines left and then we knew: we had twenty-one more bottles to collect.

We returned to Kathleen's house to unload what we had. Sonny then remembered the junky yard on the road up to the cemetery and we headed for there where we found eight more bottles.

Again, Betsy drew lines in the dirt and came up with thirteen more bottles that we needed. We had no time to have fun in the cemetery so we shouted to be heard from a distance, "Hi, Mr. Rip! Bye, Mr. Rip!" Then we headed down the rocky road.

The rough road made our bottles do a lot of clinking in the wagon and we had to hold them in place to keep them from breaking. Suddenly, Sonny stopped pulling the wagon and we looked in the direction he was looking, at a pile of empty bottles at the side of the old, gray hermit's shack. This was a very grave, scary situation so we huddled together to discuss how to get to those bottles? Sonny and Bubber, being tough boys, were chosen to do the dreadful job of asking for thirteen bottles.

The four of us girls stood back, trembling, while Sonny and Bubber walked the wooden plank to the broken screen door of the old, gray shack. They knocked, the hermit came, we heard a grunt, the door opened, and the boys went in! Scared and jittery, we did not know what to do, run for help or stay?

Bubber stuck his head out the door and he hollered to us, "Com'on! It's safe."

When reaching the door, we could see that Sonny and Bubber were not tied up. Instead they were sounding excited over things they were looking at so we went in.

The shack was one long room of gray walls and smelled very strong of old cheese. On shelves were objects and when Sonny noticed our puzzled expressions, he let us know, "These are inventions! He made them!"

We were all fascinated over the great assortment of inventions making me wonder, how could such an old, gray hermit have such an imagination? I liked the mouse trap best; it could trap a mouse without even killing it.

Bubber pinched Betsy's arm with a giant tweezers that was for pulling pickles out of a jar. I soon began to like the hermit, who smelled of old cheese, and who grunted lots in response to our interest.

Once we were outdoors again, the gray hermit grunted and grunted while watching us pluck thirteen brown beer bottles from the heap at the side of his shack. The wagon and our arms were full as Sonny carefully pulled the wagon away. We all shouted a final "Goodbye" to our new friend as he grunted and waved "So long" to us.

When we left Kathleen's with each of us carrying our own bag of six bottles, we scurried along the railroad tracks to reach Front Street and Stan's Bar. Stan, looking surprised, held the tavern door open to let us in. "By golly, you kids are really on the ball!"

While walking along the railroad tracks with coins jingling in our pockets, Bubber announced, "Here comes our Uncle Sam." I looked ahead to see "our uncle" who used his long cane to guide himself along the tracks.

This tall and skinny old man had white hair and a white beard; a very good look alike to the real Uncle Sam, the one I did not know about. What I did know was that Bubber made his Uncle Sam, my uncle, and uncle to the others, too, making us all happy! As we passed "our" Uncle Sam, he acknowledged our greetings with his cane pointing at us along with a friendly nod of his head.

When near my house, I dashed away from my friends in a hurry to get home. I had to go to the bathroom real bad!

I darted into the house and past Mother and Grandmother drinking coffee as I moved with speed for the bathroom down the hall.

After I sighed from the relief, I folded the four squares of tissue as taught to do. When lifting myself off the stool, I spied a spider in the bathtub! I ran up the hallway hollering, "Motha, Motha, thewe's a daddy long legs in the bathtub!"

Mother pushed away from the table and as she moved down the hallway, she did a wiggly dance while singing a ditty, "Can't wash daddy long legs down the drain or tomorrow it will rain." Then she sang the ditty again when coming out of the bathroom carrying a wad of tissue in her hand. She took the tissue out the front door and shook the ishy spider off onto the peony bush.

Thinking of spiders made me shiver because I stepped on one once and it made a gruesome popping noise. I remembered, too, when Bobby chased me with a fat, popping spider on the end of a stick, but he could not catch me.

The warm sun the next day filled Lila, Julia and me full of vitality as we left our homes for the coyote farm. We walked along the railroad tracks on the crusty, cinder strewn ground until out of town. The main set of rails took off in another direction and we followed a lone spur that would pass in front of the coyote farm.

There was a sweet smell in the air from the green of early summer and a gentle breeze was making the wild grasses sway as though to a rhythmic sound of a meadow lark.

After walking a good stretch, we could see ahead of us an all-black, awesome looking, monster-like building called the roundhouse. The opening looked like a big mouth that was ready to gobble us up!

When we reached its gaping mouth, what I saw inside was scary: three big, black locomotives that looked so powerfully strong I thought they might charge us if we should walk in. We walked along its outside and when beyond, I looked back into its other gaping mouth at the back of the locomotives. Then, I saw a giant round plate with tracks on it. I knew then that the round plate of tracks turned the locomotives around to head back to town. I gave a hop and a skip having learned all about the roundhouse.

When coming upon the stockyards, there was a hop and a skip in all three of us as we pinched our noses shut while hurrying past the bad smell of cow manure. Far ahead we could see the coyote farm and when approaching the farm house, a boy and a girl came running from the house to greet us. Lila already knew Lola and Carl and after the initial getting acquainted for Julia and me, I asked, "Can we see ya coyotes?"

Carl led the way to a mess of wire pens. The handsome, golden colored coyotes that I had hoped would like me did not seem one bit interested in me or the others. They paced constantly and a sickening sweet smell made a strong instinct tell me, most definitely, not to stick a finger through the wire. Carl wanted to play and hollered for us to follow as he took off down a path. We left the wild animals and ran to catch up to Carl who'd already reached a wooded area down by a creek. The creek had enough water to wade in and after we had enough of that we ran and played until it was time to head back to town.

Standing in front of their farm house and about to say our goodbyes, Lola said, "Wait, I want to show you something." She ran into the house and returned carrying a small box. Nestled in a wad of gray batting in the box were three itty-bitty, pink baby mice.

After Lola explained that their mother got killed in a mousetrap, I could not hold back my motherly compassion and had to ask, "Can I have them?" Lola shoved the box at me as though happy to get rid of the baby mice as Carl laughed while saying, "Hey, they're going to die, you know!"

I cradled the small box in my arms all the way back to town. I said, "Goodbye" first to Julia, then to Lila, and hurried into the house to show Mother my surprise.

I found Mother in her bedroom putting clean linens on the bed and when I showed her what I had she backed up while screaming, "Uff da! Uff da! What do you plan to do with those?"

I sensed what I hadn't expected; she was not happy with my surprise. In a pitiful tone, I answered "But Motha, they don't have a motha, she got kilt in a mousetwap. I hafta be theiw Motha now."

As though she understood, her expression changed as she said, "I see, but it would be kind of you to keep your babies in the wash porch, please?" I nodded an okay, then carried them away.

There was a low shelf in a corner of the porch that I knew would be a good place for my three pink babies. While clearing a spot to put the box on, I felt the presence of Mother. She had in her hand a shoe box with lots of clean white cotton in the bottom for a new clean bed. The mice, each no bigger than the end of my little finger, I rolled over onto my palm and set them down on the new cotton.

Mother took the old box, pinched between two fingers and carried it out the door. When she came back in, she suggested I get my dolly's milk bottle so I could feed them.

I ran to my bedroom and rummaged through stuff on my closet floor until I found my dolly's bottle. Mother warmed a bit of milk and as she filled the bottle for me, I felt a strong sense of togetherness with her helping. I knew I would be a good mother, too.

I sat on the floor in the wash porch with the shoe box on my lap, but feeding my babies was difficult. Their mouths were just tiny slits and each time I put the tip of the bottle's nipple to a slit, a big pool of milk would cover its whole teeny head. I had to then dab the pool away with a wad of cotton each time.

When I had fed all three baby mice and they were sleeping, I cradled the shoe box in my arms as I talked, rocked and sang softly to them, "I love you, 'wock-a-bye baby in the twee top, when the bough bweaks the cwadle will fall, and down will come baby cwadle and all,' but I won't let you fall, nosawee!"

Just then my grandmother walked in and she told me that Mother said I had something to show her. When she saw my baby mice she said, "Nice," then shuffled back into the kitchen.

When Patty saw what I had she patted me on my shoulder. "You're a good mother."

Dumb Bobby said, "Your mice are grossly ugly."

My dad laughed as he patted me on my head when saying, "That's my Tootse."

For two days I gave my three baby mice lots of love with still time left over to play with my friends. The afternoon of the third day, I found all my babies lifeless! Dead! I was shocked and hurt; my emotions created a terrible struggle within me. I did not want it so; I wanted to make them alive again. I became so overwhelmed with sorrow all I could do was cradle the box in my arms and rock back and forth as I cried.

Mother came and sat quietly beside me until she said, "I am sorry. You were a good mother to your babies. But now that they are in heaven with God and their real mother, maybe in time, you can feel happy for them." Mother then left me to be alone in my sorrow.

As the day passed, seeing my babies still in their box, I began to think about what Mother had said. *If they awe in heaven with God then how come I can see them?* I believed they might still be alive, but I touched and all three were very cold and stiff.

Mother returned with a lid to the box and Bobby was right behind her. Bobby asked if he could help me bury the box? For such kindness coming from my brother, I cried more tears, then handed him the covered box to let him do the job in the backyard.

I was sitting in the wash porch feeling very sad when a sudden thought made me run out to the corner of the garden where Bobby was knelt. He had already smoothed a pile of dirt over the box, burying it. I screamed, "Did God get my baby mice?"

Bobby hesitated, then said, "You can sure bet they're in heaven now!" Bobby made me so glad and was so nice as he tied a stem from a leaf around where two twigs joined, making a cross. After he stuck the cross in the ground, I picked a hollyhock flower and laid it down by the cross and the grave became the prettiest grave we'd ever seen.

While still on our knees Bobby said in a perky voice, "Show me your snake!" I was so surprised over his sudden interest I jumped up and ran to the front yard with Bobby following. I searched and searched for my pet snake calling, "Hewe snakey, snakey, hewe snakey, whewe awe you?"

Not finding him, I pouted on the swing which hung from a branch of our cottonwood tree and while my head was drooped, I saw him! My green snake was in the green grass at the base of the tree all curled up, sleeping. I called out to Bobby who was going into the house, "I found him!"

Bobby knelt beside me at the base of the tree and watched as I said to my pet, "Hello, mista snakey, how awe you today?" My sleeping pet lifted its head and waved it about. "See!" I said, "He talked to me."

Bobby had a look of disbelief so I asked my pet another question, "Do you love me?" My pet again lifted his head and waved it about.

Bobby then admitted the snake was my pet, but when Bobby headed for the door I overheard him utter something awful.

I puffed up my chest and I shouted, "I hate you!" I looked down at my green pet all curled up and asked, "You wouldn't have liked eating my baby mice like Bobby said, would you?" My pet lifted his head and waved it about, and that meant, "nope"!

Later that morning, Mother answered the ring of the telephone. She hung up, then called Dad at the garage to tell him the chickens were in at the post office. I tugged at her arm to signal her I wanted to go along to get them. She asked Dad, then said to me, "You must hurry."

I ran out the back door and all the way up the two alleys to the garage where Dad worked. Dad was in a pickup waiting for me and I hopped up and in to join him. As the pickup motored along, I rolled down the window and hung my head out to feel the air moving across my face.

Dad parked in the back of the United States Post Office and we walked around to the front of the important looking building to enter. I was greatly fascinated over its stately look. The walls and floor were made of shiny marble and on one wall was a giant painting. Glancing away from the painting to look about, I saw a poster near the door, a surprise that was bewildering to me. I was seeing for the first time a picture of our Uncle Sam!

But in the picture he was wearing a top hat and pointing his finger at me instead of his cane. As Dad waited his turn at the window, I tugged at his arm to get his attention. "How come his pictcha is thewe?"

Dad explained, "Uncle Sam is wanting men to join the army."

I said, "We see him lots of times when crossing the twacks."

Dad frowned, then seemed to sink into a spell of deep thinking until uttering, "A white goatee, too! By devil, a dead ringer for sure. l will have to let your Mr. Uncle Sam know about this great honor you have bestowed upon him."

I felt so proud! And I knew that our Uncle Sam had to be a "mista" to Dad cuz Dads don't have Uncles, just kids do. Dad's broad grin made me feel so happy, and smart, too, that he'd learned from me about our Uncle Sam's picture being here.

After Dad told John, the postman, what he'd come for, we followed John to a back door. When we entered a large area there was a strong odor of chicken feed and I heard lots of peeping coming from boxes stacked in one corner.

The boxes had little round holes all around and I could see the color of yellow. I stuck a finger in a hole and the little peepers pecked at my finger.

Dad carried one big box of peepers out the door and set it down on the bed of the pickup. Dad looked at me and guessing what I wanted to do, said, "Hop aboard so you can watch over them."

I rode in the bed of the pickup, comforting the tiny yellow balls of fluff that were all peeping. Dad stopped the pickup when we got to the back yard gate. I hopped down to hold the gate open as Dad carried the box through and to the chicken coop.

Mother and Patty and Bobby joined Dad and me in the coop. Then Grandmother came, but she stood outside looking in. Dad left us to return to work.

We lifted the yellow fuzzy babies out of the box to set them on the ground, except the last one, I wanted to hold. I cupped my hands about its little body and held it next to my cheek to feel its softness.

A warm, wet sensation was sensed, and after setting the chickie on the ground, I saw a white glob of poop on my palm. I wiped it off on a weed, then saw Grandmother holding a hanky to her mouth to muffle her chuckle.

Mother made us leave the coop so the chickies could rest. Standing outside, the little peepers, like little yellow balls, all rolled together for warmth, and needed sleep after such an exhausting trip on the train.

It was noon time and I heard the Skiddoo coming! I ran to wave to Mr. Engineer and all on my train. Then I called Kathleen. I told her of the exciting news of getting chickies! I knew if I asked Mother if I could show my friends the chickies she would probably say, "I'd rather you not." When Kathleen arrived, I whispered to her, "We have to sneak to the chicken coop."

Sneaking is fun; if you've made it without being seen, then you've won the game. We left the house by the front door, then snuck around to the backyard and darted from bush to bush until we reached the chicken coop. We made it inside.

When sitting on the ground with the chickies, they pecked at our legs, tickling us. After a short time with the cute, yellow, fuzzy balls, we decided to do something else to pass the afternoon away.

It had been planned that when Kathleen left to go home I had go with her and spend the night. As we left my house we saw ahead between the warehouses a boxcar on the tracks. When we got to the tracks we discovered what we feared, there was a long line of boxcars connected to a locomotive. With a locomotive ready to pull the train we knew what the rule was, we'd have to go way up to the people crossing.

Kathleen and I frowned because we did not want to have to walk that far around to get to the spot straight across from where we stood.

I realized when looking at the locomotive a great distance away that it was not making a ch-ch-ch-ch-ch sound, it was quiet. With it looking like a harmless toy I knew it could not cause us harm. Kathleen and I discussed the situation and knew our problem could be solved if we crawled under the train to get to the other side.

We first looked about and saw no one on our side of the long, great wall of boxcars who would see us, and we forgot to think of anyone being on the other side. To keep from cutting our hands and knees by the cinders, we simply stooped over and shuffled our way under the coupling between two boxcars.

Popping out on the other side two shoes, shiny and black, stood firm at the track. We looked up to see the LAW OF THE RAILROAD! His steely eyes made him look mean, then his thunder roared, "Next time I catch you kids doing this I will CHOP your *heads* off!"

There was such a force of power in the words spoken by him, we stood frightened and shaking. Then Kathleen and I took a hold of each other's hand, and slipped away from the law of the railroad. After a safe distance away, the powerful force of his "CHOP your heads off!" words, caused by us breaking a rule, caused me to feel not well . . . because we now had another thing to worry about . . . our parents finding out. We made a big promise to keep what we did a secret, even from Sonny.

At Kathleen's house her mother was busy cooking supper and she did not ask us about our day. Not even during supper, nor during our chore of clearing the dishes away were we forced into having to remember the bad thing we did. Sonny, Kathleen and I then went out to play with Betsy and Bubber.

In the fading light from the evening sun about to go down, we played our favorite games that we played when I lived on the same side of town. Then a full moon came up, giving us still enough light to play until quite late.

We then heard a call from Kathleen's mother, "Come on in now, kids, bed time."

As I expected, from my memory of the days when I lived close by, I knew Sonny would call back, as he did, "Ah, Mom, it's not that late yet."

I knew from before that it would work and she answered, "Okay, but not for long, you hear!"

With so little time left of the night, and to stay close to home, the five of us squatted on the ground and, believing some frightening thing could be lurking about in the dark, put us in a whispering mood to tell stories.

Although I enjoyed this other memory of being out late at night with my best friends, the drone of storytelling caused my mind to drift away and I shuddered from the return of the forceful words Kathleen and I heard that day, "CHOP your heads off!" When the last call came, "Come in! Now!" I was the first one ready to go in.

On our way to the house with Sonny dragging his feet to make the night last longer, I felt an overwhelming need for sympathy because of our encounter with the law of the railroad. I broke the promise Kathleen and I made; I told Sonny.

Sonny stopped and instead of an expected understanding, he called us, "Dummies!" Then, so bossy like, he put his two cents worth in scolding us, "Doncha see? If that train would have moved, the wheels could have chopped your heads off!"

I spoke up to defend what we did, "But the engine wasn't wunning."

To try and excuse what we did did not cut any ice with Sonny, he was mad!

Kathleen and I became very fearful he'd tell our parents, so in very tearful voices we pleaded, begging and begging until Sonny promised he wouldn't tell on us.

The next morning when awake very early and lying in bed next to Kathleen, I watched the frilly curtains swaying from the morning's fresh air flowing in. A rooster crowed.

Then, a whinny of a human horse was heard and the patter of feet!

Kathleen, whom I thought was asleep, jerked up and pushed me against the wall as the human horse bolted into the bedroom and belly flopped on the bed. A pillow fight ensued until a couple of feathers floated free from a pillow and that caused us to settle down out of fear of getting into trouble.

Sonny was fun again, he was not mad at us like he'd been the night before.

At breakfast, since I was company I got the first fluffy pancake. It was as big as my plate. Then we went outdoors in the warm rays of the sun to play with Bubber and Betsy.

Mostly we played like we used to and when close to noon time, wound our way to the railroad tracks to stand in wait for our train, the 12 o'clock Skiddoo.

After a bite to eat, we decided to hit the trail for the open prairie. When passing the last house we had to do a high spirited run to keep from being stung by humming bees around their beehives.

While strolling along, Betsy pulled a fistful of bubble gum from her pocket to share with each of us. Once our chewed gum was ready to blow bubbles, we tried blowing a bigger bubble than the one that popped.

All but one stopped blowing with Bubber wanting full attention pointing to his bubble thinking he could become the champion of all bubble blowers, and it did grow big as we watched in "awe" until the biggest bubble ever EXPLODED!

Watching Bubber flinch as he picked gum from his nose, hair and eyebrows, we did not laugh, for the same happened to each of us at some time. It hurts!

After crossing the highway we hiked around the dairy farm to come in the back way to the cemetery. We greeted Mr. Rip, then walked about. The boys, this time, helped to steal flowers, bunches, to make the dry ground around the little graves become like a garden of many colors.

After leaving the cemetery we visited with the old, gray hermit to see if he had any new inventions. Although there was nothing new, the old ones were still fascinating, like using the pickle pinchers to pull a pickle out of a pickle jar. It was so easy, and the crunchy pickles were so good.

When our day came to an end, I had a great wish that all my days could be like the days when I lived in our old house, nearer to my old friends. Yet, when tripping across the tracks for home, I was anxious for the next day to come to tell my other friends all about my fun on the other side of the tracks. Telling them the story about Bubber and his bubble, I felt as happens, with Bubber not with us we could laugh about it popping all over his face.

Chapter 3

When I arrived at home after spending the night at Kathleen's, and playing with my best friends, I figured I would find Mother in the kitchen preparing supper, but she was not there. I found her out in the chicken coop with all the baby chickies.

As she held a baby chickie in her hands she had such a worried look on her face, I had to ask, "What's the matta?"

"I don't know, this little chicken is losing its feathers." I grabbed for her wrist and pulled her hands down in order to see. I saw a bald spot on its rump. Mother put the chickie down, then we went into the house.

When sitting around the table at supper time, I became overly stimulated telling what I had done with my friends across the tracks. Mother interrupted to tell me to slow down and chew my food well.

Bobby whispered to me, "You're supposed to chew your food forty times before swallowing."

Patty piped up and corrected him. "Don't you believe him; you have to chew just twenty one times before swallowing."

It was then that my compulsive behavior of counting to twenty one when chewing my food began. I counted to twenty one, then swallowed. When I got to fifteen on my next bite of food, Mother brought up the plight of the little chicken. Grandmother explained that the chick must be a rooster and that other roosters were pecking its feathers off. Becoming serious caused me to lose count of my chews. *Why would a baby woosta peck the feathas off anotha baby woosta?*

With another bite of food I got to six chews when Dad broke the rhythm of my counting when telling Mother, "You'd better bring the chicken into the back porch if the situation gets worse."

I shared a startled look with Patty and Bobby over Dad allowing a pet in the house! Then recalled and thought about my other gran'ma. *Once she had ha chickies in a box by ha stove to keep them wawm, and they had all theiw feathas!*

The next morning when I awoke I heard a lot of peeping and mumbling of voices. I jumped out of bed and found everyone in the wash porch, but not Grandmother. In a box on the floor was a completely bald chickie! It looked naked, and so skinny. It even had a neck! I fell to the floor and cupped my hands about the poor peeping baby. It liked the warmth and stopped peeping.

Patty left and returned with a handful of cotton she stuffed into a corner of the box. I set the chickie in its new bed and it stayed. Dad left to get ready to go to work and Mother returned to the kitchen to fix breakfast. Then, Grandmother shuffled in. Patty and Bobby tried to think of a name for the bald chickie and came up with, "Baldy." Grandmother agreed that it was a good name.

For all to be sitting around the table at the same time on a Saturday morning was unusual. Bobby said, rather seriously, "Geeze, we got up with the chickens just like a farmer would."

Mother sneered; she did not like getting up as early as the chickens.

While counting my chews, I focused on the day ahead, then told everyone, "We git to see Woy Wogas and Twigga today cuz we collected bottles, lots!, to git money fwom Mista Stan at his baw."

The one who seemed to be listening was Dad as he said, "Stan was telling about a prompt delivery of bottles from kids." He laughed as he added, "I should've known who it was."

I liked knowing a grown up Dad knew. I started counting with number one with another bite of food.

Baldy had my full attention the rest of the morning. After lunch it was time to head for the movie theater. I met up with Julia first and feeling happy, we greeted our fellow money making buddies with, "How-de-doo!"

It was noisy and fun inside the theater as we traipsed down the dimly lit aisle to take our seats. Bubber and Sonny separated themselves from Betsy, Julia, Kathleen, and me with two seats between them and us. When the curtain began to pull open, the lights went out and a loud cheer rang out from the young cowboy fans. We watched two comedies, a serial, then the matinee began.

I clapped, too, when Roy Rogers came on the screen singing a cowboy song while riding Trigger, his horse. I really clapped and hollered, too, when later, Roy Rogers, the good cowboy caught the bad cowboys. When Roy Rogers sang to the pretty lady, I did not boo like the boys did and I was really glad he did not kiss the pretty lady or the boys would have hissed! Boys don't like that stuff. Trigger was a smart horse; he counted in the dirt with his hoof to show off to the pretty lady, it was so exciting I clapped, too! The End.

Leaving the theater, we hit the trail along the tracks to get home. Our Uncle Sam, letting the tracks be his guide to town, met us with his cane pointing at us as a greeting.

That reminded me of his finger pointing at me in the post office and I said to my friends, "I saw his pictcha!"

Kathleen said, "You did!" And while Sonny had his mind on being a good cowboy, Bubber "frowned" as though not believing me!

I figured he hadn't seen the picture yet so I explained, "At the post office! I did!"

Bubber curtly replied, "No you didn't!"

I said back, "I did too see his pictcha thewe! Just ask my dad!"

Bubber repeated, "Not our Uncle Sam! You didn't see him in our post office!"

Sonny heard just enough to now want to be a soldier, and he shouted, "Hut-two-three-four! Uncle Sam is wanting men to join the army!"

I perked up saying, "My dad said that too! See Bubba, Sonny believes me!"

The strutting soldier, when noticing Bubber glaring at him with a mean look, stopped with a, "Whoa!" Like a cowboy, and baffled, he asked Bubber, "Why are you mad at me?"

Bubber kicked at the cinders as he snapped at Sonny, "Shit-o-dear! Ol' poopy-doopy pants was talking about our Uncle Sam we just passed!"

The last heard when leaving my friends at the tracks was Betsy scolding her brother, "You cussed!" And Julia scolding, too, with a, "Shame-Shame!" Sonny went silent looking "kooky."

On the step of our house was a hobo eating a sandwich. I avoided him by going around the house to enter through the wash porch. Baldy was fast asleep in his box.

When entering the kitchen Mother saw me and suggested that I take my bath. Not wanting to take a bath and feeling stirred up from Bubber's frenzy about our Uncle Sam, I told her, "That hobo needs a bath moe than me!"

When Mother said, "Git!" I took off for the bathroom. When hearing her expected message, "And don't waste the water!" I knew what she meant, as times before she would say, someday there will be no more water in the ground if we waste it.

In the bathroom, before getting into the bathtub, I made sure there was no daddy longlegs wiggling around. I plugged the drain hole, sat down, and turned the faucet on. When the warm water just about covered my legs, turned it off. Not using so much water made my bath go faster, and knowing my dad would soon be home from work and take his usual after work bath, I felt glad I had saved enough water in the ground for him.

Lila and I watched from a hidden spot, a new family move into Osterberg's apartments. A boy, a little bigger than us, was helping his mother and father. His name was Howard. We heard his mother call him that.

Our curiosity over the new boy almost got Lila and me into trouble with Mrs. Oister, the battle axe. We planned playing knock on doors and run so we could knock on the new kids door just for fun. What Lila and I did not know was that the new kid was up to our game. He'd caught us sneaking up the stairs and overheard us giggling over knocking on his door.

After our knocks and flying down the back steps and to the old heap, we discovered the new kid, Howard, was right behind us!

Having realized we got caught, we were shocked over more than just him! He did not understand the trouble about to appear at the upper door.

Lila grabbed his arm and pulled him down and with our fingers to our lips, he understood to be quiet. Just then we heard the expected bark, "You kids stop that; you just got me up from a nap!"

It was a nice way to get acquainted with our new friend, Howie. That was the name he wanted us to call him. I had to show Howie my pet snake, but my pet seemed bothered and it slithered away to hide under the peony bush, I guessed, because it was so very hot.

We hadn't noticed a big, black cloud rolling over us and when we were about to show Howie our neighborhood, heavy drops of rain fell so hard they popped when hitting the hot sidewalk.

We ran for shelter into the old, rusty heap in the alleyway that had hidden us from Mrs. Oister. It had a roof, no tires, and all but the front and back windows were broken out, yet it protected us from the heavy drops hitting the hot metal that caused steam to rise up.

Howie sat behind the steering wheel and roared like a motor: "Brrrruuuummmmm-Brrrrruuuuummmmm." He took us to the town he left way back down the road and we got to meet all his friends he knew best. I especially liked Andy.

Lila then had to have her turn. She got behind the wheel and gave it a good spin taking us on a wild ride, but when she did not get to where she was going, I insisted on having my turn!

I took us on the only road I knew, to my gran'parents house in the country. I drove and I drove until the humid air and patter of rain made me fall into a sleepy mood. No one asked if they could take over; the other two were also mesmerized by the falling rain.

Then, a loud, CURRRACK!!! scared us out of our wits! We heard someone running and quickly turned to see before the someone disappeared.

I screamed, "Fwankie!" He'd set off a firecracker under the old heap.

Howie yelled, "Who's Fwankie?"

I snapped, "You don't know Fwankie?"

He yelped, "I just moved here!"

Lila shrieked, "He's mean! We don't like him!"

Howie laughed and acted so sensible when he let us know, "There's no mean kid I'm afraid of."

So I let him know, being sensible myself, "Becuz ya a boy! We awe gawls!" The black cloud had floated away and we left the cozy, old heap to show Howie more of what we thought he should know.

Early morning of the Fourth of July, I saw Dad coming in a black car and ran to the curb just as the car pulled up. We were all going to our gran'parents in the country to visit them, all except my other grandmother, she was away visiting my Aunt Margaret.

After Dad got out of the black car, he walked around to the rear to unlatch a heavy iron grate, then eased it down. Setting on the boulevard was a big washtub. Dad placed it on the iron grate and secured it with a rope.

I hopped aboard in the front seat with Dad and we drove around the corner to the icehouse. It'd been a busy morning for the iceman and he was ready with his giant pinchers to lift a block of ice and set it in the tub. Back at the house, Mother now had pop, beer and watermelon setting on the boulevard. Once all was packed around the chunk of ice in the tub, Dad wrapped a heavy blanket over it and tied it down.

When we were about to leave, Patty and Bobby pulled a trick on me. They called me into the house saying I forgot something. I did not know what it could be as I had not forgotten my box of clothes. When I ran into the house, Patty and Bobby ran out and jumped into the car to sit next to the windows and I got stuck in the middle, over the hump in the floor!

Although I pouted, the middle was best for me; the hump held my knees up making it easier holding my box of clothes on my lap. I had plans to stay a whole week at my gran'parents, but the others had to return home at the end of the day.

After many miles of seeing nothing but the tops of telephone poles from the middle, I pushed forward with my elbows on the front seat to see more out the front window. Yet, the harsh horsehair seat caused my elbows to burn so I sat back. I folded my arms over my box and I gave Bobby a dirty look; he deserved it making me sit in the middle! He grinned a dumb smirk making me so mad.

When passing a little town, Mother said, "Don't blink or you will miss it." Then the car turned off the smooth pavement onto a gravel road. The ping-ping of rocks hitting the car underneath had kind of a pit-a-pat musical beat as we passed flowing fields of grain.

A grove of trees far ahead marked where a farm was. We passed it, then came upon a horse on the other side of a long fence line.

I jabbed Bobby in his ribs as a signal to roll down his window. I pushed over the top of Bobby causing him to groan, as I yelled, "Hi, haasey-haasey!"

The horse picked its head up, perked up his ears, and picked up his legs to race neck and neck with the car. It was breathtaking watching the majestic black beauty running so free with its tail and mane flowing in the wind. Then it slowed and stopped when the fence line came to an end.

Bobby groaned again when I pushed away from him to scoot up on my knees to look behind the car to get a last look at the beautiful horse, but I could not see through the rolling dirt being kicked up by the car.

The fields of grain rolled by and by then Mother said, "There's the halfway mark."

I knew the church was the halfway mark and pushed forward to see the little white church with its face and hat. The door was its nose, the steps its mouth, the windows its eyes, and the steeple its top hat. I sang a ditty with my fingers intertwined, "Hewe's the chuch, hewe's the steeple, open the da and hewe's the people." I wiggled my people under Bobby's nose and he slapped my hands to make my church fall apart.

Patty then said her piece, "Sit Still!" I did, for a while.

The flowing fields of grain rolled by. Flowed, and rolled by, flowed, and rolled by making me have to turn my head away; I was getting sick. I rested my cheek against the harsh horsehair seat and sat motionless. Then, a smell from the horsehair made me more sick. I swallowed and swallowed to try and keep down what was wanting to come up. The car began to slow to come to stop. Mother knew with me being so quiet that I was getting car sick.

When the car stopped Bobby bolted out screaming, "Don't you dare puke on me!"

Mother walked with me around and around the car until the fresh air cleared my head of its motion sickness. I then got to crawl in the front seat between Mom and Dad.

My stomach was made to feel much better with the sweet gum Mother had given me, and I got to see a whole lot more from the front seat.

In one corner of the sky dark streaks were coming down and Dad made the comment, "Looks like Harchanko's getting rain."

I knew what he was talking about; I, too, could see the streaks and was glad we were not going in that direction. A whirlwind in a field of all sod caught my attention to watch until it whirled away to nothing.

Then Patty pointed to what she saw, "There's the Melon farm." When I saw, too, the trees around their farm, that meant it was not far to the store and house of our gran'parent's.

When the car made a sharp right turn then motored over a small hill we could see my gran'parent's place. I Knew what to do and pushed forward to get ready to wave when close enough to see Gran'ma at her kitchen window watching for us.

Ahead, on one corner of a crossroads in the road, was our gran'parent's house and store all under the same roof. Next to Gran'pa's store was the large one room brick schoolhouse. On another corner was the big Penner farm, and on the other corner was the blacksmith shop and a house. The last corner was all a wheat field like the rest of the countryside.

I saw my gran'ma and waved and waved until I could no longer see her when Dad pulled up to the crossroads to turn. To keep the dust down Dad eased the car up to the door of the store as our gran'parents were coming out the door to greet us.

Gran'ma, her dark gray hair pulled back in a bun, was wearing a bibbed apron, and Gran'pa, with his thin white hair, large belly, cigar in his hand, wore a friendly smile.

When the car stopped, I scrambled over the top of Patty to be the first out. I wrapped my arms around Gran'ma who smelled so nice of sugar and cinnamon. She asked, "Vell, how vas da vide?"

I answered, "Fine!"

Gran'pa put his cigar in his mouth, and with a warm hand he held mine as he said, "Yup," and with his other hand patted me on my head as he repeated, "Yup."

The bell over the door rang "ding-a-ling" as we entered the store. We then passed the shelves of bread to reach Gran'pa's very important United States Post Office, and with a curtain pushed aside, entered Gran'ma's kitchen.

I dipped the dipper into the water bucket for a drink, then reached high into Gran'ma's cupboard for a cookie I knew would be there. I went from the kitchen into the living room, then through a doorway into the bedroom where I knew Felix, their cat, would be. He was curled up in a ball on the bed. Felix could be very mean and when his ears went back I stopped petting him.

I opened another door in the bedroom and like going in a circle, was again in Gran'pa's very important post office. He had lots of important papers and books stacked in wooden crates along the wall and his desk had a chair that could spin around and around.

A bigger, overstuffed leather chair, Gran'pa's favorite, was part of his office, too. I saw in his trash box lots of cigarette rolling papers. They were still in their packets which meant they were brand new! I wondered if I dared ask Gran'pa if I could have them, but I wouldn't want him to think I wanted them for rolling cigarettes.

I felt a sudden urge to go to the bathroom and when beating it out the kitchen door, bumped into Bobby coming in from the outhouse. I dashed along the wooden plank making the clucking chickens in my path scatter. Once inside and done, I looked down both holes to check on what was below.

When leaving the outhouse I saw Bobby at the pump pumping the handle to fill the drinking pail for Gran'ma. Across the way to the Penner farm, I could see Mrs. Penner at her kitchen window. I waved, she waved, then she disappeared from her window.

Gran'ma was busy at her stove fixing food for us. Dad and Gran'pa were sitting in the post office talking and smoking cigars. Mother and Patty were browsing around in the store, and I joined them.

The store was full of lots of things; hanging from the ceiling over tables were saws, rope, lanterns, buckets, and other farm items. Under the tables were kegs filled with different sized nails. On the tables were pots and pans, and lots more household utensils. Wooden crates stacked along two walls were filled with small farm tools, work gloves, axle grease, salve for animals, Band-Aids, matches, and more.

I watched as Mother thumbed through fancy ladies things in a showcase. She found a hanky she liked, it was so pretty and delicate you could never use it to wipe a wet nose.

Underneath the showcase, Gran'ma told me once what was hidden there in boxes; ladies underwear, stockings, and girdles. Next was where the cash register was at, and best of all, boxes of candy.

Mother left to help Gran'ma in the kitchen and Patty followed her. I stayed to play store lady. From the many boxes of candy, I sold lots and lots, to me! Each time I dropped a candy bar in a paper sack I punched a key down on the cash register to see the money sign pop up in the little window.

Behind the sales counter and me there were more shelves with soap, flour, and that kind of stuff; there was a cooler room for smoked meats, grandma's eggs, and now our full washtub.

"Soups on!" was a signal from Mother, it was time to eat. After I placed my full sack of candy where it would be safe, I joined the others at a table set up in the living room.

Once seated, Gran'ma composed herself, and while in silent prayer, Dad said, "Pass the potatoes."

Patty and Bobby wanted to giggle, but did not dare.

Gran'ma lifted the platter of fried chicken to pass to me and I felt very special when she said, "Da chicken leg iss va you."

When we were all done eating, Dad retired to the bedroom for a nap and Felix took off for outside. Gran'pa went to his office and after hearing the crackle of his leather chair, a strong smell of cigar smoke drifted into Gran'ma's kitchen. When the tea kettle on the stove made a loud whistle, the hot water was ready for Gran'ma and Mother to do the dishes.

Patty, Bobby and I needed exercise and we headed for the school playground. I couldn't keep up in a race with them so I slowed to a walk.

The wind blowing across the prairie was singing a ghostly sound, not a sound to be afraid of for it made me feel like the horse that day, running so free. Though I had lost the race to the playground, I picked up my pace to grab a swing.

I pumped so hard on the swing my feet touched the sky and I took many trips down the slide. Bobby and I teeter-tottered until Bobby jumped off making my end plop very hard to the ground making me bite my lip! I chased him up the steps of the schoolhouse and all the way inside where Patty'd already gone.

Standing in the cloakroom, I forgot about Bobby as I smelled chalk, books, and polish. In the classroom our echoes gave the room an interesting sound, and I snooped to learn what school was all about.

When I had reached a piano in a corner, I sat and played as though I knew how; plinkety-plink, plinkety-plink, plink-plink. Bobby joined me and with his fist he went boomety-boomety, boom-boom! boom-boom! making me so mad, I punched him on his arm! Then I ran pell-mell out of the schoolhouse and back to Gran'ma's.

Bobby caught up, then Patty, and Gran'ma said, "Vell, da vatermelon iss veady to eat." Mother and Gran'ma joined the three of us eating watermelon on the back steps. It was a nice time.

The chickens scurried around to peck up each black seed we spit on the ground. When done, we set the rinds on the ground and waited for Bobby to get the sparklers. Bobby had to leave his firecrackers home knowing Gran'ma would say, "Dat vould scare my chickens so day vould not lay eggs."

Bobby gave me my share of sparklers and I stuck them into a watermelon rind. Once lit, we oh'd and ah'd until the spitter and the sputter petered out with the last spark, *ftttt!*

It was later in the day and with no wind on the prairie, it was quiet. In the sky were white puffs of clouds and we played a game finding an elephant, a bird, and George Washington in the clouds! Then Dad came to the door and said, "Last trip to the outhouse before we have to go."

The sun was casting a golden glow across the land all the way to the horizon and that caused a melancholy, lonesome feeling in me. I knew I had time to change my mind and go home with my family, but that was just a passing thought, I really wanted to stay.

My dad, mother, sister and brother got into the car to drive away as I stood close to my gran'ma and gran'pa. Then I ran to the edge of the store to keep waving to the dark figures waving back until the car disappeared over the hill.

Gran'pa moved his cigar to the other side of his mouth and uttered, "Yup."

Gran'ma said, "Vell, dey are gone." The ding-a-ling of the bell "velcomed" us back into the store.

I had not forgotten the packets of cigarette rolling papers in the trash box. I asked Gran'pa if I could have them. He said, "Yup, yup, take all you want, yup."

I grabbed a sack and I filled it, leaving the rest to be burned. I hadn't figured out yet what I could do with the brand new packets as I placed the sack next to my sack of candy.

I found Gran'ma outside putting her chickens to bed, then followed her around the store sprinkling sweeping compound over the wooden floor. She locked the door of the store and while Gran'pa finished his important work at his desk, I followed Gran'ma to the living room. She picked up her crocheting and I watched her crochet in the light from the lantern hanging from the ceiling.

When it became very dark outside, it was time for bed. Gran'ma made a bed for me on the studio couch in the living room. After I crawled in, Gran'pa reached up and turned the knob on the lantern. I watched as the glow in the lantern faded to dim, then went out.

The rooster woke me early in the morning, "Cock-a-doodle-doo! Cock-a-doodle-doo!" From outside, I heard the hens clucking and Gran'ma talking to them.

I jumped up and stood at a window above the studio couch to look out. When seeing the golden glow across the wheat fields from the rising sun, I was filled with a peaceful feeling, different from the setting sun the night before.

I saw Gran'ma with her chickens, then I heard the squeak of Gran'pa's chair at his desk and I knew he was up, too!

I hopped from the bed to the floor, then looked in at Gran'pa from the kitchen door. I said, "Good maaning, Gwan'pa."

He cleared his throat, peered over the rim of his round glasses and said, "Yup, it is a good morning, Tootse."

Then outside I smelled the goodness of fresh clean air as I said to Gran'ma, "Good maaning, Gwan'ma."

With her hens clucking about her feet, she asked, "Did you sleep vell?"

I answered, "Shah did." On my way to the outhouse I hopped from heel to toe on the wooden plank to avoid the many white and black globs Mother called "Calling cards." The globs were just plain chicken poop and I was barefoot!

On my way back from the outhouse I waved to Mrs. Penner across the way, then went inside to get dressed to help Gran'ma in the store. I held the dustpan while she swept the mixture of sweeping compound and dirt into it, then dumped it into Gran'pa's trash box.

At the breakfast table, there was no rush to get going with no place to go and I ate slow enough to count my chewing twenty one times each time I took a bite of food.

After the dishes were washed and put away, I was ready to help Gran'ma by playing a store lady like her. Before we could get past the curtain and into the store the ding-a-ling of the bell announced a customer had come in. I rushed in to see Punky with his dad. Punky was a farm boy my age who wore cowboy boots.

The two had come to pick up the mail that had piled up in their postal box. Punky's dad said to me, "I see you've come all the way up from the big city to visit us farm folks."

I did not like anyone calling me a city kid; at my gran'parents I wanted to be a farm kid just like Punky. As Gran'ma filled a small order and the big men talked about the weather, Punky and I stood staring at each other.

When they left, I was sad to see Punky go, but the bell rang again with Punky coming back in.

He asked if I could go back to their farm with them? Gran'ma said, "Dat vould be nice."

Punky and I got to ride on the running boards of his dad's farm truck. Punky had a tight grip on his side of the cab and I had a tight grip on the post to the window on my side.

As the truck picked up speed to reach a rumbling roll, I felt the ride to be exhilarating with my body pushing through a blast of warm, dry wind. Then we rolled through a flying path of grasshoppers so big they smacked hard against our skin! I had to keep my mouth and eyes closed tight until the truck slowed to turn on the road to their farm. As the truck approached the barn then stopped, a big cloud of dust engulfed us. I hopped down from the running board excited to be a real farm kid for the day.

Punky had to finish his morning chore of picking rock, with me helping. Following Punky through a pasture of soft sod, my shoes filled up with dirt, and I knew then why farm people wore cowboy boots.

When we reached the hired hand in the tractor that was pulling a wagon, I sat down and emptied my shoes. In the field there were lots of rocks of all sizes, and I, feeling like a strong farm kid, picked up the big ones. Choosing the size was easy, it was struggling to lift them up and onto the wagon that was hard!

When my arms began to ache I became a smarter farm kid like Punky by picking up the smaller rocks. It was a dirty job and lots of work, but as the wagon filled up with rocks I felt proud that I helped.

Our chore had come to an end when the hired hand said, "Kids, let's call it quits and go eat lunch." I got to ride on the tractor all the way to the farm house.

We washed, ate lunch, then Punky had a 4-H project he wanted to show me. We ran from the house to a pen to see the pig Punky was raising. Punky said before going in the pen, "We have to beware of my pig for she can be very mean if she wants to be."

After climbing over the wooden enclosure, I took his warning seriously; I stood ready to climb back over in case the pig got mean. Punky said her name was "Lady Grace." He called, "Come Lady Grace, come Lady Grace."

The sleeping duchess lifted her immense body up and lumbered towards us. She was nice; she let us pet and hug her as she snorted and rubbed against us. Punky was happy I liked his pig, and so surprised me when he asked, "Can you go to our 4-H meeting day after tomorrow?"

A 4-H meeting was important stuff for a farm kid, and I, a city kid, asked to be a 4-H member for one day, my mind exploded with great honor and I yelped, "Yes!" Then asked, "Will you take Lady Gwace?"

He said, "No, but I have to give a report on her." Lady Grace must have felt she had enough attention; she lumbered away snorting and snorting. Then Punky full of spunk, cried out, "Come on! Let's climb the windmill."

As we approached the huge structure the great noise it created mixed my feelings; I felt weak, yet strong. It was not at all like a windmill built from tinker toys where a gentle blow of one's breath made it work, the power of wind was what made this giant work as it rotated its blades that made a pipe go up and down inside another pipe; the noise it created was a loud, CLANG-CLANG!

I got behind Punky climbing a ladder to a wooden platform halfway up. We were in the blue sky and could see across the flat prairie to the ends of the earth.

I felt Punky sink to sit down, and I did the same. He crossed his legs, I did, too. And up so high with the clean air blowing across my face made me feel like a bird soaring so free over all I could see. Then Punky, in a whisper, said, "I do this lots of times to dream of faraway places seen in picture books."

After a pause Punky asked, "Have you ever seen the Statue of Liberty?"

I answered, "Once, in Patty's school book."

Punky said, "My dad told me it is higher than this windmill and you can climb all the way up to the top, way inside the torch over her head." My heart leaped a scary beat thinking of being higher than we were. Then he added more, "When you stand inside the torch, my dad said, you can see New York City. Over there!"

I looked, and saw a golden wheat field. Then, with a swipe of his arm taking in the whole farm, he said, "You can see the ocean, too, and ships!" I tried hard to imagine all of this.

Then when telling how he was going to sail on a whaling ship someday, I then felt smart, and told him,"My gwan'pa did that."

Punky sucked in a surprised "gasp" to listen as I added, "He was on a whaling ship lotsa times, he told my dad that."

Punky asked, "Did he ever get a whale?" Not knowing, I simply answered with a shrug.

Punky's eyes then took on a fixed gaze, looking out into the sea of blue, and with his hands cupped around his mouth, he hollered, "Ahoy, shipmates! Seen any whales?"

As though the shipmate said, "Yes," Spunky stood up and threw an imaginary fishing line over the edge of his imaginary whaling ship. He then shouted, "I got my whale!"

While pulling his great whale aboard his face twisted in pain when straining so hard, and as he grunted while pulling, I felt I, too, wanted to grunt and groan. When he yelled, "Get back! Get Back!" I did, to the ladder, just in time, with no room left with the giant whale aboard I had to go down to the ground. Punky followed with his toil at sea all over.

I learned Punky had lots of picture books. When we climbed the big haystack, we became flying airplanes in a war. We stretched our arms out as wings and with our motor mouths revved to a roar, we ducked, then soared to keep from getting hit. But once hit, our planes went into a dive as we slid down the haystack to the ground. That was great! I liked playing war just so we could slide down the haystack and a few times more until Punky decided our planes were plumb out of gas.

We ran for the inside of the barn. Punky said while pounding his chest, "Me! Tarzan; you, Jane!" There was a rope hanging from the hayloft and Tarzan and Jane played like the hayloft was a tree.

When swinging on the rope, we dropped onto a pile of straw while bellowing our cries just like Tarzan, "Ah ~ ah ~ ah ~ ah ~ ah." We did it again and again until my hands became so sore I had to stop playing and I dropped to the straw below.

From being such a busy farm kid, I plopped back on the straw for a rest; Punky did too. The comfort felt was great, though made me sleepy.

I heard then the clanging of a cow bell and the barking of a farm dog bringing the cows home. Coming home, coming home, barking, clanging, barking, clanging, the cows are coming, the day was over, and I had to pick myself up and go home, too.

That first day with Punky was fun. I liked being a farm kid, especially when I went to the 4-H meeting with him. All the kids treated me like I was a real farm kid, except I was the only one not wearing cowboys boots.

Soon my week of fun with my gran'parents was almost over. How I was getting home turned out to be a big surprise! When the bread man came in with his delivery of fresh bread, I overheard Gran'ma ask him, "Vhen next time you come vill you give her a vide?"

When he answered, "Yes," Gran'ma said, "I vill give her money and she vill vide the Skiddoo the vest of her vay home."

My heart jumped with joy. I had made a wish a long time ago when standing at the tracks, to someday take a ride on the Skiddoo—the next day my wish would be coming true!

In bed, in the dark, all snuggled in my blankets I was thinking good thoughts of what my train ride would be like. My imagination grew and showed me a picture of what I wanted to have happen.

I would be on the Skiddoo, the only passenger, and Mr. Engineer would come to take me by my hand to ride with him in his mighty engine and let me pull the cord to make the Skiddoo's whistle go, Whoooooo-ah! Whooo-oooah! *When I see my friends I will wave so they will see me! They won't believe and I will have to shout, "It's me! It's me!" Then I will pull the cord, again, to whoo whoo the whistle. Boy, oh, boy are they going to be surprised!*

My imagination gave me such pleasure, I retraced every mile of my train ride so I could see the surprised looks on the faces of my friends. My fun ended when my train stopped at a place called slumberland.

In the morning, after helping Gran'ma feed the chickens, I helped to sweep the floor in the store. Then I sat in Gran'pa's leather chair waiting for the bread man.

At my feet was my box of clothes and two paper sacks, one filled with candy bars and the other with the packets of cigarette rolling papers. I thought about my days with my gran'parents. When I played "store lady" Gran'ma had let me ring the money up in the cash register and had let me give the change back.

Gran'pa had given me a job stuffing mail into the post boxes and one day when he went someplace, I played with his typewriter as Gran'ma watched. When Gran'ma made her doughnuts, I got lots of doughnut holes. Gran'ma read to me from her Bible and she taught me how to crochet.

I heard the bread truck and jumped off the chair to be ready. After the fresh bread was delivered, we were on our way. I waved back at my gran'parents until I could no longer see them. The truck made a sharp turn and we were on the stretch of gravel road headed for the tiny town where the Skiddoo would be waiting for me.

The bread man did not talk much, nor did I, and the trip seemed to be taking so long I truly believed my train came and left without me.

When the tiny town came into view, I bounced forward to see if I could see the Skiddoo. I could not; we were still too far away. I felt so very worried, but when we were on the depot road the bread man said, "I see you will be the first one here."

That meant I was early!

The bread man was very kind to help me with my box while I carried my sacks, and kind, too, when waiting to make sure I got my ticket. Then he left.

I sat on the wooden bench on the wooden platform with my box and sacks at my feet. I held my ticket tightly in my hand out of fear it could drop through the cracks in the boards at my feet. If I lost it, I knew I could not ride on my train.

A farm truck pulled up to the platform and I watched as the farmer unloaded milk cans to be picked up by the Skiddoo. A man appeared and stepped up to the office window to buy a ticket, two more people came behind him, and then four more. With the space filling up with mostly men, and two ladies, people I did not know, I did not want to be noticed so I sat perfectly still.

When hearing a whistle blow, though it seemed far away, I knew it was the Skiddoo! Then clickedy-clack-clickedy-clack-clickedy-clack, and another, Whoooooah! Whoooooah! it came into view. As the mighty engine eased up to the platform it let go of a long, chuuuuuuuuuuuuuuu, while spitting white smoke in the air.

As the mighty engine eased up to the platform, the squeal of brakes brought its peak of power down to a purr. The call then came, "All aboard! All aboard!"

I felt so very small and not important when being smothered by the people around me, all pushing me along. I did not think of them as people me and my friends would wave to, nor did I think the engineer would see me. I forgot all thought of this train being "my train."

At the steps the train man in blue called me, "Young lassie." I had seen him many times, but now he seemed like a stranger as he helped me up the steep steps. Standing alone at the door of the passenger car with my box and two sacks, I could see the other passengers filling the seats on each side of the long aisle.

A suitcase from behind booted me along, but I could not guess where to sit until I got to the last seat, and there I stepped up from the aisle to sit by the window. I set my two sacks beside me and my box at my feet. My ticket I held tightly in my hand.

I heard a clunk, clunk and I hugged the window to look out and down in time to see the last of the milk cans being heaved aboard, clunk!

The man in blue pushed up the step, waved to the engineer, then jumped up on the train. A chuuuuuuuuuuu sound with, too, the spitting of a white cloud of smoke, the train jerked, jerked and jerked again along with another chuuuuuuuuuuuuu sound, then a ch-ch-ch-ch-ch-ch-ch-ch, chchchchchchchchchch, Whooooooah! Whooooooah! And we were on our way!

I heard, "Ah-hum," and I turned from the window to see the man in blue looking at me. He asked, "Young lassie, do you have a ticket?"

I opened my hand, having forgotten about it. When handing the crumpled ticket to him, he smiled kindly when seeing it. Again, I focused my attention out the window as the train rumbled, rattled and rolled with great speed in the wide open spaces.

Far across the way was the highway where cars looked like toys and the telephone polls like toothpicks. We whistled past the back of a small farm with ground too rocky and dry for cows and sheep, but I clearly saw the goats. Having gone a far stretch, we came upon a creek bed with a trickle of water in it, a small forest of trees lined its bank. Then again we were in the wide open spaces.

I saw the buildings of another farm that belonged to Mrs. Gouge, a lady Sonny and Kathleen knew well. The whistle of the train sounded before we rocked and rolled around a bend. As the train approached where my friends might be, I forgot to look, but once past that spot I looked back, and saw no one at the tracks.

The train then slowed to a ch-ch-ch-ch-ch-ch-ch-ch sound when passing my house, then it spit out a puff of white smoke with its last chuuuuuuuuuuuuuuu sound as the final Whooooooah! Whooooooah! was heard. Then the squeal of brakes brought the train from its peak of power to a purr at the depot, my destination.

Stepping down to the aisle, I felt, yet, the motion of the ride in my head, and to get me to move along I was being pushed from behind.

The man in blue at the bottom of the step took my box and handed it to my mother who was waiting for me. Then he put his hands under my arms and lifted me down to the ground with ease.

Mother was in a hurry to get home and she moved me along. I still felt unconnected to our train; I had been a passenger, that is all. Then, after taking a look back at the mighty engine, I began to feel much better knowing I had my friends to tell all about the trip. I hopped along to keep up with my mother.

In the house I found nothing had changed while I was away, except the house smelled spic and span for the ladies who were coming that night to play bridge.

I dropped my box of clothes on my bedroom floor, then hid my candy bars and my packets of cigarette rolling papers. I thought of my pets and skipped out the back door to find Baldy first, but Baldy found me!

Before I had left for my gran'parents, Baldy had grown to be a big, nice rooster with lots of feathers, yet now he was mean! He kept pecking with fury at my feet and I had to do a jig to avoid his sharp beak!

When Mother came out to empty a garbage can she saw what was happening and explained, "You've been gone a week and Baldy now thinks you are a stranger. He will get used to you again."

I did not like Baldy thinking of me as a stranger so I ran to the front yard to find my pet snake. He was asleep under the cottonwood tree and I fell to the ground on my knees and asked, "You wememba me don't you?" He picked up his head and waved it about and that meant yes!

I ran back into the house and called my friends to let them know I was back. Kathleen wouldn't believe me when I told her, "I got to wide on the Skiddoo." I had to say, "I am not a fibba! When you come ova tomowwow you just ask my motha!" I was so glad I had my mother for proof. She will tell my friends, it is true!

Bobby came bounding into the house and he bellowed, "Hey, you're back! Boy, was it peaceful around here." He then snapped his fingers for me to hurry when he asked, "Come on, share some candy."

I ordered him to stay put while I ran to my bedroom. I closed the door, and when Bobby shouted, "Get me an 'Oh, Henry'!" I knew he had been peeking through the keyhole and I called out, "You bugga! You saw!" After I gave him an "Oh, Henry," I plugged the keyhole and I hid my candy, again.

Not long after Mother's ladies came to play bridge, I went to bed. The sound of cards, the murmuring of voices, and gay laughter lulled me to sleep. The next morning the house still had that party look and upon discovering a few cigarette butts in the waste paper basket, an idea popped into my thoughts.

I scooped up the bigger butts and snuck to my bedroom closet; I dropped to my knees to slit each one open. I dumped the tobacco out onto a hanky and tied the ends of the hanky together, then left.

I ate my breakfast and while in the kitchen with no one looking, reached up into the match holder and I dug out a few matches. I took them to my bedroom to leave with the tobacco pouch.

When Julia came to play outside with me, I had an idea. I shared my idea by asking, "You wanna play gwown-up and smoke a weal cigawette?"

Julia liked playing grown up and asked, "You mean you have real cigarettes?"

I answered, "Kind of. We have to woll ah own."

I told her to stay and snuck back into the house to get my stash of secret stuff. As I was leaving, Bobby bolted out the door and in passing us said, "Got something up your sleeves?"

I scowled, wondering if he really knew what we were about to do. He said nothing more as he darted to the tracks, always in a hurry to get to his buddy Billy's place.

Julia and I picked a good spot to hide under the lilac bushes. I dumped the cigarette making stuff out on the skirt of my dress. After we sprinkled tobacco on the papers we started rolling, but it was difficult keeping the tobacco on the paper–much fell out! When we had enough tobacco to make a roll, we licked the paper to make them stay rolled. I picked up tobacco with my tongue and I reacted by spitting, "Pa-tooey! Pa-tooey!"

Before lighting our cigarettes, we made believe we were real genteel ladies. We crossed our legs, and acted highfalutin' when talking big lady talk. "Miss Julia, can I paa you a cup of coffee?"

Julia tipped her head and with eyelashes fluttering, answered, "I really would prefer a cup of tea, my dear. My, but the weather has been nice."

"Yes," I answered, "But I heww it may wain tomowwow." Then, I asked, "Miss Julia, how awe ya child'wen?"

She answered, "My children are fine, thank you, almost grown up now." I handed her a pretend cup of tea and we pretended to sip our tea until we grew tired of pretending.

The time had come to do a real thing–to light our cigarettes. I struck a farmer's match on a rock and the burst of flame was so great I had to hold it away! When lighting our cigarettes, the twisted paper on the end burned red hot! We had to hold the cigarettes away until their flame died to a glow.

It was time to take a puff. Like sucking through a straw, we sucked in a big drag making our throats burn like fire! We coughed so hard Julia thought we were going to die. It was an awful experience! We crushed our creations into the dirt and knew we never wanted to smoke another cigarette ever again!

I pulled Julia into my house and to my bedroom to share a sweet candy bar with her; a second bar made us feel much, much better.

Kathleen came to join us in play. When we told her we smoked real cigarettes, she shamed us and threatened, "I wiww teww your mothers." I shared a candy bar with Kathleen so she'd promise not to tell; splitting a second bar with her sealed her promise. Kathleen opened up with a secret. "The boys are going swimming in the river and cuz it's so hot they're going swimming without their cwoozes on."

Julia piped up with a thought. "Let's go climb the dike and spy on them."

Spying meant we had to be sneaky so as not to get caught. After darting past the junky cars in the alley and reaching the icehouse, we crouched low to let the weeds along the icehouse hide us. The ice truck was gone and we dashed across the road. We scooted to the top of the dike and fell on our bellies. The river below could be seen for a long ways and we searched for the boys down by the riverside. There appeared to be movement in the brush and when two blurry figures jumped out we quickly formed an "O" with a finger and a thumb, yet saw nothing more than a blur as the boys took a giant leap into the cool, cool milky river.

Absorbing too much heat from the hot sun while lying on the rocky dike was sufferable. We slipped down from the dike and went back to the icehouse, where we scraped sawdust around to find chips of ice. To cool our bodies down, we rubbed the first chips on our arms and faces and the second chips we sucked on while walking to the alley.

Once in the alley, our attention was drawn to the sound of a "hum" of voices coming from in front of my house. There were lots of people standing in the street, all looking in the direction of the railroad tracks.

I squeezed between people who showed me their concerned looks, and found my Mother. I tugged at her arm to get her attention, then asked, "What happened?"

She looked at me with a troubled expression and in a grumpy tone spit out, "The old man with a cane got hit by a train. Now get back to the house!"

The only man we three knew with a cane was our Uncle Sam! We were so very saddened; I thought he was dead, but when Kathleen asked, "Did he git kiwwed?" I was not sure if he was dead or just hurt. The message I had gotten from Mother was, "This was no place for kids," so we squeezed through another part of the crowd to get a closer look.

Mrs. Oister near us was in a big sweat over the heat, causing her to say to Howard's mother, "This awful heat must have paralyzed the old man."

Another person said in a disturbed tone, "They claim bits and pieces of him lay all over the tracks." That meant he had to be dead. Sad, again, but curious, we wanted to see more. We moved in closer, but a policeman caught sight of us, and ordered, "Scat, kids.

The awful heat and the accident caused everyone to be in a grouchy mood so we sat on the curb to wait for everyone to leave. This had been the first tragic death we ever heard of, and we became absorbed in thought over blood and guts, so much so, we did not hear Bubber and Sonny creeping up from behind.

When two of us got goosed in our ribs, we jumped! The boys who'd scared us wanted to know what the hubbub was about. The three of us girls rambled on so over what happened, we confused the boys. They thought we were full of nonsense talk. They disappeared into the crowd, but were quick to return. The policeman had sent them back before they found out on their own what happened.

When the last person was seen leaving, we took off at a dead run to find what was left of our Uncle Sam along the tracks. Not finding even a small speck of blood or guts, it was as though nothing had happened.

Bubber, acting disgusted, uttered to Sonny, "Those dippy girls, pro'bly was a dog that got hit!"

The boys ignored our arguments that day, though they had to accept the fact, for we never met our Uncle Sam along the tracks again. And Bubber won about Uncle Sam's picture at the post office, cuz Sonny, the big traitor now, took Bubber's side! I never mentioned our Uncle Sam to them ever again.

Monday was wash day and I talked Mother into letting me help her. I watched as she added soap shavings left over from Bobby's soap carving to the agitating water, then the bluing to the rinse water. The white sheets went in first and as they agitated, I waited to do my job. When ready, Mother pulled out the corner of a sheet and handed it to me.

I knew the wringers were strong enough to pull my arm through and crush it, so I carefully aimed the corner of the sheet to the two spinning wringers and when the wringers grabbed the sheet, I yanked my hand away. After the sheets were done in the first rinse water, I put them through the wringers again to drop into the next tub of rinse water, then into the basket and that was it! I had to help out at the clothesline, too, by keeping Baldy away from Mother's feet.

When the wash was over and Mother was mopping up the wash porch it was lunch time. Hearing the back gate squeak open I looked out to see Dad coming.

What I saw surprised me! I yelled to Mother, "Come see! Huwwy!" What we both saw was Dad carrying Baldy!

When Dad got far enough into the yard, he set Baldy down and when he came in, Mother said, "I see Baldy has taken a liking to you."

Dad said in grumbling words, "Damn old rooster, meets me at the end of the alley every day at noon! How the heck does he know what time it is!?"

I had to tell Patty and Bobby about Dad carrying Baldy, but they wouldn't believe me. Patty told me I had a pipe dream.

When they asked Mother for proof of what I saw she did not want to make a big "to do" about it, so she simply said, "I guess it happened."

I wanted to prove to Patty and Bobby I was right! The next day when the time on the clock was getting close to noon I got them to follow me. We crawled into a shed next to the alleyway in the neighbor's back yard.

There were cracks in the wall for each of us to peek through, but the two, still not believing me, wouldn't bother to watch at their cracks. I had to signal for them to look just in time to see Baldy strutting up the alley to where he stopped at the end to peck at the ground. After a moment or two, Baldy started doing a strutting dance.

We looked up the alleyway and saw Dad crossing the street to reach our alley. The words we heard were very faint, yet clear enough to hear Dad say to Baldy, "Hello, you old rooster."

What followed was a war between Dad and Baldy. As Dad walked, Baldy pecked at Dad's heels, and Dad would shove Baldy away with his shoe, but Baldy strutted back to peck more at Dad's heels. Dad again gave Baldy a push away and again Baldy returned to peck at Dad's heels.

Dad finally gave up and while grumbling a few bad words, bent over and picked up Baldy. Dad tucked Baldy under his arm and as Dad walked, stroking the head of the, "Damn old rooster." The two had made peace with each other.

Bobby was flabbergasted! Bobby, not wanting to be heard by Dad, rolled on his back while gleefully kicking his feet in the air over what he'd seen.

When it was safe to talk, I looked at Patty with a smug expression on my face. "See! I did not dweam of pipes like you said!"

Patty was speechless for a moment, then said, "Dad can never know what we saw today." We had to then make a pact "to keep owa secwet locked away, that owa dad weally, weally did like pets, especially woosters."

Julia and I were going to our first carnival. Waiting outside for Julia and her dad to pick me up, I began to pace up and down the sidewalk while enjoying the sense of pleasure I felt from the warm evening breeze.

It did not take long, though, to become greatly perturbed. Julia had said once, "If you step on a crack you'll break your mother's back," and there were so many cracks in the sidewalk, and believing I could break my mother's back, I stepped up onto a fork in the tree on the boulevard to sit and wait.

As I waited, I wondered about something that caused me to feel nervous. It was kindergarten; it was about to start. Not long ago when playing with my friends on the other side of the tracks, I told Betsy, "Julia and I will be going to kinder-gar-ten togetha cuz she is my fwiend."

I asked Betsy all about kindergarten, again, and later told Julia, "I guess I asked Betsy too much about kin-dergarten, because cwabby Betsy got mad at me."

When the familiar pickup came into view, I hopped down from the tree. Once in the pickup the motor sputtered and metal clattered as we drove up the street and out of town to the fairgrounds. Julia and I jumped with excitement over what we saw out the window. Over the top of a wooden fence we saw the grand sight of colorful lights, lighting up big, big rides!

When the pickup stopped at the gate Julia and I hopped from the running board to the ground, and while racing for the gate, we heard the screams, gay music, and laughter! Inside the fun packed arena, we looked and we listened. In the gaily lit booths, dangling from strings, were lots of dollies dressed in feathers, clay elephants, horses, and clay doggies of all sizes, sailor men, pins and pennants, ashtrays, and balloons. Such a sight!

Men wearing top hats beckoned for all to "Come play the game! Come play the game!" A musical blend of chimes and pipes drew us to a marvelous machine called a merry-go-round. The fancy, colorful horses with eyes of fire were taking little riders up, down and around to the sound of the calliope music.

Julia and I traded our dimes for a ride, then raced for the horse most beautiful to us. When our whirling ride was over we laughed over the dizziness still in our heads. Then we continued on.

A giant ride, too big for the two of us, had our interest. It was called the ferris wheel. The colorful lights and screaming riders went clear up to the sky then back down, up to the sky and back down. Then we walked on until we came to another giant ride. The screaming riders were in swings that went way, way up and way, way out while whirling around and around.

With a crowd of people on the ground waiting their turn, or just watching, we left the ride to mosey along. We weren't far away when our fun of seeing more was interrupted by a great cry of awful screaming coming from behind us. We turned and saw a lot of confusion on the ground at the swings with spectators bumping into each other while holding their heads. We did not know why. Two men were stumbling about, laughing hysterically, trying hard to catch a breath to explain to others what caused the strange behavior under the swings.

One man controlled his laughter long enough to tell us all, "That ol' gal threw up when up in that swing!"

The other added his big hoot of more laughter before he cried out, "Yah! And those below got it all!" The two men, weakened from laughter, had to brace themselves against the wall of a ticket booth to keep from collapsing to the ground.

From watching the two, Julia and I were caught up in the laughter over them. Then we went on to see more of the carnival.

The sight of pink puffs of cotton candy on sticks and the smell of sugar made us want one. We watched a man with red hair and beard whirling a stick around in a tub to catch the spun hair. The cotton candy cost one dime and we walked up to the jolly looking man with pink fluff in his red hair and beard and we each bought one.

As the sweet fluff melted in our mouths, we walked about to watch the throwing of balls, the pulling of strings, dimes being tossed, and rings whirling through the air. A few people won, most did not, some kept trying, and some gave up.

A tap on our shoulders from Julia's Dad got our attention; he'd come to take us home. As we strolled away from the heat of the lights into the chill of a dark night in the parking lot, we could still hear the laughter and gay music.

Once home and in bed, a vision of colorful lights, rides, cotton candy, and the sound of chimes and pipes still filled my head until Mr. Sandman came and I went to sleep.

Howie was in the hospital because he was playing in a tree and fell and broke his leg. Lila came to tell me when he came home from the hospital. Lila and I had never seen a broken leg before and the two of us visited Howie to see his broken leg.

He looked terribly uncomfortable with his leg all wrapped up in what Howie called a cast. Howie wanted to talk a lot and we listened until his mother said to us, "It was nice of you to visit with Howard, but he needs his rest so you must leave now."

Howie whined, "Mom, I'm not tired."

She looked at Lila and me and said, "The girls can come back tomorrow."

The next day when Lila and I became tired of playing, we went to Howie's apartment to see if we could visit him.

His mother let us in, but she said, "Howard must stay quiet." Then she suggested we play monopoly.

I had never played monopoly and learned on that day I did not like monopoly. Neither did Lila; we could not read what the cards said. Howie would read the cards for us and we were always stuck in jail! Howie's cousin then came to visit him and we did not see Howie again until he was able to hobble outside with his cast on.

As I left the house, Mother said, "Have a fun day in kindergarten."

I waited at my gate for Julia so we could walk together to the schoolhouse. The words from my mother to "Have a fun day," helped to ease the fright I felt as Julia and I, hand in hand, climbed the stairs to enter the building.

Once inside, Julia's hand in mine squeezed tighter when we met a stern looking lady with her arms crossed at her chest. She studied us a moment then asked, "Kindergarten?" I replied with a nod of my head to mean yes. She said, "Downstairs."

When looking down the stairs and seeing the cold, gray of the basement's concrete floor, I did not want to go down, but that was where we were supposed to go. When our feet landed on the concrete floor, a nice lady met us. She told us what door to go through to enter the kindergarten room.

In the room, seeing others the same size as us, I felt better. Julia and I, still holding hands, stood and stared at those staring at us. When the last came into the room, our teacher closed the door and introduced herself as Miss Coleman. After we were told to take a seat at a desk, Julia and I dropped each other's hand. I wiped the sweat from my hand to my dress, then picked a desk next to Julia.

After Miss Coleman called out our names and made a check in her book, she let us have free time to get to know what was in the room to play with and to get to know each other.

Julia and I, hand in hand, shuffled to the big doll house. Suzi and Kay reached the doll house at the same time and Carla joined us, too. We had fun rearranging the tiny furniture and as we played house, I saw what the others were playing with.

Gail, Sherman, JoAnn, Myrna and Tom were at the big toy box. Charlotte, Bob and Rita were walking about in the corner of the room where the store was. Betty was playing with the cash register and putting play money in the drawers. Darlene was talking into the telephone while Janice waited her turn. Julia left me to play with clay with Marlene, David and Gary.

When our play time was over, Miss Coleman clapped her hands to get our attention and her instruction was, "Please take your seats." Back at our desks, Miss Coleman explained what we'd be expected to learn, "Good manners, how to share, and to clean up after ourselves after playing with the toys, clay, or color crayons."

Then she explained about our schedule during the day which included a rest, what I remembered Betsy telling us about, a nap that wasn't really a nap, but just a rest. Then, Miss Coleman had us tell a little bit about ourselves. I told everyone my name and how old I was and that was about it.

We had recess on the playground and played on the swings, slide, teeter totter and the merry-go-round, then went back into our kindergarten room. Teacher read two stories and then we played. I was smart at being a store lady. I had already learned how when I helped my gran'mother in her store. After putting things away we had been playing with, it was time for lunch. We paraded out of our room and into another basement room where we ate our lunch before the bigger kids got in there. After a walk around the school grounds twice, it was time for our rest.

The colorful braided rugs that hung from a bar on the wall were what we had to use to lie down on. I spread mine out on the floor next to Julia and I lay down for my rest. The ceiling looked so far, far up, and the lights hanging from the ceiling looked like they could come tumbling down on top of us. The desks from underneath weren't polished like on the top sides. The round table that had short legs looked bigger from the floor, and teacher at her desk looked like she was hovering over us.

I saw a leg lift high in the air and heard a boy ask, "Is our rest over yet?"

Miss Coleman looked at the clock. "You have three minutes left."

After our rest, teacher read another story, then we played with whatever we wanted to play with. Again, we had recess outside and inside again we played with clay and colored. Then kindergarten was over for the day.

Each day of kindergarten was as much fun as the day before and when the day was over, Julia and I would stay a little longer to play on the playground.

One day we stayed much too long and we were still playing when the first three grades got out. Mean Frankie was one of them. Julia and I fooled ourselves into thinking he did not see us when we took off for home. Going down the last alley, Frankie jumped out from behind a garbage can and scared us so bad! To get away from him chasing us, we ran real fast! Once we were safe at my house, Frankie went on. Then Julia left out the front door of my house to go to her home. After that day, we made sure we left the playground before Frankie got out of school!

Julia, Lila and I had been playing tag with Howie, and when Howie had to go with his parents someplace, we girls went to my yard to rest. It was an unusually warm Saturday afternoon so when I saw my pet snake curled up sleeping under the cottonwood tree, I knew it needed a rest, too, so I did not bother it. After getting a glass of kool-aid for each of us, we sat in the shade under the lilac bush near the cottonwood tree.

As we talked about lots of things, we had a clear view to the end of the block in the direction of town and we saw the Robinson boy coming. Seeing us, he acknowledged us with a nod of his head. Then his attention was drawn to what he saw at the base of the cottonwood tree. He dashed into the yard, grabbed my pet snake by its tail and like a whip, he smashed and smashed its head on the sidewalk. Then with a heave, he threw it out onto the street and walked away.

The horror of seeing what we saw, the tragic death of my pet, happened so fast I sat stunned for a moment. When what happened became a reality, I jumped up and ran to the street. My snake looked like an old green jump rope. I could see no head; in its place was a bloody mess. He was dead! I ran from my friends for my house, for my bedroom, and my bed.

I hated that boy! I hated him! I hated him! And I hated myself! If I would've bothered my snake to wake, he would've slithered under the peony bush and would still be alive. My snake had been sleeping. He was just sleeping, that's all. I could not understand and my sorrow was great. I cried and I cried.

The next day, feeling numb yet from my great loss, I walked out of my yard and looked into the street to the spot where my snake laid the day before. He was not there. I stood motionless and silent. As a gentle, warm breeze began to blow across my face, I knew then that my snake was in heaven with my baby mice, though I felt yet terribly haunted by the way my snake died – that hurt so deep so bad.

╫╫

It was early fall and a big chore had to be done to get the house ready for winter. The screens on the windows and doors had to come down and the storm windows and doors had to be put up. After Dad had worked to get the old putty off the windows, Patty and Bobby's chore was to clean them. I was too little to help except I did so when Dad called out, "Someone get this damn old rooster away from me!"

Baldy had been pecking at Dad's heels and I ran to help by chasing Baldy away from Dad, but Baldy would find some way to return and I would have to chase Baldy again!

Later in the morning, before Dad left for the garage, he instructed Patty and Bobby to have their work done by the time he got home so he could put up the windows.

When it was time for a quick lunch for Patty, Bobby, Mother and me, Mother put bread, butter, and peanut butter on the table for us to make our own sandwiches.

At the table, Bobby was in a jovial mood and started humming a tune, a tune to words that would make Mother so mad!

She scowled a hateful look at Bobby when he started singing the words with Patty chiming in, "The worms crawl in, the worms crawl out, the worms play pinochle on your snout; your body turns to slimy green and the puss runs out like whipping cream."

With the awful expression Mother had, Bobby wanted to tease her more, and started singing the ditty again, but only got to, "The worms crawl in," when Mother lashed out in fury, throwing her slice of buttered bread at Bobby. Bobby ducked and the buttered bread sailed past, hit the wall, and stuck there. Slowly, it came loose and fell to the floor, leaving a greasy butter smudge on the new wallpaper.

Mother reacted with harsh, scolding words. "See! See what you kids made me do!"

It had started with Bobby's ditty, but we worried we'd all be in trouble when Dad got home and saw the big grease smear on the new wallpaper. We quickly ate our lunch to get back outside so Patty and Bobby could get their chore done. When Dad came home, he was pleased with the two for doing such a good job.

At supper time, with us seated at the table, Patty and Bobby ate with good manners, very fearful of when Dad would notice the grease smudge. I was so scared and nervous for them, I forgot to count the chewing of my food.

Then, when we were just about done and ready to run, Dad gruffed, in a loud and clear tone, "There is a grease spot on the new wallpaper! How the heck did that get there?"

I had thought Mother would squeal on Patty and Bobby, but instead, she said, "Yes. I have figured that there must have been a grease mark there before we wallpapered and it is just now coming through."

Shock and surprise had Bobby, Patty and me marveling over our dear, sweet Mother. Bobby never sang the "worms crawl in" ditty to Mother ever again, and certainly not when we were at the dinner table.

Gusts of wind fouled Halloween. The day came and was gone with only a memory of a howling night. The chill of late fall and getting darker earlier meant our evenings would be spent mostly indoors.

After supper, after Dad had had his rest in his favorite chair, he got ready to go out for the night. He did his toothpick trick when kissing Mother, then, before going out the door said to us kids, "Enjoy your radio programs." As he left, a gush of cold air rushed in before he could shut the door behind him.

Mother turned the radio on and listened to "Fibber McGee and Molly." I could hear it when playing with my pick-up-sticks and felt sorry for poor Fibber McGee when he opened the closet door. Such a noisy clatter was heard of lots of things falling to the floor which caused Molly to remind Fibber McGee, again, that he had to clean out that closet!

The next radio program was "Charlie McCarthy with Edgar Bergen." It was so funny the way Mortimer Snerd talked. When Bobby came in I said, "Maatima Snud talks like you!"

Bobby said back, "You are a wooden dummy! Just like Mortimer Snerd."

I did not know that Mortimer Snerd was a wooden dummy and thought Bobby was spoofing, but when I asked Mother she confirmed that he was a wooden dummy and that it was Edgar Bergen doing the talking for him. I could not understand how someone else could do the talking, nor could I visualize Mortimer Snerd as a dummy. I was confused and preferred to believe that Mortimer Snerd was a real person who just talked funny.

The wind continued to howl on another cold night. With Dad gone, Bobby scooted about, turning off the lights to make the front room very dark.

Patty, Bobby, and I sat on the floor in front of the radio to listen to "Inner Sanctum." The dim yellow light from the radio gave Patty and Bobby's faces a ghostly look. I was glad when Mother joined us by wiggling herself between Patty and me, and just in time.

The deep voice on the radio beckoned, "Come ~ into ~ the ~ world ~ of ~ Inner ~ Sanctum. Join ~ us ~ in ~ the ~ dark ~ if ~ you ~ dare!" Then the quivering voice said, "Lights ~ out," and I shivered as an eerie sound just like the creepy old hinges on our back door went Screeeeeeeeeech!

Beyond that door, the voice took us on a scary journey in a dark world of the unknown. Overwhelmed with great fear, I felt we were not alone in the pitch dark world of our front room. I looked about and found that the tall floor lamp looked scary, like a monster, and could come after us. When the horrible tale grew even more frightening, I glanced at that floor lamp to make sure it was still there!

Bobby's hand dropped on my shoulder causing me to scream bloody murder! This scared Patty and Mother so bad Mother made Bobby sit where we could all see him! After the radio door closed with its eerie scrreeeeeeeeeeeeech sound I left my family and got ready for bed.

Once settled between the cold flannel sheets, I could hear the "The Phillip Morris Show." I giggled, hearing the name "Ishkabibble," and ducked my head under the covers. My warm breath warmed my sheets, and I could still hear the mellow, soothing radio voice of a boy named Johnnie as he sang, drawing out the words, "Call~for~Phillip~Morris. Call~for~Phillip~Morris."

In kindergarten a new boy named Leighton made our morning more fun. Miss Coleman gave us extra free time to show Leighton what we had in the room to play with. Then we had to take our seats. Miss Coleman handed out a coloring project for us to do. The stiff paper had the outline of a turkey. I did a good job staying inside the lines. I colored the body brown and one tail feather I colored green, another yellow, one purple, one orange, and the dingy hanging from its neck I colored red. I thought my turkey was the best one of all.

Teacher read us a story about the very first Thanksgiving, then she let us participate in telling of the food the Pilgrims and the Indians shared. It made me think of the food we would be eating at my gran'parent's place in the country. But my Gwan'ma neva has conn; she has peas and potatoes with lots of gwavy. Dad said if it does not snow, we will go to my granparents for Thanksgiving Day. When the story was over, teacher taped our turkeys to the wall in the room and they stayed there until the day before Thanksgiving.

When that day came, as we paraded out of the kindergarten room with our paper turkeys flapping in our hands, teacher wished each one of us a very happy Thanksgiving. Julia and I did not stay to play on the playground; we were afraid we might lose track of time, then Frankie would chase us, making us ruin our turkeys. Although the air was cold there was no snow yet.

Mother was very pleased with my colorful turkey. She taped it to the window next to the two pilgrims Patty made a long time ago.

Bobby never'd made it home with his artwork from school before, but on that day he did! A turkey, too! He poked fun at my colorful turkey calling it, "A dumb looking one."

When he was taping his next to mine on the window, I saw what he did and I screamed for help, "Motha! Bobby made my tukey fall to the fla!"

Bobby said, "It was an accident!"

I barked back, "Baloney!"

Mother let out a sigh, picked up my turkey and taped it to the window again, but far from Bobby's.

When Mother praised Bobby for his good job of coloring, Bobby turned to me and said, "See! My turkey looks real, not dumb like yours." I made a fist and I hit him lots on his arm as he laughed and repeated, "Bug off, bug off, bug off."

Thanksgiving morning there was not a white flake of snow on the ground and I got stuck in the middle over the hump when riding to Gran'ma and Gran'pa's in the country. The telephone poles zipped by, then the tiny, tiny town. The gravel made its pit-a-pat sound under the car as the barren flat land rolled by, and by, and by. After passing the church, the halfway mark, more flat land rolled by, and by, and by, making me car sick. I had to have my walk around the car, then I sat in the front seat chewing my gum the rest of the way.

The ding-a-ling of the bell "velcomed" us into my gran'parents store. After warm hugs, Gran'ma asked, "Vell, vas da vide nice?"

Gran'pa moved his cigar to the other side of his mouth and said, "Yup, yup."

After getting a cookie from the cupboard, I found Felix on the bed. Then I went through Gran'pa's post office to get to the store part. I snooped about before playing store lady, buying myself lots of candy. When I heard, "Soups on," I knew it was time to gather around the table.

There was a bountiful amount of food on the table like what the Pilgrims and the Indians ate, only instead of corn, we did have peas and instead of turkey, we had chicken. I got the leg. For dessert, I ate my pumpkin pie with lots and lots and lots of whipped cream because I did not like the taste of pumpkin.

After our big feast, Dad retired to the bed for a rest and Grandpa to his favorite chair in his post office. I wanted to go to the playground at the schoolhouse and did not want to go alone. It was cold out and Patty got out of going by saying she had to help Gran'ma and Mother with the dishes.

Before I asked Bobby, he knew already what I was going to ask and said, "No! Cuz it's freezing out!"

I figured with Patty helping Gran'ma with the dishes I could get Mother to go with me. When I asked, she sneered, then turned to Bobby and pleaded with him to give in.

Bobby then made me happy because he could not refuse Mother, but when we got to the playground, Bobby bellyached over the swings being too cold, the teeter-totter, too, and he yelped loudly when feeling the cold through his pants when going down the slide. I followed him back to our gran'ma's house.

When dusk loomed outdoors, Thanksgiving with our gran'parents was over; it was time for us to leave. We hugged our gran'ma and gran'pa, then waved and waved as we motored away.

Before we reached the halfway mark, it became very black outside the car, nothing could be seen except the two yellow beams of light on the road. I sat forward and when I focused my sight on the beams of light, the road appeared to be in motion.

I studied the mystery until it became clear, there were lots and lots of field mice scurrying every which way. I thought of the car's tires squashing them and looked away from the yellow beam of lights. What then appeared to be a ghostly phantom far away in the black night was a light flickering from a farmhouse. I sat back in the seat, listening to the beat of the rocks and the hum of the car, and with Patty's warmth on one side of me and leaning my head on Bobby's warm shoulder on the other side, fell fast asleep. I slept until the hum of the car stopped. We were home.

The house was freezing cold and after Mother gave the key to the floor furnace a twist, we huddled over it to feel its comforting warmth. Then we went to bed. The next morning I plugged the keyhole to my door and I found a good place to hide my sack of candy bars from Gran'pa's store. Later that day I did share one candy bar with Bobby, and on Saturday I shared with my friends, and with Bobby again because he made me believe that another candy bar would help heal an "owie" that he had on his "poor" thumb.

Monday morning with still no snow I had to keep a watchful eye on the cracks in the sidewalk as Julia and I walked to the schoolhouse to attend kindergarten. Not wanting to break my mother's back, I had created another compulsive behavior that I sometimes made into a fun game like playing hopscotch.

We had many more days of the freakish dry weather, and that meant there was no white covering on the sidewalks to hide the many, many, many cracks, and my "fun" compulsive behavior to not break my mother's back began to become most exasperating!

Chapter 4

It was December seventh, a cold Sunday afternoon, and not a flake of snow had fallen. The bunch of us at Kathleen's house were feeling very humdrum as it was out of season to have to play another game such as "Ante-i-over." It was Julia's turn with the ball and she gave a good effort to throw it over the roof to Sonny and Bubber. After Kathleen, Betsy and I shouted, "Ante-i-over!" the ball hit the roof and rolled up to the tip, but stopped too soon, then it rolled back. We had to then bellow out, "Pig's tail!"

Bubber's voice with a great shout from the other side ordered, "Com'on you weaklings! Throw it over!" Wearing a warm heavy coat with burdensome sleeves, it was difficult to throw the ball to get it over the roof!

Julia tried again and this time the ball hit a window pane creating a terrible noise.

Sonny's mother then suggested we play something else.

Kathleen expressed her idea of a game when she said, "Et's pway hide and seek!"

Sonny suggested another game, "Who will draw the frying pan?" Bubber perked up thinking that was a better idea!

We ran to a shed next to the alleyway and I was the first to hide my eyes. I closed my eyes real tight and leaned my forehead against the shed so someone could draw a frying pan on my back.

I felt a finger drawing a big circle and recognized the voice to be Julia's as she said, "I'll draw the frying pan who will put the weenie in?"

I had to guess who that would be. The voice was disguised as a froggy sounding voice that said, "I will." Then that finger poked me so hard on my back it made me yelp, "Ouch!" I turned and scowled a mean, mean look at Bubber as I shouted, "That was you Bubba!"

Bubber puffed his chest out as he asked, "How'd you guess?"

Between two boys it was not hard to guess and smart like I answered, "Cuz I am smawt!"

Bubber now had to hide his eyes. Kathleen stepped forward to be the one to draw the frying pan on his back and I stood ready to give him a good poke! Like he gave me!

But Sonny beat me to it. We held back our snickers so we wouldn't give away who'd poked him. When he guessed it was me, he was wrong and he had to be "it" and hide his eyes again.

Bubber grumbled and wanted to quit playing what he called, "A stupid game!"

Betsy pushed him against the shed and said, "You have to!" Betsy was going to take her turn drawing the frying pan when suddenly we were startled over hearing a loud bang!

We turned to see it was Kathleen's mother who had thrown open the storm door so hard it banged against the house. She stood outside shouting, "Pearl Harbor has been bombed! Pearl Harbor has been bombed!" Then she went back in without further explanation.

We looked about to see who she could have been shouting the message to and finding no one but us, we found the news to be pretty exciting! I did not know where this Pearl Harbor was, but such important news meant it must be very, very close to our town.

The announcement of this place being bombed created a new game to play: war! Bubber took off at a run and the rest of us jumped in behind to form a line to snake about with our arms out like we were airplanes. We all roared loudly imitating the leader, then swooped when dropping our bombs while shouting, "Boom! Boom! Boom! Boom! Boom! Boom!" Up and down the alley we flew, snaking about until we became tired of playing our war game.

When I got home I wanted to tell of my fun news of this Pearl Harbor being bombed, but was abruptly hushed by Mother. She and Dad sat near the radio listening very intently to President Roosevelt talking about the bombing of Pearl Harbor.

I already knew that! When our President said, "War has been declared!" I wanted someone to listen to the war my friends and I declared. No one, not even my grandmother, was interested in listening to me!

The next day in kindergarten Miss Coleman asked if we knew what this bombing of Pearl Harbor meant? Before I could tell of what I knew, Tom jumped up from his desk seat and while swooping an imaginary sword about, he answered, "It means war!"

Miss Coleman said, "You are right. Because Pearl Harbor has been bombed, war has been declared." Her hand reached up to unroll a map and she pointed to where we live in the northern part of the United States, then her finger went way,

way out to a tiny speck in the ocean, to this Pearl Harbor. I was now confused, the fuss seemed too great for such a tiny place so far away.

The next day the fury of a snowstorm hit. It created a lot of good cheer in all of us with the kind of war we played, building our snow forts and having our snowball fights.

Harold, the delivery boy from Yondell's Grocery and Bakery store, was heard stomping snow off his boots in the wash porch. Mother held the kitchen door open for him to carry the box of groceries to the cupboard. Harold then said to Mother, "Mr. Yondell has instructed me to tell his customers he will not be giving away Christmas trees this year because the Boy Scouts will be selling them to earn money."

Mother said to Harold, "Please tell Mr. Yondell that is fine. Bobby will be one of the Boy Scouts selling trees."

On the day of the Boy Scout's money making project, it was understood Dad would be the one buying a tree from Bobby. Dad got the message from Mother over the telephone that I wanted to go, too. At noon I met Dad and as we left the garage, I knew the rule: children were to be seen and not heard. I did not say one word as I kept in perfect step with my dad all the way to the empty lot on Front Street that was now full of Christmas trees.

Bobby, in his Boy Scout uniform followed Dad and I around as Dad picked up each tree and gave it a spin. While looking it over he mumbled like he was talking to the tree. Returning to the first tree he said to it, "Looks like you are the best." Dad told Bobby he'd done a good job as he paid the good salesman fifty cents for the tree.

As Dad carried the tree down the street to our house, I helped by holding up the top end. Mother had a bucket ready and when Dad plunked the tree in it, they filled the bucket with sand to hold it in place. Mother turned the tree about until she was satisfied the best side was showing.

The house was filled with a wonderful new aroma, a fresh pine smell from the fir tree. After the lights, ornaments, and icicles were hung ever so perfectly on the green branches, we all agreed it was the most beautiful tree we'd ever seen. The angel at the top appeared to glow from the shining lights. This made me feel she, too, was enjoying the reflection I was seeing in the silver teardrop ornaments, everything so tiny.

On the night of the Christmas program at church I sat with my Sunday School class; we were the little singing group. Patty and Bobby were in the manger scene. Patty was an angel, the prettiest one of the six angels who paraded in to stand at the back of the altar. Then Joseph and Mary walked in to be by baby Jesus in his manger and that is when my group sang very loud, "Away in a Manger." The older kids followed with, "It Came Upon the Midnight Clear" and "Hark! The Herald Angels Sing."

The first of the animals appeared from behind a curtain. Bobby was on his hands and knees wearing long ears and a long tail. He was a funny looking donkey.

When my giggling was heard over other giggles, Mother looked at me with a frown. I had to pucker my lips to keep from giggling more.

Two more boys crawling in caused another twitter of laughter from everyone. One had a fuzzy white rug draped over his back making him look like a lamb, the other had a long tail and a brown rug wrapped around him. Hearing his brother in the audience utter a "Moo," the "cow" gave him a dirty look. When the shepherd boy took his place, the older kids sang "The First Noel."

Then, three camels came crawling in with stuffed gunny sacks for humps with three kings beside them. The song sung was "We Three Kings of Orient Are." Parts were read, more songs were sung, then our Christmas program was over and everyone sang, "Silent Night."

My group was the first to go down to the basement and when the bigger kids were coming down, I heard Patty whisper to Bobby, "You were the best ass I have ever seen." When Bobby's feet hit the concrete floor, the donkey chased the angel all around the basement until our parents joined us. We were each given a Christmas sack bulging with an orange, a red apple, a popcorn ball, peanuts and curly candy.

Christmas Eve, after supper, when it was time to hang stockings, Patty, Bobby and I raced for our dad's sock drawer. Dad's big hunting socks made the best stockings to hang. As we grabbed for a stocking, Bobby grabbed the same one I did and we pulled, stretching the sock so badly Bobby screamed for help, "Mom!" It was too late; I found its mate. I pinned mine to one arm of the daveno like Patty did with her sock at the other end. Bobby's deformed sock hung from the arm of the overstuffed chair.

The rule for opening gifts was to open them Christmas morning, but our anxiety became so great Mother gave in to opening just one! I poked, squeezed, rattled and guessed until I opened a gift from my aunt Margaret. It was a pretty blue and white, knitted neck scarf Mother said my aunt made for me. I watched as Patty opened her gift while Bobby was deciding between two he had in his hands.

Feeling full of good cheer and excited over the expectation of what Santa would bring during the night, I went to bed earlier than usual. The rhythmic words to "Away in the Manger" that told of, "The little Lord Jesus asleep on the hay," lulled me to sleep.

Very early Christmas morning I hopped out of bed and ran to the tree. My joyful screams aroused everyone! Santa Claus thought I needed a pair of clamp-on ice skates. Patty got tap dancing shoes and Bobby got an electric train set.

I made a dash for my bedroom to put my shoes on, then dashed back to the tree. I slipped my shoe into the first skate and tightened it to my shoe with the key and buckled the strap around my ankle. Then I did the same with the other skate on my other shoe. I stood up and had no trouble walking with the double runner skates on, my first pair of ice skates.

When Mother walked in from the kitchen and saw what I was doing, she got mad because I was marring her linoleum. I still had gifts under the tree to open so I crawled about until I found them.

When all the gifts were unwrapped, the room was a mess with paper, ribbon, and presents scattered about. Patty's stocking and mine were as deformed as Bobby's was the night before. They were stuffed with the same treats we got in our Sunday School sack, except instead of a popcorn ball, we each got a box of Cracker Jack.

When the excitement of opening gifts was over, I crawled to my bedroom, eased my door shut, and played like I was really on an ice skating rink, while at the same time being very careful not to mar the linoleum.

For two days after Christmas I left my ice skates hanging on the hook in the wash porch next to Patty and

Bobby's fancy ice skates. Since Christmas Day, it had been snowing so hard it was drudgery to walk and it was so cold we did not want to go out if we did not have to.

On the morning of the third day I could see from my bed the glow from the sun coming through my window shade. I crawled to the foot of my bed and I gave the shade a tug; it zipped out of my hand flipping on its roll. Jack Frost had left a spectacular show of glistening magical patterns on the window pane. I was so captivated I used my fingernail to trace around a beautiful pattern of ice crystals. Looking through the scratch mark I saw a crown of brilliance on the snow, tiny gems sparkling in many colors from the bright sun.

When I got out of bed it was so cold in the house I had to stand over the floor furnace to get warm. Bobby joined me and butted me off! Mother was busy in the kitchen so I joined her. While eating my cereal I heard a fight between Patty and Bobby over the floor furnace, then Patty, too, joined me to eat her breakfast.

When passing Patty in the kitchen after I was dressed in my snowsuit, she said to me, "If you wait, I will go with you." I did not want to wait; I was in a hurry to go ice skating, so I said to her, "Meet me thewe." When I entered the wash porch it was freezing cold and I gave my new scarf another wrap around my neck. I grabbed for my new skates and went out the door. The bright sunshine and nippy air was very invigorating!

Instead of plowing through deep snow, I stepped in the big boot prints Dad had made when he walked up the alley to go to work. Once out of the alley and in the street, I walked in the tracks made from tires.

I could not see the ice skating rink that was a short distance ahead because of a bank of snow created by a tractor I could hear going, "chchchchchchchchch." I climbed to the top and could see the tractor scraping the last of the snow off. I slid to the bottom, sat down, and ripped my boots off to clamp my double runner skates onto my shoes. I scooted on my seat to the ice and pushed myself up, but I wobbled a little, walking on ice was not as easy as on Mother's linoleum. I held my arms out for balance and focused my eyes on the ice below, out of fear that if I looked up I would fall.

A pair of hands grabbed my hands. Patty had come to help me. Although she skated backwards pulling me along, my fear kept me focusing my sight on the ice below. Once around the rink, Patty asked, "Are you ready yet?" I tightened my hold on her hands to let her know I was not ready for her to let go! Now and then I felt the swish of air from others skating on the rink, but I dared not look up to see who it was. We glided again around the rink, then Patty's hands slipped out of mine and she skated away.

I was on my own and doing fine until I stopped. When I tried to get started again, I lost my balance and sat down hard on my rump! I struggled to push myself up and once steady on my skates, Patty glided to a halt next to me and took a hold of one hand only and we skated side by side. This time I learned how to lift one foot then the other like on my roller skates. When Patty let go I was truly ice skating! I made it around the rink several times.

After such a pleasurable feeling of accomplishment, I wanted to be like the bigger kids and use the warming house for a rest. There was a hot potbellied stove in the middle of the room, long benches lined three walls and under the benches were boots and shoes. I sat on a bench and watched skaters come and go. Most walked on the tips of their skates going click, click, click, click across the floor. This fascinated me. Then I noticed how quiet it was; I was all alone. A boy and a girl entered. I thought they were trying to hold each other up, but when they sat down on the bench across from me and were whispering in each other's ears I knew they were being lovey-dovey. I was so embarrassed I wanted to leave! I stood up and rolled up on the tips of my skates so I could click, click out the door, but I learned that did not work with double runner skates. I lost my balance and made a loud thud when I sat down hard on the bench. The two looked at me and giggled. I felt so alone and silly I had to get out of there! I walked out like I had walked in.

Ice skating was getting rough, what with too many wanting to play crack the whip while I was trying my best to learn to be a good skater. The rough play caused me to fall too much so I figured it was time for me to head for home. As I walked along, a silver sky that made the sun disappear made me feel a very deep chill through my snowsuit. Once in the house, warming my body over the floor furnace, I felt happy; I had learned how to ice skate.

After Christmas vacation, I came down with pink eye. When I awoke after a night of sleep, I could not open my eyes! They were sealed shut with gunky stuff. Mother soaked my eyes with wet cotton balls to loosen the gunk. It was like dried boogers when I peeled it away. Expecting to go back to kindergarten, after a weekend of rest, Mother thought I needed to stay home one more day.

With nothing to do I was bored and followed Mother around as she gathered clothes to be washed. I wanted to help, but because I was supposed to be sick, Mother said, "The wash porch is too cold."

I pouted, then played with my tiddlywinks until I heard the whistle of the Skiddoo. I jumped up and pressed my nose to the cold window pane. While gazing across the fluff of snow to the tracks, a lonesome feeling had me deep in thought about how far apart my train and I had become with me so busy in kindergarten. As my train came into view, I waved by simply wiggling my fingers as the Skiddoo passed. Knowing that no one could see me, I sighed, and went back to playing tiddlywinks.

When Mother brought the sheets in from the clothesline they were frozen stiff. They filled the room with a heavy scent of fresh air as Mother set them up like tents around the floor furnace so they'd thaw. I crawled in and out of each tent. After they were dry, folded and put away, Mother brought in an arm load of pants, Dad's and Bobby's. After each frozen pair of pants was propped against the table and chairs, it looked like the room was filled with invisible people who were wearing just pants.

In the month of February, warm chinook winds blew across the land melting the snow into slush. Then March came in like a lion with a cold wind and more snow and, fitting the pattern, the month went out like a lamb in time for my sixth birthday.

I had a birthday party in the afternoon, and after supper with my family still sitting around the table, except for Dad who was settled in his favorite chair, Mother gave me a present. When I opened the soft gift, it was a special dress that I had not expected, a Shirley Temple dress!

For my birthday, I would always get a new dress to wear for Easter, but a Shirley Temple dress was extra, extra special. It had a big collar in the front and back and soft pleats hung from the collar to the hem. It was all white, except for the names of girls embroidered in many colors all over the dress.

Patty read the names for me until I recognized one and screamed, "Patty!" Her answer was, "Right!"

When she continued I interrupted again, pointing to my name and shouting, "Mawie!"

After Patty had read all the names, she came up with one more, "Poopie!"

With a surprised expression I looked at Patty and when she laughed, I knew she was kidding.

Bobby overheard and knowing Dad had left the house, bellowed out, "You are the poopie!"

I hollered back, "I had watha be a poopie then a boobie like you!"

Bobby hated being called "Boobie." In anger, he called out, "You shithead!"

Mother was then heard loud and clear. "If I hear another word like that you will all get your mouths washed out with soap!"

I zippered my lips shut. When taking my new Shirley Temple dress to my bedroom, I had to pass Bobby and he gave me a dirty look. I closed my bedroom door and whispered softly through the keyhole, "Boo-oo-bie-ie."

The age of six means you are older than five, five sounds babyish, six sounds grown-up. Grown-up meant I was big enough to go to big kid's school and do big kid's things like learning how to swim.

While playing with paper dolls with Lila, and feeling so grownup after my birthday, I asked Lila, "Don't you wish you wewe as old as me?"

Lila frowned, then got huffy and said, "I am older than you!"

I was very dumbfounded over her statement and shouted, "No siwwee! I am olda than you!"

She yelled back, "My birthday comes first! So there!"

When I remembered she did have a birthday before mine, it made sense that could make her older than I, yet I knew what I had been told! I scowled a mean look and let her know, "My motha told me I am olda than you!"

She placed her hands on her hips bossy-like as she snapped, "Ya! You lie! My birthday comes first!"

I had no words to add to prove I was right so I shouted, "I'm going home!" And I stomped away.

I looked for Baldy before pushing open the gate. He was getting so mean, attacking anyone's feet with his sharp beak! I carefully pushed the gate open to keep it from squeaking. I did not want Baldy to know I was coming through. I made a dash for the door of my house and made it without Baldy finding my feet to peck at.

I found Mother in the kitchen and asked, "Am I bigga than Lila oe she bigga than me?"

Mother seemed to be thinking over what I had asked, then answered, "I guess you are both the same size."

I felt greatly distressed and cried out, "I mean! Is Lila olda than me oe am I olda than Lila?"

Mother, acting distressed, too, said, "How many times do I have to explain? You are older than Lila!"

It was a great relief to know I was right, but it was not enough to make Lila believe me. I had to know what made me older. "If Lila's bithday comes befa mine why isn't she olda than me?"

Mother paused, thinking and frowning, before answering, "It is not whose birthday comes first, but what year you were born. Lila was born a whole year after you; she is still five years old!"

I understood! I have to be older because I am six years old! Yet to explain to Lila I had to be prepared to tell Lila the very same words Mother told me.

By the time Lila and I got together later that day I had become so befuddled repeating, over and over, what I was going to say that I no longer cared who was the oldest. I was glad when Lila did not say one word about it. We played like we always did, as good friends.

After Easter, and searching in my Easter basket for one more candy egg that might be hidden yet in the grass, the telephone rang. I hopped off the chair to answer it, but Mother beat me to the telephone. I could tell from the sound of Mother's voice that it was a bad call. The conversation seemed to be about Grandmother. She'd been away visiting and was expected back soon.

After Mother hung up she told me, "Your grandmother died on the train." Mother then picked up the telephone to call my dad.

I remembered Julia's bad luck story and had to slip away from Mother to go to my bedroom to be alone. The haunting guilt over what I did when it last snowed, had returned with this awful news about my grandmother.

Julia said a long time ago, 'If you step on a gwave someone in the family will die.' I did, I stepped on that gwave, but I could not help it! The snow was so deep in the cemetewy I did not see that gwave. I could not help it! Is Gwandmotha dead cuz I stepped on that gwave?

In my confusion I suddenly needed to be comforted, to be with my mother!

Mother was resting in the overstuffed chair. I dared not speak of my guilt. *No-no-no.* I carefully thought over the words I could say. "Why did Gwandmotha die?"

Mother's eyes looked very tired as she looked at me, then she said in a sad way, "Your grandmother died because her heart was old and worn out."

I lay my head against Mother's chest, loving her so much for making me feel better. She patted my head and with a whisper said, "Now your grandmother is in heaven with your grandfather and other loved ones who've gone before her."

On another day, we were getting ready in our best clothes to go to a funeral. I had never been to a funeral before and I did not know what a funeral was, except to know it had something to do with my grandmother who died. I got to wear my Shirley Temple dress and felt so pretty.

Patty was next to show up dressed and ready for this funeral and she was wearing the funniest hat I had ever seen. It was a red straw hat shaped like an upside down ice cream cone tipped just a bit. Around the fat part of the cone shape was a shiny, colorful ribbon with the ends of the ribbon falling down the side of Patty's face.

I was dumbstruck over what Mother said to her. "Patty, you look very nice in your new hat." Patty grinned and feeling pretty, did a hoity-toity walk around the front room. Mother's very, pleasing response to what I thought was a silly looking hat made me want a hat, too, to wear to this funeral.

Bobby was heard stomping down the stairs. He had not worn his best clothes for a while and kept tugging at the seat of his pants that looked like they'd shrunk in the wash. When Dad was ready, and with us all dressed up, it was like going to a party when we left the house to go to this funeral.

In the car, Bobby did a wiggling jig trying to get comfortable. I sat ladylike, like Patty. The car motored to a part of town I hadn't been to before and stopped in front of a church unfamiliar to me. A few relatives and people were standing outside. When seeing my cousins and other children, I scrambled over Patty to be the first out of the car. I ran to join the other kids and we chased each other around and around the grounds of the church.

When it came time for something to happen, Mother grabbed me by my shoulders to guide me along as everyone paraded inside the church. I could smell flowers and looked around a tall person to see what I could see. Way, way up front were baskets of flowers, some with big fancy bows. There was also a long silver box with very pretty handles sitting on a cart with big wheels.

Going down the long aisle, keeping in step with a cousin in front of me, I accidentally stepped on the heel of his shoe making it slip off. When he had to hop along to get it back on, we giggled.

The people sat down in the empty pews they came to, but I was taken to the very front pew. Mother let go of my shoulder and directed me in to sit with the cousins a bit younger than me, except one. Patty and Bobby were at the far, far end of my pew and Mother sat behind me with my aunts and uncles.

There was plenty of room on the pew for my cousins and me to spread out, but it was more fun for us to bump and squeeze together, except the one cousin older than me who seemed too sad to want to be squeezed.

The room darkened when the big doors at the back closed. I looked behind and saw lots of people; they appeared to be very sad. When the soft music of an organ started playing, I searched up on the altar for it, but could only see the pretty flowers and that long silver box. A minister came through a door and walked to his special place. He paused when looking at all of us, then bowed his head and when saying a prayer, I closed my eyes real, real tight! I knew that was expected of me.

When the prayer was over, the minister said nice words about my grandmother, but he kept talking so much I became fidgety. For something to do, I eased my hand around the back of a cousin next to me to poke one next to him, making that one look behind to see who poked him. He did not know it was me. I tried to do my poking trick again, but someone poked me first. It was my mother. I got the message from her frowning expression that I had better sit still.

I tried sitting still and I did listen when hearing about Jesus. When the minister spoke of "Jesus who died on the cross for the sins of the world," I remembered baby Jesus in his manger and wondered, Why did Jesus have to die on that cwoss? And what is a sin? I felt very troubled because the minister said, "Jesus washed away our sins when he died for us." The word "sin" seemed awfully bad. Then he talked more about my grandmother and I suddenly felt very sad.

I was hearing a lot of tearful sounds from all around, especially from the cousin who was bigger than me. When

I leaned over and peered down the row at her, she was sobbing very hard. I figured I had better cry, too. I frowned to feel very sorrowful; I blinked and blinked my eyes until they became watery. I was crying, but not as hard as my cousin. Then the minister said another prayer and I had to close my eyes real tight again. When he said, "Amen" I figured this long funeral was over.

I looked around and saw not one person get up to leave. I sighed; I wanted to be outside in the sunshine playing with my cousins and new friends.

The organ played again and two men appeared in the aisle. They slowly stepped up to the altar to that long silver box and carefully removed the beautiful bouquet of flowers that had been laying across its top

The box had a lid and they opened it! The inside of that lid was full of pretty white tufts of satin and that was all I could see, yet I sensed there was a reason for opening that box. When looking for something to change my sudden mood, I saw another man pop into view at the end of our aisle. A flip of his hand was a signal for us to stand up.

Once in the aisle, my cousins and I became intertwined with the bigger people all inching forward up the steps towards that long silver box. I watched those who looked in the box. Their expressions were very grim and I felt the need to look for my mother. She was far behind holding the arm of my aunt who was crying. Dad, Patty and Bobby were too far from me and then I was there at the long silver box.

I lifted up on my toes to look in. What I saw I had to quickly accept, it was my grandmother! I felt very confused as I pondered over what I had been told by Mother and the minister, too, who said about my grandmother, "She is now at peace with God." Remembering the tears and the words spoken about my grandmother, I had to trust my mother. I figured, Gwandmotha had to be hewe fa this funewal. Aftawads, God can take haw to heaven.

I felt the touch of a gentle hand on my shoulder to make me roll down from my toes and move on. As I walked down the aisle, I wanted to forget all my thoughts of this long funeral. When I reached the door, I bolted out into the warm sunshine. Seeing other kids already chasing each other, I ran to join them. We chased each other around and around the church until we were made to crawl into the cars we came in.

Our car followed a long black car with no window in the back. The other cars were all behind our car. When I hopped up on my knees to see them, I knocked Patty's hat off. She became miffed and ordered me to, "Sit down and sit still!"

I asked, "Whewe awe we going?"

Bobby, in a disgusted tone, uttered, "Geeze!"

Mother answered as though I should know, "To the cemetery!"

I was so surprised, I blurted, "You mean evewy-body?"

Mother seemed to understand what my thoughts were, with other kids there, as she ended any idea I had when she let me know, "And I want you to behave!"

As the trail of cars approached the cemetery, I wanted so badly to show my cousins and the other kids what I knew about Mr. Rip, the little graves, and all, but once beyond the brick pillars, the long black car drove to another location where we never played.

The cars stopped near a large gray tombstone with our last name, BAKER, engraved in big letters on it. That was my grandfather who died once; I never knew him.

When we got out of the car, Mother's hand rested on my shoulder, again. Setting on the ground in front of the tombstone was a frame made of gold bars with big balls on each corner. There was a dark shadow in its middle and as Mother guided me closer, I saw that the dark shadow was a deep hole. My dad and uncles pulled the long silver box out from the back of the long black car. Their legs wobbled as they carried it and I guessed it was especially heavy because I heard the men grunt and they set it on the gold bars over the black hole.

This was much too much fuss and too serious. I felt, then, a jolt of what was real. It had to be, it was true, my grandmother was still in that box! As I was growing up, there had been a gradual acceptance that graves were more than funny names on tombstones. Until now there was no need to think about it.

I looked about with a new mind full of what our cemetery was all about, and I felt the willies. I began to believe, when thinking, Maybe this is whewe ghosts weally live, and spooks too! Sonny has said so, but Sonny likes to tease, I know that.

My aunts, mother, and others cried when the minister said a prayer, then very kind words about my grandmother, the same words he had already said at the church! I was getting tired of this funeral. I had figured out all I needed to know, God is full of magic. He will get grandmotha out of that box when he is weady to.

The long silver box remained resting on the gold bars as the cars rolled slowly down the lane and out of the cemetery. When we got home, we found someone had left lots of food on the dining room table and the relatives and some friends who followed us home stayed to eat the food. It was like a big party and no one cared how much cake I ate and I ate the kind with thick, thick frosting. I then went outside with my cousins and other kids and we chased each other around and around the house. The day of the long, long funeral was full of surprises and it ended with a lot of fun.

One week after kindergarten was over, Bible school started. The smell of more crayon wax after kindergarten made me not like Bible school. I wanted to be outside playing, forgetting that the friends I would be playing with were in their Bible schools.

On the very last day, when coloring, I thought about plans Kathleen, Sonny and I had for Saturday, the next day. We planned on hiking to Mrs. Gouge's farm. I had never been there before. Sonny says she has a fun farm.

I colored the sheep on the sheet of paper different colors instead of all white because I was tired of coloring. My teacher praised me for doing, "A good, creative job."

When I awakened Saturday morning, I got right up and dressed for hiking. I was alone in the kitchen, and when standing on a chair pushed up to the cupboard so I could reach for a box of cereal, I felt a sudden chill from cold air rushing over my body. It had come from the stairwell, but when I looked, expecting to see Patty or Bobby, I saw no one. A spooky feeling made shivers run through me.

Strange things had been happening. Mysterious sounds were being heard upstairs when there was no one up there. Mother figured there had to be a logical explanation. She tried to keep Patty or Bobby from scaring me with foolish stories, yet I could not help overhearing when someone would be wanting to know who was walking around upstairs? Or why was Grandmother's trunk sliding across the floor? Or who knocked the lamp off the dresser?

While pouring cereal in my bowl, my hair fell over my cheek and when brushing it away, a prickly sensation made me scream, "Ouchy!"

The day before when I had a peach in my hand, Bobby told me, "If you rub that peach on your cheek its fuzz will tickle you."

I believed him and when I rubbed it on my cheek it stung like a thousand stickers pricking my skin. The only thing that helped sooth the stinging was cold water. Yet when I would forget and rub my cheek, it still would sting like there were lots of stickers left in my skin!

Eating my cereal in haste before the flakes could become soggy, I recalled what Bobby told me the other day; he tried to convince me we have a ghost by saying, "Probably it's Grandmother, back from the grave."

Ghosts were "scawy" and I knew Grandmother could never be a "scawy" ghost. Remembering what Mother told a neighbor lady, I shouted at Bobby, "Pwobly it's a boogla!" Then he made big fun over my burglar idea. I scooped up the last cereal flake, looked at the clock and it was time to leave for Kathleen and Sonny's.

In the country, as Sonny, Kathleen and I were hiking, the warm sunshine and the wide open spaces made me feel out of reach and safe from ghosts, and I decided to share the fun of having a "scawy" ghost in my house.

I got Sonny and Kathleen's attention by asking, in a perky voice, "Guess what?"

In unison the two asked, "What?"

I said, "We have a weal ghost. No spoofing!"

Kathleen asked, "A reo one?" I nodded my head confirming that we do while Sonny jerked his head back and forth.

He was convinced I was spoofing, and said, "Nah. Ya don't either!"

I told him, "We do too! Bobby said so!"

Sonny looked at me from the corner of his eyes as though to think, if Bobby said so it could be true. Then he said, "What do ya do, keep your dumb ghost in that crawlspace upstairs?"

I hadn't thought about that place being where a ghost could hide, and imagining a real one there, I no longer wanted to have a ghost in my house! I covered my mouth as I let go of a snicker that let Sonny think I was really spoofing!

He got so mad he kicked a pebble making it fly as he said, "See! Ya don't have a ghost, do you?"

I needed to save my skin the best I could and began to explain, "Bobby weally believes we have a ghost in the house, but Motha thinks it's a boogla." I then raced ahead; when the other two caught up, the subject of ghosts had been forgotten.

We came to a fence line and in the middle of the pasture, on the other side of barbed wire, stood a mean looking bull. He lifted his huge head and took a hard look at us with his steely eyes. He was looking for the color red that would make him fierce and want to charge us. I was the only one wearing red; it was in wee patches on my shirt.

Sonny said, "We can do it; we can cross if we run real fast." The three of us crawled under the barbed wire and stood motionless, testing the bull. It ogled us, then dropped its huge head to eat more grass. Sonny whispered, "On the count of three, run!" Crouched in position to push off on the count of "Three!" Kathleen and Sonny ran!

I couldn't. The fear I felt was so great it was like my shoes were nailed to the ground. The big bull did not try to charge the others; I knew it was waiting for *me*! I was the only one wearing the color red. When Sonny and Kathleen were safe on the other side and saw that I was where I was, they chanted, "Com'on! Com'on!"

The feeling of being separated from my friends was worse than the fear of the bull charging me. I pumped myself up with lots and lots of confidence, then pushed off, running lickety split across that pasture. Hearing the cheers from my friends made me believe I was going to make it. I dropped to the ground, rolled under the barbed wire and scrambled to my feet. I looked back and I saw the bull still in the same place munching on grass. I was so happy it did not charge me, I said to the other two, "Shah is a dumb bull."

A stream of water was ahead and we made a loop around it, to the road and back to where we could see Mrs. Gouge's farm. There was a weathered, white house with dark green trim and behind the house was a pig pen and an old, red barn. I had already seen much of the farm from the Skiddoo when it passed by real close and knew the white specks all about the grounds were chickens.

A few sheep, a cow and two horses were grazing behind the barn, and near the barn was a tractor, and an old wagon falling apart. With such a short distance left, we raced down the hill to get there.

Sonny knocked on the door. When no one answered, Sonny pushed the door open and called out, "Mrs. Gouge, you home?" We guessed she did not hear us, or was not at home. Knowing we would be welcomed, we walked in.

She was not in her kitchen, nor was she in the other room which was her front room and bedroom. Sonny knew there was a soft feather tick mattress on her bed and wanted to show Kathleen and me how much fun it was to lie on it. The three of us, with a great sigh, sunk into the cuddly comfort of the mattress. While we were enjoying our rest, we could hear someone come into the house through the kitchen door. We waited quietly to surprise Mrs. Gouge.

When she appeared in the doorway, I saw her close up for the first time. She was wearing men's work clothes. I figured because her husband was dead they were his overalls and work boots. She had short black hair that caressed a dark and wrinkled face. Her long neck tapered down to a small chest and she grew very wide below her waist.

We hopped down from the soft mattress to greet Mrs. Gouge with warm hugs. She acted so very happy we came to visit; we had really, really surprised her!

Mrs. Gouge's kitchen was full of work that needed tending to and we wanted to help. On the cupboard was a stack of combs from beehives. In the combs was still a little honey and we got to dig out and eat what was left.

A huge horsefly wanted the sweet honey, too, and two more buzzed about like they were mad we were eating their honey! Sonny then stacked the combs where they were supposed to be, on a box by the back door.

I saw a big chore that I could do and asked, "Can I sweep ya fla?" I licked the honey from my fingers as Mrs. Gouge handed me the broom. I started at the edge and swept three piles of dirt up to a hole the size of a jar lid right in the middle of the kitchen floor. Then, with a swoosh, swoosh, swoosh I swept the dirt down that hole! It was such a clever solution to a dirty floor. I knew if Mother had a hole in her floor, she'd never have to use a dustpan again.

I felt the floorboards vibrating from an approaching train, the Skiddoo. Then the dishes in the cupboard made a clinking sound as the Skiddoo rumbled by on its way to town.

This reminder that it was noon made us feel very hungry. Mrs. Gouge cut each of us thick slices of homemade bread. I smeared my slice with butter that smelled so very good of wild onions, then I dribbled dark honey all over the butter. The horseflies buzzing about were quite annoying; I had to keep swatting them away! When done with my sandwich, I licked my fingers clean of the sweet honey.

After lunch, we had other chores that needed to be done outside. We followed Mrs. Gouge out the door with Sonny carrying a full bucket of slop for the pigs; some spilled a little before getting the bucket to the pig pen.

Kathleen and I stood on the outside of the wooden fence to watch Sonny pour the slop into a trough with the pigs pushing and snorting to get to it. Kathleen felt mean and screamed out, "Those pigs sound jus' ike you when you eat, Sonny."

Sonny, making believe he still had slop left in the bucket, made us believe he was going to throw it at us. A big pig like Lady Grace thought, too, there was slop left in the bucket and snorting wildly, she came running after Sonny! Sonny was afraid the pig would knock him over so he ran for the fence, and when scrambling over it, in time, Kathleen and I were laughing hard. We scooted ahead before Sonny could bop us over the head with that bucket.

Mrs. Gouge had disappeared somewhere and we had an important chore to do. The barn needed cleaning. We gathered up a long rope from the floor and hung it neatly on a nail. A tractor seat, two horse collars and wagon parts had to be hung on the hooks they'd dropped from. When picking up old tools with wooden handles, we had to be very careful of slivers. The rust and grease we got on our hands from handling cans and metal parts we wiped on our pants. Sweeping the scattered hay on the floor out of the barn door made us cough and sneeze.

Mrs. Gouge, wearing her heavy work boots, could be heard coming around to the barn door. She peered in and praised us, "My, oh, my, what a good job you three have done with this old barn." Then, as she handed a bucket to Kathleen and me, adding, "I have another chore for you girls to do. You two can gather the eggs." Turning to Sonny, she told him to follow her as she plodded away in her heavy work boots.

The chicken coop was a lean-to against the barn and inside it were a few chickens. I carefully opened the wire door and the two of us stepped inside, but we were not welcomed by those roosting on poles! We shielded our faces as the roosting chickens fluttered about squawking as they found their way past us and out the door.

The only chickens left were the ones nesting in boxes nailed to the wall. The eggs we were to gather were underneath the chickens. I tried to ease my hand under one, but she became very angry and pecked at my hand. I yanked it away!

Kathleen tried her best to scare it off the nest by throwing her arms about while hollering, "Shoo! Shoo!" Not one flew out and away.

I looked down and spotted a gray rock among the many globs of "calling cards" and picked it up. I took the bucket from Kathleen and made a loud racket hitting the rock against the bottom of the bucket. The hens scolded as they fluttered out of their nests and out the door. We plucked the warm eggs from the warm straw and filled the bucket almost full. With another farm chore done, we each gripped the bucket handle to carry it out.

As we walked around the barn to head for the house, we heard Sonny from behind us yell, "Hey! See what we have!" We turned to see Mrs. Gouge and Sonny, with Sonny carrying a baby lamb. We set our bucket of eggs down and ran back to see the tiny baby lamb.

Mrs. Gouge called the lamb a "bummer" because its mother did not want it. As Sonny continued to carry the baby lamb, Kathleen and I patted the fuzzy baby on its head while Mrs. Gouge carried the heavy bucket of eggs to the house.

Mrs. Gouge heated milk on the coal stove and as we played with the soft woolly lamb we giggled and giggled as it licked our faces. Kathleen got to feed it from the bottle and it sucked so hard milk dribbled to the floor. Sonny and I made a bed in the corner of the kitchen and after the baby had been fed it was readu for a nap.

We heard the clattering noise of a pickup enter the yard. It was Mrs. Bloomer, Mrs. Gouge's daughter, who'd come to pick up the eggs and give us a ride home.

Sonny lifted up the crate of eggs to set on the bed of the pickup box next to Mrs. Bloomer's eggs. After Kathleen and I hugged the baby lamb one last time, we hugged Mrs. Gouge then crawled into the cab of the pickup with Mrs. Bloomer. Sonny crawled up to sit on the bed of the pickup box to keep the eggs from tipping and breaking on the rough, bumpy road.

We waved goodbye to Mrs. Gouge as Mrs. Bloomer turned the pickup around on the dirt driveway. We got jerked about as Mrs. Bloomer dodged the many potholes. We felt one last jerk when motoring up and onto the highway.

We were taken to Sonny and Kathleen's house first. Kathleen and I were pleased when her mother bought some of the eggs that we'd gathered. Mrs. Bloomer was so nice; she told Kathleen's mother, "Ann, I hope you let the kids come to visit me sometime. They can help me, too, with my farm chores." We jumped with excitement hoping that would be soon. Then, Mrs. Bloomer took me home. I waved goodbye as she turned the pickup around heading for uptown to deliver the eggs to the stores.

When I reached for the gate, I very carefully opened it remembering the problem with Baldy. Instead of looking for him, I felt someone looking at me. I thought it was Bobby and looked up at his bedroom window upstairs, but there was no one there. At that moment I recalled what Bobby once told me about ghosts: sometimes you can see them and sometimes not.

I made it to the door of the house without Baldy finding me, but upon opening the door and calling out for someone to be home, Baldy came around the corner of the house. With him coming after my feet with his sharp beak, I had to dance about while telling him, "Be nice, please, you have to be nice." It worked; he calmed down and was nice. When no one answered my call I sensed how deathly quiet it was in the house and could not go inside.

As I sat on the step to wait for someone to come home, Baldy let me stroke his colorful silky feathers. That helped to ease my spooky feeling, and my wait was not long before I saw Mother coming from town carrying a bag of groceries. I cupped my hands about Baldy to hold him still so he wouldn't be mean to Mother as she came into the yard.

Mother smiled, expressing her delight in seeing me. She asked, "Did you have a fun day at Mrs. Gouge's?"

I answered in a perky voice, "Ya! She has a bumma!" Mother corrected my, "Ya" with a "Yes," then asked, "A what?"

I explained, "The baby lamb's motha did not want it so it is called a bumma." "Oh," Mother said, "I see what you mean."

With my scary thoughts still bothering me I wanted to know about ghosts from Mother. Before we went into the house, I asked, "Do we have a scawy ghost?"

Mother lowered her eyebrows with a questionable expression on her face. She set her groceries down, then sat on the step beside me and said, "No, not that I know of, and if we did have a ghost, why would you be afraid of it?"

I was surprised over such a question and blurted out my thought. "Cuz ghosts awe scawy and can hut me!"

Mother tapped me softly on my forehead with her finger while saying, "Ghosts are scary because you make them so up here in your head." She stopped tapping my forehead and said, "If there really were ghosts around, maybe if you were nice to them, they would be nice to you."

I gazed into Mother's eyes expecting to see a devilish look; sometimes Mother can look that way when she is spoofing, but she was serious! Instead of wanting to know how I could be nice to a scary ghost, my thoughts turned around to what Bobby said about our grandmother. I asked, "Can Gwandmotha be ah nice ghost in the house?"

Mother jerked her head back in a startled way before asking, "Whatever gave you the idea your grandmother could be a ghost?"

I answered, "Bobby said so!"

This time Mother's finger tapped me on my knee as she said, "I bet Bobby will stop trying to scare you if you simply tell him, you are not afraid of ghosts." Mother got up and went into the house, and I followed her.

After what Mother said, I was convinced a ghost could be nice to me during the daytime and I would be safe searching downstairs, where Mother was, for the nice ghost in our house. In the most important room, my bedroom, I found only dust balls under my bed, and my dark closet had nothing more than what was supposed to be there. I did not go upstairs to search, as I figured, like Sonny had said, if we did have a ghost, it had to be hiding in the dark, scary crawlspace, and Mother was never up there when I was.

Mother was right. When Bobby knew he could not scare me with his spooky ghost stories, he gave up trying.

In time, the unexplained noises stopped and I, too, forgot about ghosts during the daytime.

At night time was when my thoughts would cause a ghost to rise up from under my bed and creep around in the dark. I believed, by my habit of looking under my bed before crawling into it every night, that'd keep me from harm, and it did!

Now that Julia and I were six years old, we could play in the city swimming pool, but until we learned how to swim, we had to stay in the shallow end. Julia and I were buddies while in the pool; buddies were supposed to take care of each other and get help if a buddy was drowning. A boy almost drowned once. He was way out in the middle of the deep end of the pool and he was beating the water with his hands. When we heard the whistle from the lifeguard, we looked in time to see her dive in. The lifeguard came up out of the water next to this kid, grabbed him around his neck and pulled him to the edge of the pool.

One day, when Julia and I were walking home from the swimming pool, Frankie jumped out from a shed in the alley and scared us so bad! When we had other friends with us, Frankie was never around to be mean. It was when it was just the two of us when he would be so scary, but we always ran faster than he did to get away. Then, mean Frankie left town for part of the summer.

I went away for a while, too, to visit my grandparents in the country. I played store lady, and worked for gran'pa in his important United States Post Office by putting mail in the postboxes. I helped to sweep the floor and feed gran'ma's chickens, I ate lots of doughnut holes and practiced crocheting, learning how to do better. Punky's dad drove the two of us to a 4-H meeting where we had a barrel of fun. Then a nice farm lady took me home.

Well now, I am going to jump to the year 2022 to tell a story about my grandparents. I must. Gran'pa Otto had died leaving Gran'ma Anna, at age of 87, to manage everything. A winter storm blew in and created a bank of packed snow between the house and the pump for water. A young man entered the store and Gran'ma asked if he could please shovel a path through to the pump. He did try, but it was too much work, and he gave up. Then, what did the best doughnut maker in the country do? She carved out steps, up the bank and down, and her bucket runneth over with water.

I now tell of a heartfelt story about Otto, my Gran'pa. When taken to the hospital the month of June, he was told he would never go home again. My mother walked into the room and told him that I planned to be home in July, and he said, "I have to live to see my Tootse." And he did. He was home when I arrived, the family and I headed for the high country for a day of visiting. And I had a very memorable time with my Gran'pa, sure did. That night he died . . . I will dry my eyes now to continue telling my childhood story.

On some summer days I crossed the tracks to play with my old friends. Sometimes we went hiking or played in the cemetery and sometimes we collected bottles in buckets and boxes from the old, gray-haired hermit as an excuse to see his newest inventions. On Saturdays, when we had enough bottle money, we went to the matinee to see a cowboy movie. We filled every day with lots to do, except one day I wanted to see a movie, a scary one, and there was no one around to go with me.

Mother made Bobby take me with him and his buddy, Billy. Bobby whined and made a fuss over having to take me along, but Mother told him he had to, and that was it!

I did not care that I had to walk way behind Bobby and Billy as I clutched my box of Cracker Jack to eat when watching the movie.

We got there too early; the ticket lady was not in her booth and a long line began to form. Bobby and Billy established themselves in the line, then did what some boys do, dropped out to join other boys sitting on the curb. Cora, a girl I knew, was alone like me so I joined her, then as friends we would sit together.

A big boy took "cuts" to join other boys his size. He started telling them a story about a cousin who lived in the country. Cora and I could not help overhearing, and when he said his cousin was going to a country school, I imagined the schoolhouse behind my gran'parents store. When he told his friends about an "outhouse full of crap" they were not words kind to our ears . . . feeling embarrassed we had to act like we did not hear! But hear we did as he continued. His cousin and a classmate placed a long board half-in and half-out of hole in the back of the outhouse, and the embarrassing conversation continued telling about the teacher going into that outhouse, and his cousin jumping on that board, whacking that teacher with, you know what! "Ah, you joke!" said one friend, while another overhearing, said, "I know outhouses and that is impossible!" Never-the-less, other boys overhearing turned the story into a rip-roaring funny one.

The rattling of keys got the attention of everyone and a great cheer rang out with the ticket lady entering the ticket booth. All the boys sitting on the curb and the girls huddled together out of line, scrambled to take their places as had been saved for them. The line inched forward and then it came my turn. I shifted my box of Cracker Jack to under my arm because I had to have a finger free to pry loose the dime and two pennies stuck to my sweaty palm so I could pay for my ticket.

Cora and I traipsed down the aisle to the first row and took our seats in the middle. While waiting for the movie to start, I shared my box of Cracker Jack with Cora and she shared her Bit-O-Honey candy bar with me.

I thought about another scary movie I came to see once, about a monster named Frankenstein. It wasn't scary, it was sad. For a split few seconds the whole of that movie took a spin through my memory. *The people on the scween in that movie wha so mean to him; he was just a dumb monsta is all. He twied hawd to get away fwom those mean people chasing him. He found this blind man in a cabin and the blind man could not see Fwankenstein and Fwankenstein could only gwunt so they became vewy good fwiends. They helped each otha. Then a fia buned the cabin down, and when Fwankenstein saved the blind man fwom buning up, those mean people found him. I cwied so hawd fa po Fwankenstein when they put him in that cawt full of stwaw and stabbed him with that pitchfak, again and again, huting him so bad! Po Fwankenstein.*

The lights blinked in the theater signaling all to take their seats. When the curtain opened, a loud clapping noise drowned out the music announcing the Newsreel. The news was of seeing our soldiers in a war someplace and we saw our President sitting in his chair in his office speaking about this war. Next, we watched two funny cartoons that created hearty laughter from everyone. After the previews of coming attractions, the movie to scare us began.

Across the screen flashed the title of the movie that I could not read, but I knew what it was about, a Werewolf! I figured it would be like Frankenstein and not be too scary. The movie began with nice people dressed in an odd style of clothing who lived in horse drawn wagons. They were happy and friendly and liked to sing and dance. A young lady with these people was very pretty and there was this handsome man from town who was very much in love with her.

After getting to know all the characters, one day, in a wooded area outside of town, these merry people were singing and dancing. The pretty lady was dancing with the handsome man from town. Another man, who had a big head, was seen leaning against a tree watching the dancing. He seemed to be nice, but very lonely and he was wishing the pretty lady would dance with him. Then the festive night ended.

The next scene was the dark of night and dreary music started playing. The man with the big head was in his room and he was acting very nervously. Then we left him and were out into the night again. In the black sky was one cloud; it rolled away revealing a full moon. The light from that moon on the fog covered ground was casting shadows of doom. The fog drifting about alerted the creative power of my mind to smell a musty odor.

Then we were back in the room with the man with the big head who was pacing back and forth. Suddenly we were outside once more seeing the shadows of doom from trees and buildings. Dreary music played that caused my keen imagination to build up an anticipation of dreadful harm. I had to pull my feet up and tuck them under me. A big hand appeared on the screen. I grasped the arms of my seat when seeing icky, grayish hair grow all over that hand! Then claws popped out! The grayish hair grew up and up the arm. Then we saw all of the man with the big head as he jerked about becoming something else.

The scene flashed away. We were in a forest of trees where the horse drawn wagons were camped. The pretty lady appeared from a wagon. Not able to sleep, she decided to go for a walk in the night. Then in a flash, we were back in that room with the vicious Werewolf! I felt the thunder of a thousand hoofbeats in my chest as a savage beast with teeth to tear, and covered all over with rotten, matted hair, howled hideously! Everyone screamed! And screamed! Me, too! The Werewolf was wrecking everything in his way. Then it jumped out of the open window.

In the foggy night, the grizzly looking Werewolf darted from building to building and in the forest, he darted from tree to tree. The hoot, hoot was heard from an owl and too, the snarling and snorting of the Werewolf.

It was getting closer and closer to the pretty lady walking in the forest. I had to warn her! I screamed, "Go back! Go back!" She did not hear me! Nor did she see the Werewolf hiding behind the next tree! I jumped in my seat! I screamed! Everyone did as the flesh ripping, hairy hand reached out to grab her, but when she heard her name ring out she moved away in time!

The call came from the handsome man who'd saved her. I had worked so hard for the pretty lady, I sank exhausted in my seat.

As the full moon began to sink over the horizon, the Werewolf shook and jerked to again become that nice man with the big head, but he did not know what he had become. Our terror ended only to return with an eerie full moon.

When it was discovered that the Werewolf was the man with the big head, he became awfully sad. He did not want to hurt anyone. A solution was considered: build a cage strong enough to hold the Werewolf during the time of a full moon. It worked! Everyone was safe! "THE END."

Outside the theater, I waved goodbye to Cora. As I caught up to Bobby and Billy entering the first alley, I waved to my uncle Carney in his barber shop.

In the alley, I noticed there were big enough objects to hide a monster that could reach out and grab me! Even though it was daytime, I was scared! I stayed on the heels of Bobby and Billy all the way to my back yard gate.

Before entering the yard, I looked for Baldy. I had a feeling about him that troubled me and wondered why I hadn't seen him around for two whole days.

When I got in the house I asked Mother, "Whewe is Baldy?"

Instead of answering, she asked, "How was the movie?"

I knew if Mother knew the movie scared me she might not let me go to another scary movie. I answered gleefully, "I liked it! It was jus' a little bit scawy." I had to change the subject and asked, again, "Whewe is Baldy?"

Mother did what she does when acting irritated, she threw her arms about as she said, "I don't know! I don't know! Everyone wants to know where Baldy is and I do not know!" It appeared Mother was mad at me for asking, but when she realized how harsh her answer was, she said in a calm manner, "I suspect someone stole Baldy to have him protect their house from burglars."

I had a funny thought, "Baldy chasing that boogla! Afta the boogla wuns away, Baldy will come back home, he will."

Baldy's disappearance became a concern as he did not come back and I had another concern over what was haunting me: the Werewolf! I was free of fear during daylight hours, but in the dark of night, at bedtime, I imagined terrible thoughts. After falling asleep, I would have a horrible nightmare that caused me to scream and wake up Mom and Dad. The same nightmare happened again and again.

When going to bed, my mother stopped saying to me, "Goodnight, don't let the bed bugs bite." Bed bugs were a bug everyone feared and she thought that might be causing my bad nightmares. I feared that if Mother knew about the monster in my bad dreams, I would definitely be prohibited from going to another scary picture show.

While the light was still on in my bedroom, I checked under my bed and finding nothing there, crawled into it. Mother came along to snap off my light and to say, "Goodnight."

In my dark bedroom the doom and gloom feeling caused me to dream up a musty odor like the smell in our dirt cellar, a place where I imagined the Werewolf could hide! This became a fear too great and to change my mood I had to scramble my thoughts. I began my bedtime prayer, but when I got to the part, "If I should die," I pulled my covers over my head and did not continue my prayer. At some time I fell asleep.

The same bad dream rolled around and I found myself standing in an open field. I sensed that something very frightening was in a forest of trees far behind me. I knew I had to hide, and quickly! I looked for protection; I saw ahead, a very old, gray barn. What was expected, then became clear. I knew what was hiding in the trees; it was the Werewolf coming after me!

My heart was racing hard as I bolted ahead for the safety of that old barn, but after running and running hard I never got further than the spot I was standing on! The Werewolf's hairy paw with skin ripping claws was coming down on my shoulder! I screamed! I screamed! I awakened myself, and Mom and Dad, again!

Mother burst into my bedroom and held me as I shook from being so terrified. When I was calmer, Mother asked, "What in the world is causing these nightmares?" I shrugged my shoulders not wanting to tell her. She lifted my chin with her hand and she was looking me in my eyes when she said, "Have I ever told you about your guardian angel?" This was an odd question I had to think about, then I shook my head to and fro. Mother surprised me with more, "You do have a guardian angel." She tapped me on my right shoulder as she told me, "Your angel sits on your shoulder right here. She protects you from harm, and especially from bad nightmares." Mother then got up from my bed as she said, "Goodnight, and sweet dreams."

My mind became saturated with good thoughts of what was new; my guardian angel Mother said I had protecting me. It was too dark to see and when I touched my right shoulder I felt only the softness of cloth, but that was expected, I knew that, because we can't see angels. To imagine her, I etched and sketched in my mind what she must look like and figured out how tiny she must be. Vewy, vewy tiny. She has to be if she sits on my wight shoulda. I knew, too, She has white haiw like the angel on awe twee top. And she looks in ha face like a gawl, like me! Oe maybe smawt looking like a, a, a teacha! With happy thoughts over what I was imagining, I pulled my covers up under my chin. Then I remembered and uncovered my right shoulder for I sure did not want to smother my angel to death.

A good measure of blithesome sleep cleared the way for child's play in my "sweet dreams." I felt something that got my attention. I twisted my head to see what was tapping my right ear. What I saw was a white blur. It floated up with a fluttering sound and it landed in front of me, on my chest. I was astonished to see what the white blur was! I bolted up in bed causing what I saw to tumble over and down to my lap.

There she sat, my wee tiny angel all crumpled, her dress a mess and dangling in front of her face was a ring of gold, her halo. She helped herself up, smoothed out her dress and in repositioning her halo to where it was supposed to be, I saw that her hair was white and her cheeks were very rosy. She did not look old, nor did she look young, but like she could be a friend to anyone.

She looked up at me, then her tiny arm with an opened palm stretched out as though beckoning. I was awestruck as I wondered, Why? Then I realized what she wanted me to do and I eased my big pointer finger down to touch her wee hand. A tingle of electricity rippled through my body that made me jiggle and jiggle. I was shrinking! When my head stopped spinning, I could see my angel was as big as me; I, too, was tiny.

The halo over her head began to wiggle and wiggle, then took a dive to again dangle in front of her. She tapped her toe as though greatly perturbed and I jumped in to assist. I grabbed the ring and gave it a spin, but I did it too hard and had to run behind my angel to catch it! Once I had it stabilized in the air over her head I felt an urge to caress her hair. It felt soft and did not cut like the hair on the angel on the tree top. Her wings looked very fragile; those I dared not touch for fear they would turn to powder dust.

My angel reached out her palm and our hands became intertwined. Her delicate wings began fluttering; feeling light like bubbles, we floated up and up; I was flying! It was a beautiful, heavenly feeling. My bed and dresser below disappeared and we were in the color of blue somewhere. Then, that too disappeared and we were in the color of green, all around. As expected, with no guessing, the green was a giant Christmas tree. What I saw hanging from a bough made my heart go leapity leap! It was my favorite teardrop ornament, and it was gigantic!

Into its shiny, crinkly indentation we flew, up, down, and around laughing over the silly faces I was making at us in the mirror's reflection. Then my angel looked at me with a twinkle in her eyes that led me to believe I was in for another surprise. She snapped two fingers and in the silvery shine, Christmas lights lit up with colors of strawberry, lemon, lime, ale, orange and sarsaparilla. They were my bottle caps! We flew around them to the very last, a root beer. Then like a flash, I was suddenly in nothingness, all alone, and lost!

A spooky sensation tingled through me when I could not see my angel; she'd vanished! Gone! Where? When I was about to really panic, I saw ground far below me. I floated down with great ease, down, down, until my feet landed on a soft dirt mound. I thought my tiny angel was simply playing a game of hide and seek and I, too, still tiny searched for her under whopping big trees of grass and weeds, flowers and things.

I heard a whistling and I set my course through a patch of mighty big crocuses to seek and find her. I could not believe what materialized. I rubbed my eyes to see and saw more clearly, my three baby mice! My will-o'-the-wisp of enchantment was filled with much merriment as we skipped and romped about until bumping into a king-sized dandelion causing it to rain cottony seeds and under all of that fluff we sneezed and sneezed.

Like a carousel of mice and me, we whirled round and round, whistling. While synchronizing, we hit a unique key and unlocked more magic, a green thing-a-ma-jig. We stopped our whirling and what had been a blur in the middle was now visible: my pet green snake! Tears ran down my cheeks. I dropped to my knees and asked, "Awe you happy?" My snake lifted his head and waved it back and forth. I knew from before that meant yes, not no.

Bursting with joy, I leapt to my feet and again whirled with my mice, round and round, whistling. My snake rose up, and up, and up to wiggle and jiggle on the tip of his tail making us giggle and giggle until our giddiness of dancing created a spell of dizziness. Once again around, then my friends were gone as though blown away by a wind.

I was once more lost in nothingness, alone. I began falling, a heavy nauseating feeling. I kept falling while calling, "My angel! My angel!" I fell and I fell and no angel responded. Instead, my soft bed appeared and I landed on it. I rubbed my hands across my covers for the comfort needed as I wondered, How did my bed find me? My head still hazy, my stomach still queasy, I wanted to forget, and I knew nothing more through the night.

Early in the morning, while still in the far outer edge of my consciousness, I heard a whistling and in a blink of an eye I weaved together the part of my dream with my mice and snake. When I finally awoke, it was the tea kettle on the kitchen stove that was whistling. In a split second, I recalled every bit that was full of color and happiness and needed to tell Mother all about it. I hopped out of bed, thrust my arms out and I flew out of my bedroom all the way into the kitchen.

I screamed, "Motha! Motha! I saw haw!"

Mother asked, "Who?"

I wrinkled my nose wondering why she did not know. I reminded her, "My guawdian angel!"

It took a moment before she answered with a simple, "Oh."

I thought I finally had Mother's attention as I acted out my dream with much enthusiasm. I told Mother all about it up to when I was playing with my mice, and I had whirled too much, causing dizziness in my head and in my stomach. While I rubbed my queasy stomach, I remembered my falling and asked, "Why would she not come when I needed haw?"

Mother was poky again in answering. She appeared empty headed when looking at me, and when she realized I said something about someone, she asked, "Who?"

I was terribly frustrated! I gave a sharp answer, "I told you! My guawdian Angel! Why would she not save me fwom falling?"

Mother set her expression in a frown, but I perceived it was a deep thinking frown before she asked, "What makes you think your guardian angel didn't save you? You woke up safe in your bed didn't you?"

Without the least delay of thought I knew what Mother meant; my angel did save me after all! With her magic she put my bed where it could catch me.

After the hot water from the tea kettle had seeped through the coffee grounds, the brewed aroma seemed to have awakened Mother. She poured herself a cup, sat down, and from the cup, she poured part into the saucer to let it cool. She heaved a nice "sigh" to say she was now ready for a new day.

As Mother and I shared the cinnamon and sugar toast she prepared, Mother related what her thought was, "It is comforting to have a guardian angel, and we must be thankful to our Father in heaven for giving us one. Now that you know your angel will protect you, you need not have any more of those nightmares." Sneering, Mother said, under her breath, "So we can all sleep through the night again!"

My mind suddenly was set on the day of my grand-mother's funeral when hearing about Jesus and, too, about "Our Father in heaven," and my attentive listening had aroused a great curiosity within me over what was meant by the word "sin."

I asked Mother, "Sin, what is that?"

She set her coffee cup down, and as she blinked her eyes, I knew the words were about to roll out, as she explained, "God gave us ten very good rules to live by and when we break one of those rules it is called a sin."

I blurted out my next question, "Have I sinned bad?"

Mother gave a perky reply, "You can bet your sweet patootie you haven't!"

As we laughed over Mother's playful comment, I could tell by her expression she was nurturing a feeling that put her in more of a good, heavenly mood, and she shared her sentiment with me, "Do you remember your Bible stories about Jesus and how he loved children especially?"

"Ya!" I answered.

Mother corrected me by saying, "Yes, not ya!" She hesitated while remembering what her thought was, then continued, "Jesus loved children especially because children are full of perfect love and so forgiving. If you are always kind to others then you will never have to worry about being a bad sinner." Mother had a smug, contented look as she picked up her cup and gulped down the last of her coffee.

I felt comforted from what my mother said. I lifted my arms way out and I flew out of the kitchen all the way to my bedroom. After I was dressed, I thrust my arms way out to fly out the door of the house to a new day of play with my friends.

At bedtime, I continued the habit of looking under my bed before crawling into it, but before falling to sleep, I would remember to uncover my right shoulder so my guardian angel could breathe. She did what Mother said she would do; she protected me by taking away all my fears when sleeping and I suffered no more from ghoulish nightmares.

Chapter 5

With school about to start, my great enthusiasm for adventure filled me full of confidence. I was six, a big girl, and ready for first grade.

The morning of that first day Julia and I reached the school grounds and found the place buzzing with older kids meeting old friends. Their cocky expressions made me realize they knew what to expect and I *didn't*. My confidence fading, I felt like the size of a wee pea, unimportant. In such a situation, Julia became very shy and I had to pull her along to get us to our first grade classroom. We were greeted by Mrs. Welsh, a friendly looking teacher, and seeing familiar faces from kindergarten helped to make us feel welcomed.

As Mrs. Welsh did the roll call, we were assigned desks so we'd be sitting in alphabetical order. I was seated behind Alexander.

As then ordered to do, we filed out of the classroom in an orderly manner to join others going outdoors for the flag raising. All six grades formed a big circle around the base of the flag pole. Watching the bigger kids across from me I imitated, placing a hand over my heart, but as soon as I realized those on either side of me had their *right* hands over their hearts, I switched! The red, white and blue flag whipped in the wind while I did my best to mimic what the others were saying for the "Pledge of Allegiance."

Afterwards, we first graders got to stay outside to march around the school grounds. We shouted louder than our teacher as we marched, "Left, wight, left, wight." She told us, this would help to get our left brain to work with our right brain, and help something else called "Whythm."

Once seated at our desks again, teacher held up a sheet of tablet paper and a pencil. "Pupils, do you know how fortunate you are to have paper and pencil to use?" It was not a question to be answered and she explained with another question. "Can you tell me what you could use if you did not have a pencil to write with, or paper to write on?"

There was total silence as she looked from one student to the other, waiting for a reply. David slowly eased his arm up as though he was not sure of his answer. When teacher acknowledged him, he asked, "Could I use chalk on a blackboard?"

Teacher's face lit up. "Yes! Good answer. What else could be used?"

Now that I knew what teacher wanted to hear from us I remembered what Betsy did, and thought, use a stick and wite in daat.

Sharon raised her hand, teacher acknowledged her, and Sharon said, "I would use a paint brush and paint on a rock."

Teacher nodded her approval then called on Louie whose hand was held high and shaking wildly. He yelped out, "Smoke signals!" That made sense because Louie was an Indian.

Teacher said, "Very good."

I was still thinking of my idea when Gail gave his answer. "We could chisel letters in a stone."

Teacher nodded, then acknowledged another's raised arm—Julia's. Julia said, "I would use a stick to make words in dirt."

I glared at her for stealing what I had wanted to say! With not another hand raised teacher said, "Those were all good answers and every idea mentioned was used before paper and pencil were made available to mankind. We must feel very fortunate and not be wasteful. Use the front and back of your paper, do not over sharpen your pencil, and please do not bite the eraser off."

Our first lesson was to print the capital letters of the alphabet. On the blackboard teacher had already diagrammed how to use two wide lines. I drew a big A again and again across the page as instructed. On the next two lines I drew lots of big B's, then C's. When working on the big D, I felt the presence of teacher behind me and that made me so nervous I pressed too hard and drew one very heavy capital D. Teacher gave me a pat of approval on my shoulder making me feel at ease again. After teacher checked the work of the students in the last row, she said it was time to put our tablets away.

Teacher then grabbed a book from her desk and flipped the pages and read aloud,

"Good Morning." Nobody responded so I guessed that must be the title of a poem. Then she read,

"Good morning, sky;
Good morning, sun;
Good morning, little winds that run!
Good morning, birds;

Good morning, trees,
And creeping grass and brownie bees!
How did you find out it was day?
Who told you night had gone away?
I'm wide awake! I'm up too.
I'll be right out to play with you!"

Then came what was best of all . . . recess.

On the playground, the second graders, whose recess overlapped ours, were already hogging the teeter-totter, slide, swings, and merry-go-round. We first graders stood back and watched.

In the afternoon when recess came again, as suggested by teacher, Bob grabbed the football for all the boys to play with.

Janice and Darlene pulled the long, long jump rope out of the toy box for us girls to have fun with. On the playground, Charlotte and Carla were first to take their turn to flip the rope. As the line worked up to Suzi jumping, I was next. I rocked until my rhythm was just right with the flipping rope and when Suzi jumped out, I jumped in.

I was in perfect rhythm, happy and having fun until someone dashed by throwing a hand out making the rope go crazy, causing me to trip and fall! I saw it was Sherman running away with the football in his grip.

I was so mad I screamed a bad word I had overheard a second grader using. "Damn you, Sherman!" Realizing I had said a naughty word I was greatly relieved a teacher hadn't heard me, yet I had to endure being shamed by Rita. After I had my turn flipping the rope with Annie, teacher's whistle blew and we had to return to our classroom.

At the end of our first day in first grade, teacher said, "We will continue tomorrow what we started today." Then we left the schoolhouse for home.

After leaving Julia at her gate I walked to the door of my house, feeling a great loss for my grandmother who died. She would listen when I told her of things I did; sometimes Mother acts too busy to listen. This had been a big day and I had so much I wanted to tell. When I found Mother, she did seem excited to hear about what happened on my first day, until she let go of a heavy sigh, then I knew she had heard enough. When Grandmother would sigh, she would say those nice words, "Oh, to be young again."

I changed to my play clothes, ran outdoors and found Lila waiting to tell me all about her day in kindergarten. I already knew about kindergarten and let her know she had to learn about first grade for when she gets bigger. Before I could tell her much, Howie was heard stomping down the back stairs of the apartment house. Lila and I ran around the back yard fence and met him in the alley at our favorite old heap of a car. We got inside with Howie grabbing the seat behind the wheel. He made it clear to Lila and me that we had to listen to him to learn what second grade was all about. After a long time of listening, he took us on a wild spin with him spitting out a loud motor sound, "Brrrrruuummmm, brrrruuuummmm." For miles and miles he steered that wheel never *once* giving us a turn! When I heard Mother calling me home, I was glad! Lila and I piled out of the old heap and left Howie sitting all by himself.

As the school days passed, my confidence of feeling bigger than a wee pea took a gradual climb. I soon knew what to expect in the schoolhouse and on the playgrounds and learned every word to the "Pledge of Allegiance."

I liked the challenge of trying to do better. With the help of teacher I could speak a few words with r's in them correctly, "Are, our, for and or." The stories teacher read were fun and some were an adventure to new places.

Printing the alphabet had to be done perfectly by each of us, and we were still working on the small letters when I taught myself to say the alphabet backwards, just as fast as Julia could! My best friend was a little smarter than me, but I was much better at coloring. When decorating the classroom for Halloween, I did a real good job coloring my witch, teacher said so.

An old problem was much worse though, now that Julia and I were in first grade—we got out of school at the same time as mean Frankie. Some days Lila would wait for us after kindergarten and on some days Howie would walk home with us, but on the days Julia and I were alone that cagey, mean kid would hide and wait for us. Taking a different route did not help, somehow he'd know, but we got away from him every time by running as fast as we could.

Two of the decorated pumpkins in our classroom from Halloween were getting so stinky Mrs. Welsh had the janitor carry them away. Of those that remained, their good smell reminded me of pumpkin pie and being at my gran'parents in the country at Thanksgiving time.

One day a big class art project was to decorate for Thanksgiving, cutting out pictures of food from magazines that we thought had been eaten on that first Thanksgiving Day. It was fun, but our fingers were made sore from using the scissors that were safe for us to use. Teacher said, "We will skip printing the letters of the alphabet. Instead, I will read a story."

Teacher walked to the middle row of desks, raised one arm high in the air until she had the attention of everyone. "I am going to divide the room in half." With that arm coming down, she directed, "This side will be the Pilgrims and this side the Indians. As I read to you about that first Thanksgiving Day, imagine who you are in the story." I was on the side of the Pilgrims but I wanted to be an Indian. Louie was supposed to be a Pilgrim like me, but he was a real Indian, and that gave me the idea I could imagine myself as an Indian.

Mrs. Welsh glanced at me and the other Pilgrims on my side of the room as she read, "A long, long time ago in sixteen hundred and twenty, a ship called the Mayflower sailed across the big Atlantic Ocean." She glanced at the Indians. "When the Pilgrims landed on the sandy beach of this new land called America, at what is called Plymouth Rock, the Indians, me!, welcomed the Pilgrims, me!, to their great land." Playing both, was fun!

All of us, Indians and Pilgrims, imagined working hard to hoe the garden to plant pumpkin seeds, potatoes and corn. *We built cabins from trees we had to saw down, but making a cabin was new to me for I lived in a teepee. Fall was soon upon us and it was time to harvest the food from the garden. The girls, all of us from both sides of the room, shared in preparing pumpkin pudding, peeling and cooking potatoes, and husking the corn. The boys, from both sides, went hunting for a wild turkey. When the food was ready, we sat together at long tables near a roasting fire and our appreciation was shown for the bounty of food and for new friends we had made.*

Teacher put her story book away and picked up a stack of white paper with a heavy outline of a big turkey like we colored in kindergarten. Eric and Percy got to hand them out. I flipped open the lid to my crayon box and searched for the color brown and the color orange for a smidgen of blending. Concentrating hard on doing a good job of coloring, I bit down on my tongue and began to daydream about that first Thanksgiving Day.

The color was of fall and there were Indians and Pilgrims all around. Food was stewing in a pot over a fire that was red hot. From yonder forest of trees I heard the voices of men and a terror-ridden "gobble, gobble" sound. I saw Indians and Pilgrims tugging at a rope tied to a turkey to be butchered. The dying fire needed more wood and the hunters left to find what they could. On hands and knees I crawled to the frightened turkey and whispered, "Be still and I will wescue you."

I untied the rope and we crept along until we were found to be gone. We then ran hard until coming upon a log hollowed out and crawled into it. Out of sight, we hugged to calm each other's fright as the ground rumbled from the thunder of many feet that passed and faded away in the distance. We sighed in relief; we were now safe!

When I stopped concentrating to search in my crayon box for another color, I released the bite on my tongue. I finished my turkey by coloring the dingy under his chin red. Our colored turkeys were much too pretty to eat; I could not think of such a thing and said in secret to my paper turkey, *At home you'll be safe with me; no one will eat you.*

At the end of the school day, Mrs. Welsh wished us all a very nice Thanksgiving. As we filed out of the classroom in an orderly manner, my attention was drawn to the second and third graders bolting out from their classrooms. They were shouting their glee with lots of "hurrays" over having a holiday from school.

The air outside was bitterly cold. Julia and I had to button our coats way up under our chins. Howie started out with us, but because he was not dressed for the frigid weather he darted ahead, in a hurry to get home to a warm place.

When I reached the back door of my house, the delivery boy, Harold, was just coming out. On the kitchen table was lots of food that Harold had left and I felt a bit unsettled over what that meant. I asked Mother, "Are we not going to Gwan'ma's tomowwow?"

"No," she replied, adding, "Your dad said a lot of snow had been dumped along the highline so we'll have to stay home." She snickered, and I saw her with a funny expression as she said, "We could get stuck up there and have to stay all winter long!"

The night before Thanksgiving as we sat at the table eating, I thought my turkey taped to the dining room window was very pretty. Patty's horn of plenty was too and Bobby's John Alden was okay, he lost Priscilla on his way home from school.

Mother made my thought turn around when she told Dad about an observation she'd made. "We are getting so many more hobos at the door begging for food."

Dad's voice became gruff as he said to Mother, "Send them up the street to the soup kitchen!" Mother acknowledged Dad's order with a simple nod of her head.

The smell of two apple pies baking on Thanksgiving morning made good spirits come alive in all of us. Bobby was so nice. When the leftover pie crust sprinkled with cinnamon and sugar was pulled from the oven, Bobby didn't say to me as he usually did, "Look over there," and grab for my share. When later we played pick-up-sticks, He didn't blow his breath to make me fumble my stick, and when lining up dominos, did not try to be the one to begin toppling over the dominos one after the other before I could do it.

When the roasting turkey was ready, Patty helped Mother by setting the table with the best of everything: glasses, dishes and silverware. I got to fold and place the fancy napkins under the forks as told it was correct to do. After the gravy was made and the potatoes were mashed it was time to set the bounty of food on the table.

As we were asked what part of the turkey we wanted, the turkey I saved and taped to the window had no resemblance to the turkey we were about to eat, so I asked for, "A dawk piece, please."

We ate until we were so full we had to save our pie for later. As we pushed away from the table, Dad retired to his favorite chair. Bobby disappeared somewhere and I got to help Patty and Mother clear the table, although I carried just the silverware; Mother knew I could not break those.

I was in the kitchen with Mother and Patty when Bobby walked in; he stood close enough to the pie so he could snitch a piece of the crust. I was about to squeal on him when the ring of the front door bell made me stop and wonder, who could be visiting on this day?

Dad was the one close to the door and we knew he would answer it. Soon after, Dad entered the kitchen and we waited for him to say who it was as he walked to the remains of the turkey on the platter. With a sheepish look on his face he asked Mother, "You suppose you could carve a little of this away for a sandwich for `someone' at the door?"

I knew it was a hobo! I quickly looked at Mother remembering Dad telling her to send them up the street to the soup kitchen! She just grinned knowing Dad, too, could not turn away a hobo who was hungry. She dried her hands from doing the dishes and made a great big turkey sandwich for that "someone" at the door. That "someone" got a piece of apple pie, too!

That night the snow along the highline blew down over our town. When getting ready for bed, I looked out the window and I saw a flurry of whirling, tiny flakes.

With every wink of sleep through the night, lots of snow-flakes fell and when I awoke and looked out at a beautiful sunny morning, I saw heaps and heaps of snow.

I ate my breakfast as early as Dad, then watched him do his toothpick trick when kissing Mother before leaving for work. As he went out the back door Mother could not help seeing the heaps of snow and she sneered, then her sneer broke into a smile for the snow was too pretty to not like.

When it was time to play outdoors, I surveyed the scene from the front step. There was so much snow, only the tips of tall barren branches marked where the shrubs were. When making my way to the tire tracks in the street, I sank so deep in the snow I had to take giant strides to save my energy for playing.

I heard a door of a house bang and saw Lila bounce out. She huffed and puffed as she struggled through the snow to reach me. Howie joined us and we skated on the packed tire tracks until reaching Julia's house to get her.

The four of us played in the snow until the whistle of the Skiddoo could be heard and we knew it was noon. Plodding through such deep snow to try to reach the train tracks took a lot of strength; we fell lots and laughed too much and could not make it to the tracks in time to wave. We took our break for lunch, then gathered again to play in the afternoon, then again on Saturday and Sunday. On Sunday night a new storm dumped more snow.

On our way to school Monday morning, Julia and I had to walk in the tire tracks in the streets all the way. Reaching the playground, lots of snowballs were flying from all directions. When both of us got smacked in the back of our heads with snowballs, we turned and spotted Frankie with a pile of ammunition meant for us. We ran to another part of the playgrounds.

Everyone was having so much fun that when the first school bell rang, we ignored it. When the second bell rang, there was a rush for all to get inside the schoolhouse so as not to be marked tardy. We carried a lot of snow in on our boots and the great hall and our cloakroom smelled of melting snow.

During reading class with our Dick and Jane book open, Mrs. Welsh left Gary's desk after helping him and sat down with me. She pointed to the words on a page and asked me to read them out loud. I quickly read, "Wun, Spot, wun!"

She looked me in the eyes, then said, "Remember, take your time and pronounce the 'r' as I have taught you."

I looked at the three words again, took my time and read, "Rrrrun, Spot, rrrun." My face beamed with joy knowing I said my r's correctly. Mrs. Welsh beamed, too, as she pulled my head into her warm bosom while saying, "That's right! Now keep practicing."

As Mrs. Welsh went on to help Kay, I repeated the words on the first page, "Rrrrun, rrrun." Then I searched for other words starting with the letter "r" and I found "Rrred" four more times. Not finding more I repeated, "Run, run, red,

red." I then searched the pictures for words I thought might have an "r" sound and I found three, "Rake, rope, and road." Realizing "car" had been a spelling word, and it had an "r" in it, I searched for words like, car and farm.

I could very easily become sidetracked studying the colored pictures as I did when seeing all the red apples on the apple tree. I knew if I ever found an apple tree like the one in the picture, I would pick all the red apples, put them in the red wagon, and take them home. I turned the pages until coming to a rainy day. I picked out new picture words to add to my "r" list, "Rain, raincoat and rubba boots."

In the picture, something seen, brought up an unpleasant memory which caused my toes to curl up. The umbrella in the picture reminded me of what happened last summer. After my friends and I had seen the News Reel at the theater showing soldiers parachuting out of an airplane, we wanted to do the same! We jumped from the roof of an outhouse using a dumb umbrella as a parachute. I landed so hard when I hit the ground it made my feet sting very, very bad! I flipped the page to erase that memory not knowing the word "Umbwella," had an "r" in it.

Saturday afternoon, Julia and I, with ten pennies between us, entered the corner drugstore to buy a funny book. There were a slew of kids inside and we had to squeeze our way through to get to the funny book rack. Julia picked out a few, then sat down on the lower shelf to decide on the one we would want to buy.

Julia opened a Superman comic book and, seeing the words were much too hard for me to read, I did not want that one nor Tarzan. When Julia said she thought I would like Dick Tracy, I simply shrugged my shoulders. Watching the kids around me was much more entertaining.

The shrill whirl of a milkshake maker drew my attention to the soda fountain. I recognized a girl sitting on a stool who I had seen doing something awful one day. I nudged Julia, pointed out the girl so she'd know who I was talking about, and told her, "She picks ha boogas and eats them!" We both acted out pukey-like expressions, then Julia became absorbed again in a funny book, Mickey Mouse and Donald Duck.

A tall boy walked in front of us and stopped, blocking my view. All I could see were his legs and looking up I saw his name was like my dad's, Ray; it said so on the sleeve of his school sweater. I looked down and laughed over how Huey, Duey and Louie were making Donald Duck so mad he was furious!

The giggling of girls drew my attention away from the funny book. Four girls near a glass showcase were looking in it while sneaking looks over their shoulders and giggling more. I looked to see what was so silly to the dopey acting girls and saw that they were looking at dumb Bobby and his buddies Jimmy, Roy and Bud who were strutting into the store. When Bobby saw me, he said, "Hi, ugly!" I ignored him, yet I liked the feeling of being acknowledged by my brother around other kids in a public place.

The shelf under us quivered from the weight of someone else sitting down. We looked and we saw Frankie! He cut loose with an awful mean laugh and fearful of him, we could no longer enjoy our fun in the corner drugstore. We jumped up and put all but one funny book back. We paid for the one we hadn't looked at yet and got out of there!

While crossing the street, the crunching noise from tires on the snow packed street prevented us from being able to hear. We had to look back to make sure Frankie was not following. Someone opened the door of a tavern to go inside and we smelled the sickening odor of whiskey and cigars. We pinched our noses while uttering, "pee-u."

On the corner of the next block, at the Shoe Repair Shop, we did not wave to the shoeman inside as we walked by; he was busy waiting on a customer. At the window of Gruder's garage, I noticed how much the red pop machine glistened, reflecting the sunshine through the window. We waved back to Mr. Gruder who was waving at us.

When we reached my house Julia came in so we could share looking at the pictures in our funny book, Archie. When through with it, we wanted to trade with Howie, yet we knew best to trade on another day. Howie preferred funny books like his favorite, Tarzan, or The Lone Ranger. We knew if we could get a hold of either one, maybe he would trade for Archie, too.

Monday morning at the door of the schoolhouse, the janitor inspected the bottoms of our boots to make sure the snow was stomped off before allowing us to enter. Later that day we decorated the windows in our classroom with cut out white snowflakes. All sixth graders, in the next few days, had to prepare their classroom for when the parents visited after our Christmas program.

That very last day of school before the break, filled us all with a joyful feeling as we students anticipated our program in the evening, and the beginning of our two week vacation from school.

We so loved making snowflakes, teacher let us make another to take home. When the last bell rang, we filed out of our room into the great hall. Although we knew we would be back that night for our program, we joined in the jubilation by yelling as loud as the second and third graders, "Hurray! Our last day!"

Julia and I held our delicate snowflakes close to our chests to protect them from being torn by the wind. Frankie, who'd been hiding behind an old shed waiting to scare us, did so! Julia and I ran so hard! After reaching my yard, I saw that my pretty snowflake was torn from whipping in the wind while running.

I hated Frankie, and my ruined snowflake, too! When I got in the house, I was about to crumple it and throw it into the trash can when Mother grabbed for it. She thought my bad attitude was only because of my ruined snowflake. She commented on how beautiful it was while using tape at the tear when taping it to the window.

That night, dark and very cold, it was just Bobby and Mother walking with me to attend the Christmas program. Inside the warm, brightly lit schoolhouse, everyone glowed, as we did, with rosy cheeks and smiles. Then, when all attending had arrived, the songs of Christmas filled the great auditorium during our fun program, and the festivity lasted through the visit to my classroom. Julia and I let our mothers mingle with other parents while we mingled with our classmates.

When Gary was overheard talking to David about Toyland, going to Toyland became the topic of conversation with everyone. It was to be the next night in a furniture store uptown. Julia and I had never been to Toyland before. With all our classmates talking about it, we figured this would be the best time to ask our mothers if we could go.

We glowed with excitement when they both said, "Yes."

The first day of Christmas vacation was spent waiting for the expected night of fun at Toyland. The great suspense over what to look forward to and being alone uptown after dark made Julia and me become overly giggly. At supper time, too, I let my excitement be heard with bursts of giggles and forgot to count the chewing of my food.

Later, with my coat on and my nose to the window, I waited for my ride with Julia and her dad. Outside, the night was oddly daytime almost from the light of a full moon reflecting off the snow. Along with feeling gay and happy I also felt myself drift into a comfortable spell of dreaming as I wondered about the many toys we would see that night.

To me, a wagon, bike, sled, scooter, and skates were far too important to think of as toys. A ball, yo-yo and jacks were toys, and Sonny's tinker-toys were toys. Reminding myself of Sonny's toys, I thought also of his tiny, cute farm animals. He didn't catch us playing with those, nor did he know it was me who wound the key to his toy car too tight, breaking the spring. Kathleen saved me; she hid it.

Suddenly I was startled by Mother screaming, "Get your nose off that glass!"

Seeing the fog left from my breath on the glass, I tried wiping it away with my coat sleeve and only made a bigger smudge. I looked back to see Mother angrily sneering, then the ooga, ooga sound of a horn signaled me that my ride was pulling up to the curb. I ran for the door!

As Julia's dad drove the pickup along Front Street, Julia and I, in a jovial mood again, giggled and giggled. When the pickup came to a stop in the middle of the block across from the movie theater, we jumped to the ground, avoiding the slippery running board. Waving goodbye, we saw a few kids we hardly knew waiting for the door of the furniture store to open.

Julia began acting shy and I had to pull her past the kids to the glass door where we could peek inside. A dim light from a showcase glowed enough so we could see a partition of walls enclosing an office in the middle of the store. On both sides of the walls an aisle was formed with a heavy twisted rope to keep us kids from bumping into the furniture. There was total darkness at the back of the store where we imagined the toys must be.

Julia and I became numbers "eight" and "nine" in the waiting line. We stood motionless staring at other kids staring at us until I became aware of a darkness all about. I peered up at the sky and saw nothing, not a moon or stars. For a need to be comforted, I searched for any light, and the common, visible source became the lamp posts up and down the streets. In a dream-like thought, they became rows of soldiers using their halos of light to protect us. Then out of the cover of darkness, with a halo of light reflecting off it, one puffy, fluffy snowflake floated into view over my head. It floated down, down, down to my feet where it joined others that earlier had ceased to exist as one. More puffy flakes appeared floating towards my face and I did the usual thing—stuck my tongue out to catch one. Julia and the other kids also dropped out of line to position themselves with their tongues out under a falling flake. As I caught one, another hit me in the eye! I felt someone tug on my coat as I was wiping my eye dry with my mitten. I turned and I saw Kathleen!

Although Kathleen, Sonny, Bubber and Betsy had been expected, Julia and I acted surprised to see them and became silly with giggles again when greeting our special friends. As more and more boys and girls jumped in line, we girls were being entertained by the many clowning boys horsing around and I almost forgot why we were there.

Those of us at the head of the line heard a jingling of keys at the door and alerted all the others that Toyland was about to begin by clapping our mittens together, making a thumpity "puff" "puff" sound. Those further down the line cried out with great shouts of joy!

The door opened to a now brightly lit store. Hearing the sprightly musical tune of Parade of the Toy Soldiers, I put a "get up and get there" step in my walk as we made our way along the rope draped aisle. At the rear of the office was a flight of stairs. Up the stairs was Toyland! It was all tinsel, glitter, twinkling lights and sounds of toys wound tight. Wonderstruck, I was drawn up, and up, and up like a puppet on a string to the big floor above. Then I saw, on the other side of a circling, white picket fence, all the toys in the world.

I forgot about my friends as I stood at the picket fence to see the electric train that was set up. The black locomotive was revved to a steady "chchchchchchch" sound as it pulled a heavy load of teeny weeny Christmas trees. It chugged across a bridge over fake water and pulled into a tiny town where tiny clay people stood with a doggy scratching its ear.

I got nudged and pushed along the picket fence and saw a cabin made from building blocks, a fort made from Lincoln logs, and swings, and things made from tinkertoys. A hobby horse came next, a scooter, trike, and bike were placed side by side. Then I braced my feet to make others pass me when I saw a whole kitchen made my size. The table was set with dishes, like Patty's that I could not play with, but I did not care about those, or the sink, or stove, or refrigerator. I liked best the cute, tiny wicker basket made just like Mother's big one and more fascinating, were the teeny clothespins on the clothesline; they really worked!

Baby dolls, the kind that cry when tipped upside down, were tucked in a buggy and cradle. A stuffed teddy bear was sitting in a highchair. Then I looked up to a shelf that held other toys, and saw *her*! Propped up in a box was the most beautiful doll I had ever seen! Puffs of golden ringlets stuck out from her bonnet made of white fur, like the muff her hands were tucked into. Her soft velvet, scarlet colored coat was form fitting to her waist, then flared out and down to her white stockings and shiny black shoes.

The beautiful doll had made a place in my heart before I was forced to move along. A toboggan, so big, so big all my friends and I could fit on it, hung from a hook on the wall. Two sleds, one big and one small, hung beside the toboggan. A long board on sawhorses had an entire play farm on it.

There was a dollhouse bigger than the red barn and every room was filled with tiny furniture. There was a tractor and lots, and lots, and lots of toy farm animals. Next, marched an army of four toy soldiers wound tight. A lady wound up a mouse and let it go. The mouse bumped a toy soldier causing it to knock down others. The expression of frustration the lady had was funny as she fumbled with their moving while setting them up.

Another lady made a colorful top spin and she pushed the push toys along. She made a plane fly on the floor by winding its propeller tight. A red wagon was filled with stuffed animals and there were games, skates and more. Then I found myself at the end of the white picket fence looking downstairs to the floor below.

I felt the warmth of Julia's hand slip into mine. Together we tripped down the stairs to the tune of Jingle Bells and traipsed along the rope draped aisle to the door where two ladies stood. One reached into a large cardboard box and pulled out a surprise. Wrapped in colorful cellophane were popcorn balls! She handed one to each of us while uttering her wish, "We wish you two a very Merry Christmas."

Outside, the night seemed so dark and cold we felt sad to have left the warmth and glitter of gay lights and the toys inside. Ahead, waiting, was Julia's dad in his pickup to take us home.

In my house, warming myself over the floor furnace, Mother asked what I had liked best at Toyland. I felt the need to keep quiet because we believed that if we revealed our wishes they would not come true. I simply cocked my head and smiled. Mother shrugged her shoulders and walked away.

When ready for bed, I stood again over the floor furnace until my pajamas felt very hot. Then I made a dash for my bed so my warm pajamas would warm my wintery sheets. My good feeling of Toyland brought to mind the smell of green boughs and the sound of sleigh bells. At that moment I made my wish for what I had seen and liked best because I believed only Santa Claus needed to know. Then I imagined the beautiful doll was really mine and told her, "I will take good care of you, neva would I take ya clothes off and neva would I cut ya haih. I would keep you special foreva, and eva, and eva." After I pretended to show her off to my friends, I went to sleep.

The next day my neck felt sore. When I complained to Mother, she suspected I was coming down with the mumps and that I probably got them from Lila. I said, "Howie has them, too!"

Then Mother said, "Well, maybe you got them from Howie." The next day I definitely had the mumps, my neck was so swollen I had no neck at all. It was our Christmas vacation from school and I couldn't play.

Bobby had no business teasing as he did when he looked in at me in my bed. He laughed over what he called my, "Grotesque disfigurement." That sounded so ugly and though it hurt to talk, I did cry out for help with one word, "Motha!"

After his scolding, Bobby still teased, but in a quiet way with a smirk-like expression, making me so mad! The second time when I called for help, Mother made me feel so sorry for myself when she got mad and screamed, "For cryin' out loud! Ignore him!"

Mother made a bed on the davenport for me because she said I was calling for her too much! This helped, as Bobby could not get close enough to tease without Mother seeing him.

Feeling not so good I slept a lot. When asleep my thoughts turned into a dizzy spin. Coming at me were odd shapes growing big, then small, then big, and not going away at all. Then all went away when I heard Mother ask, "Would you like a bowl of soup?" At that moment, Patty took a crunching bite from an apple and being reminded of its tartness, it made my neck ache real bad! Mother could tell from my frown I was not hungry so she walked away.

Maybe it was because I slept a lot because when awake, my mind seemed especially clear and sharp. I could catch a thought and hold it steady without other thoughts messing up a picture in my head. This would help me learn something about our train. When I heard the whistle of the noon Skiddoo, "Whooooooah! Whooooooah!" I had recognized for the very first time something different about the whistle. What was it? I held the two "Whooooooah's" steady while thinking, then moved the sounds to the back of my mind, to make room for the next clear thought.

I pictured my friends and myself at the tracks waiting for our train. When the Skiddoo came into view, the whistle blew, "Whoooooo whooooooah!" I compared the two whistle blasts with the two in my head and they did not match. One whistle blast had the "ah" missing. That was it! All along there had been a special message in that whistle just for us kids! A tremendously tender, cuddlesome feeling warmed me as I knew then that not only did Mr. Engineer and our train love us, but the adorable whistle did, too!

I now had a great discovery to tell my friends as soon as I was over the mumps, not realizing that they might have heard a sound different than I had, or hadn't thought about the whistle at all.

I fell asleep and awoke when hearing the click of the radio. It was too much of a struggle to stay awake and I heard only parts of Mother's program, Ma Perkins. Then marching music announced that the news of the day was about to begin. The newsman was so loud he kept me awake listening to his talk about a war. He spoke of what our President Roosevelt said about it and where the generals said our troops marched to the day before.

This war sounded bad, especially when the newsman said, "Our soldiers, our boys, will be spending Christmas in a foxhole, cold, hungry, and lonely as they fight this war." I pulled my blanket over my head to hide from my thoughts of the lonely soldiers who were so very cold and hungry.

The next two days, I waited to hear the whistle of the Skiddoo. I had to make sure, without us there, there were "ahs" when the whistle blew. I needed definite proof so that I could tell my friends of my great discovery.

Christmas day passed and although I was feeling much better, Mother didn't think I was well enough to play outdoors in the cold, cold weather.

Lazy like, I sat back in the overstuffed chair. I had one leg draped over the arm of the chair and the other on the new doll buggy I got from Santa Claus. I rolled the buggy back and forth with my leg as I pouted over what I did not get: the secret wish I had kept between Santa and me, the beautiful doll at Toyland.

I knew someone else got that doll because mother told me once, "We do not always get what we wish for as someone else might be wishing for the same thing."

My wish now was that the girl who got my pretty doll would take good care of her and never cut her hair off. My lips tightened when I imagined she might, Boy, would that make me mad! I then hated that girl and took my anger out on my new buggy by giving it a hard push. It rolled, banging into the wall! I then felt bad and I gently wheeled my buggy about while softly saying to my baby dolly in my buggy, "Hush, hush."

The next day I got to go outside and Julia and I, pulling our sleds, headed across the tracks for Beaner Hill. When close, we heard the gleeful screams from Sonny, Bubber, Betsy and Kathleen already sledding. That made us hurry along and when joining in the fun, I forgot all thought of my great discovery, the Skiddoo's whistle.

Bubber, after a great spell of going up and down the hill, yelled to Sonny, "Let's lose the girls and head for the cemetery!" That was his way of teasing us, yet with so many more kids taking over the hill, it was time to move on.

The two boys got a big head start on us girls and we caught up to them near the top of the cemetery road. Leaving our sleds at the brick pillars, we blazed a trail through the snow to get to the stone monument. After greeting Mr. Rip, we heard smart-alecky Bubber bellow out, "Wonder what all the ghosts are up to?"

We girls knew he was trying to scare us so Betsy bellowed back, "Shut up, you dodo!"

Then Kathleen, so not to be heard by the boys, whispered, "Are there reawwy ghosts here?"

I simply added a wise comment before her fear became my fear, "Ghosts don't come out during the daytime."

High and mighty Julia blurted out, "But if you have been bad, ghosts can come out during the daytime to punish you!"

This time I certainly did not want to believe her and I said loud and clear for all to hear, "Ghosts can be fwiendly ghosts! My motha said so!" The boys, with their dumb laughter, were making a fool out of me, so I made up my next statement, "And if the ghosts are mean, there are enough of us to fight them off!" The boys liked tough talk and that ended all discussion about ghosts.

Sonny pointed as he yelled, "Hey, let's hightail it over there to play fox and geese!"

I was careful to plod along in the trail in the snow made by the ones ahead of me. That kept me from making another mistake by stepping on a grave. I never forgot Julia's bad luck story, a reminder of where my grandmother's long silver box was left. I was glad we did not explore that part of the cemetery; somehow it did not seem right now to play there.

When reaching the area for our game of fox and geese, we found the place partly filled with a flag pole and new tombstones. We plopped down on the cushion of snow. The two boys fell back and quietly rested. I was enjoying the wintery scene of glistening snow about us as we listened to Betsy sharing her thoughts.

The distant sound of the Skiddoo was then heard, "Whooooooah! Whooooooah!" and I remembered my desire to share, with my very special friends, that particular subject about the "adorable whistle," and yelled, "Hey guys, the whistles!"

Bubber groaned from his prone position, "The ol' Skiddoo's whistles? So what?"

I snapped back at him, "Don't you wanna hear what I have to tell!"

He demanded, "Tell what?"

I had to explain what they needed to learn first before the next whistles would be heard. "You guys, rememba those lotsa times we met the Skiddoo? Well, we are here now when hearing both whistles end with ah's, but if we were there now you wouldn't hear an ah in the first whistle."

From their dead silence, I knew I had to explain better, "I tell you, when it sees us it goes just 'Whoo-Whoo-ah.' Doncha see, the first whoo has no ah ... it whistles with no ah ... it does!"

Bubber had a strange look on his face as he said, "Has no, huh?"

Then Sonny responded with, "Whistles with Noah?"

I smiled at Sonny for understanding before I exclaimed to him, "Ya! No 'ah'!" Then I frowned at Bubber for being so dumb and I added a more sensible explanation for him, "You see, there is an 'ah' that is missing in the first whistle!" Expecting the next whistle to blow at any time I said, "Shhhhhh," and whispered, "Stay quiet now and listen to the ah's in the two whoo's of the whistle, but rememba, we are not there!"

Then clear as a bell the whistle blew, "Whoooo-ah! Whoooo-ah!" Kathleen had a sweet smile—she understood. Betsy looked to be seriously thinking, Julia, too. Bubber, though, was acting kooky, rolling his eyes and shaking his head, and Sonny, now a traitor, acted dumb looking like Bubber.

My heart had raced with excitement, wanting them to learn of the special message from our "adorable whistle." It seemed so easy figuring it out on my own, but I was baffled on how to educate them more—to make them all understand. Then it came to me. "I have a plan!"

Boys especially like forming a plan. It worked! Bubber was so curious he sat up and said, "Tell me your plan."

I laid it out then. "Let's meet at the twacks tomowwow."

Bubber did not care what for, he took over and set the exact time and the very spot along the tracks to meet. Then he made us all seal the pact we'd made for his plan, with a pile up of hands.

Sonny wanted to leave the cemetery because he was getting hungry. The rest of us followed him out and we whizzed down the road on our sleds. Then we parted to go to our homes.

The next day, as planned, Julia and I met to get to the other side of the tracks. It was very important to be at the exact spot at the exact time, but we did not have to count nine rails past the grain elevator as Bubber had ordered, we could see the others already at the exact spot.

We had a bit of a wait for the Skiddoo and gave ourselves good running starts to glide on a slippery rail. Gliding up, then back, gliding up, then back until we heard the signal, "Whoooooooah! Whoooooooah!" We then leaped into our smudged boot prints already made in the snow, to wait.

Around the bend it came, the mighty black engine in the lead. My friends beside me made it so much fun and the power I felt made me feel big. When Mr. Engineer saw us, he did what we expected, he waved. Then I saw what I had forgot, he pulled the cord to make the whistle blow, Whoooooo whoooooooah! That was when I knew, I had lost my senses believing it was the adorable whistle that loved us, too. The special message of love, with the first "ah" missing, was made by Mr. Engineer, not the whistle.

I felt so, so glad I hadn't tried to educate the boys more that day. For sure they would've made fun over my mushy, mushy talk about a silly whistle.

As our train zipped by, we had to stop waving to cover our faces from the freezing and turbulent air it created. The boys, then wanting to move about to warm up, were first to take off.

I knew the Skiddoo would be nearing the depot soon and as I had trained myself to do, I listened. When the whistle blew again, as before without us there, the distant sound was, "Whoooooooah! Whoooooooah!"

A big and unexpected surprise came from Betsy as she said to me, "That whistle was different from the one we heard when the Skiddoo passed us." With Betsy understanding part of what I had tried to tell them, I responded with a "giggle" and we girls ran to catch up to the boys.

Our Christmas vacation over, in cold, blizzard like weather, Julia and I reached the schoolhouse and joined the pack of kids waiting for the big doors to open. In the freezing wind we stood huddled together, all wishing the janitor would let us in early.

A snowball hit me on my back jolting me forward, then Julia got hit! The mean laughter was coming from Frankie! I was too cold to care, and too cold to giggle when someone complained, "Geeze! You couldn't smell a fart in this wind!"

After the bell rang, the big doors opened and the warm air was a welcome relief as Julia and I climbed the stairs inside. When I got to the top step, I tripped and fell and lay sprawled out on the floor of the great hall. Feeling like a clumsy bear I wanted to roll into a ball and pull my coat over my head to hide. Especially so when I heard Frankie's ugly laughter coming from somewhere nearby making me feel more embarrassed! My face felt red hot when lifting myself up and the laughter followed me all the way to my classroom.

Mrs. Welsh stood at the door with a happy smile welcoming us back. When roll call and the pledge of allegiance was over, teacher asked each of us to share our experiences of Christmas. Instead of starting at my end of the room which she usually did, she started at the other end with the very last kid named Yager. This gave me the time

I needed to think of what I wanted to tell about. Yager, and a few after him, spoke of who visited, where they went, what they ate, and what they got. When oh's and ah's were heard over what they got, it then became just a roll call of presents the rest told about.

That is how I learned that Sharon got my pretty dolly! While feeling sorrowful for myself again, it came Campbell's turn behind me and my heart began racing because I was next. I became so befuddled that when I stood up I said what I had not planned to, blurting out, "I had the mumps!" A ripple of groans from around the classroom was funny, making some laugh. This gave me time to get into control, and I said what I had first wanted to say, "I got a doll buggy, a game, mittens, and a war bond stamp book!"

One pupil asked, "What's a war bond stamp book?" Another said, "I got one too!" Teacher clapped her hands to end the disruptive talk and to give the last student her turn.

After Alexander sat down, Mrs. Welsh looked directly at me with a serious expression. "Would you please explain to everyone what a war bond stamp book is for?"

I stood up, hesitated a moment, then after forming a square with my hands I explained, "It is about this size and it has lots and lots of pages with little squares that are for stamps. One stamp costs ten cents and my motha told me when I get eighteen yas old I will get seventeen dollas and I will be rich!" Then I sat down.

My teacher thanked me, then said, "I would like to explain further. With each stamp we buy, we are loaning our money to our government, our President, to help end this war so our soldiers can come home." I then felt great excitement over my important gift, while thinking, If I fill my book, maybe President Woosevelt can stop this war, then our soljas won't have to be so cold and hungwy; they can come home, like teacher said!

The rest of the day in school the weather outside remained bad. At the end of the day when Julia and I left for home, the sleet was like needles pricking our faces. We pulled our scarves up over our noses, huddled close together and let instinct guide us to my house. I felt sorry for Julia having to buck the wind the rest of the way alone, but I was glad for myself!

When I entered the vestibule, I kicked my boots off and burst through the door into the living room. Finding the house dark and cold, I remembered Mother had started her new job that day. I snapped a light on, darted to the floor furnace and turned the key to make a burst of flame erupt below.

As I stood on the grate getting warm, it was so quiet I imagined the presence of something else in the house. I kept my coat on ready to run outside just in case I had to. When I became too warm, I finally had to remove my coat, but stayed over the floor furnace where I felt safe.

When I heard Patty and Bobby bursting through the door of the vestibule, I ran to my bedroom, my hot shoes sticking to the floor all the way. I knew if Bobby saw me he'd try to scare me about spooks in dark places. The noise of Patty and Bobby fighting over the floor furnace sounded comforting; I no longer felt alone and fearful.

After waiting long enough, I left my bedroom, but found Bobby still on the floor furnace. I had to walk by him and he said to me, "Hey, scum ball, didja find any spooks under your bed?" I felt certain he'd peeked through the keyhole in my door; it made me so mad!

I shouted back, "No! You bird turd!"

Bobby snorted a short smart laugh, "That's turd bird, you drip."

I barked back at his nonsense, "That's silly! I'm telling you, a turd bird is nothing! It's bird turd!"

Bobby shouted, "You sheep dip! Bird turd means . . ." he jabbed his chest with his pointer finger, giving me a lesson, "I am a turd of a bird!" It took two seconds of thought for Bobby to realize he'd pulled a goofy joke on himself. It took one second for it to dawn on me and that gave me one second to dart away up the stairs for safety with Patty!

Hearing Bobby's angry yell, I had to explain to Patty what happened and the two of us rolled on her bed trying our best to hold back the sounds of our laughter.

Mother's new job was at Yondell's Grocery and Bakery Store. The store was closed on Sundays, and Mother took Mondays off to get her work done around the house. When coming home from school on Mondays, I would feel the warmth from freshly ironed clothes, from food cooking on the stove, or fresh baked bread.

Patty had to help with a few chores on the days Mother was working, and Patty let me help. She'd let me scrub the potatoes to be baked, then with the oven lit I stood back to toss the potatoes in. When I got to set the table, Patty would praise me for doing a good job.

One day when Patty was in her bedroom, I thought I would surprise Mother by waxing her furniture. I did not know you weren't supposed to use floor wax on furniture and Mother had to work awfully hard removing the floor wax as she repeated in disgust, "It is a good thing this is old furniture!"

Like Mother, I found a job outside the house. Once a week, after school, I worked at the garage where Dad worked. The office lady, Alice, paid me a whole dime to pick up papers that had fallen to the floor. I bought stamps for my war bond stamp book with the dimes I earned, but filling my book was slow going. Bobby was on his second book, when I had only a few pages filled in mine.

Some days after school I ended up at Yondell's store to be near Mother. If Mr. Yondell was making cookies in the back room, he'd let me help cut them out and when he looked away, I would snitch a piece of dough.

When lots of ladies were shopping, Mother made me stay out of the way by making me sit on a wooden crate. I observed the ladies visiting while they shopped. One grumbled a lot over having to fool with the little red tokens needed to buy flour, sugar or coffee.

Noticing the sack of flour she was paying for with money and tokens reminded me of when Mother once said, a sneer on her face while sifting flour into her cookie dough, "The sifter was not meant to sift flour finer, but to sift these good-for-nothing bugs out!"

The new delivery boy, Larry, let me go with him to deliver groceries, if Mother said I could go. This was exciting fun for me as I got to see parts of our town I had never been to before, like exploring, and if Larry had more than one box of groceries to deliver from the truck, I helped carry them up to the house.

Another job in the store Larry had was candling eggs. There was a box with a lit flashlight propped up in it and a crate next to it that Larry sat on. He'd hold an egg from another crate up to the light to see if there was a chickie inside. Larry let me help with this job and I became very good at candling eggs. Then one day I sat on the wrong crate and smashed a lot of eggs that created a slimy mess on the floor. Mother told me I had have to grow bigger before helping with that job again.

My Valentine cards from my school party were so pretty. We made them heart shaped and they opened like a store bought card. In order to get them to stand up on my dresser, I had to put them on their sides and the mirror's reflection made it seem I had twice as many. One card toppled over and caused a few others to fall with it.

When picking them up I read each one again. "ROsEs R RED ViLETs R BLu sKunKs sTinK anD sO DO Yu fRUm tOm." The next from David read, "2 kutE 2 B 4 goten Yrs til I.D.K." The next had a lot of hearts drawn all over and it had no name. Gail's card was not nice, "Roses aR Red vilets aR blu i kild my hous caus he loked like U." I liked the next one best because it was from my good friend, "You arr verry fun to flut with me yur frind RITA." The one from Kathleen had a kitty on it that she drew. Once I had the cards all standing again, like the mirror, my mind reflected on the Valentine party at school.

Teacher let us bring a younger sister, brother, or a friend to school and Julia and I took Kathleen. The first half of our school day Kathleen sat with me at my desk. After lunch she sat with Julia. Our art project was to cut out heart shaped cards from red paper for our party. With my white crayon, I made lace around the edge of all the hearts, then I drew stick people and printed what teacher had on the blackboard, "BE MY VALENTINE."

To begin our party, teacher picked two postmen to deliver our cards. We had pink frosted cookies and cherry kool-aid, then our party was over. Remembering our fun, I sighed and a puff of air from my sigh caused a few cards on my dresser to topple over again.

Late in February the warm chinook winds melted the snow into slush, then early in March it turned cold, but there was no wind; it was as quiet as a lamb. I knew then that March would be going out like a lion, and it did. The night before my birthday, near the end of the month, the wind was blowing so hard it sounded much like a lion roaring!

When I awoke on the morning of my birthday, I was suddenly seven. I remembered what Mother had told me the night before, "Six will disappear forever and you will never be six again."

I thought about being seven years old, seven seemed too important to be just a number. Seven has made me more gwown up, I am now catching up to Patty and Bobby!

I was too old for a party, yet when supper was over my family remained around the table as Mother surprised me with a cake Mr. Yondell baked. It was so pretty.

I made a wish, then blew out all seven flames with one breath. After Mother cut me a piece, I ate the spongy cake part first, leaving much of the frosting for the last good bites.

Bobby tried to trick me so he could steal my frosting, but I was too smart for him when he baited me with, "Look over there!" Instead Patty stole his last bite when he was looking at me. It took Bobby a moment to figure out if he'd eaten it, but upon remembering, he scowled a mean look at Patty while the rest of us laughed.

Mother cut Bobby another piece of cake after she handed me two presents. The one gift, a pair of pink bloomers, was embarrassing and I quickly stuffed it under me on my chair. The next gift was a fancy pink dress. Then my birthday was over.

At the end of the first week of April, spring had sprung. The warmth of the sun was welcomed by all. As Julia and I walked to school we saw the first robin of spring. We made a wish by licking a thumb then sealing our wish by stamping it on a palm of a hand.

Good weather also caused a bad memory of an old threat. After school, Julia and I figured mean Frankie would be waiting for us for sure. Thinking we could make him give up and go home we walked very, very slowly and stopped to rest at the garage where my dad worked. Later we made it down the first alley and part of the second, feeling Frankie's presence behind every garbage can, shed, and fence, making us fear him more than ever.

When near the back of Gruder's Garage, we detected a movement behind a big tractor wheel and were already running when Frankie jumped out! The sound of his thumping feet getting closer made me try to run faster and I fell hitting the dirt alleyway on my knees. I quickly leaped to my feet and ran to join Julia on the other side of my back yard gate. Frankie climbed on the gate, and looking like a mean ape, he shook it! He then hopped down and headed up the alley.

I felt a burning sensation and looked down. My brown stocking covering a knee was torn, and drops of blood could be seen. After Julia left by the front yard gate I hobbled into the house. I caught the scent of a good smell to remind me Mother was home and as I hobbled to my bedroom I cried out for her help! I sat on my bed, unlocked the garters holding my stocking up and eased it down over my "owuie." With my knee exposed, I could see tiny bits of gravel embedded where the blood was. I dabbed the blood away with my ruined stocking and I picked the gravel out with my fingernail.

When Mother came and saw my hurt knee she left and brought back a wet washrag. When she draped it over my knee it burned, making me scream, "Ouch!" I told Mother how it happened.

She thought about what I had said and asked, "Why do you let Frankie chase you?"

I answered, "Becuz! He is so mean!"

Mother asked, "Has he ever hurt you?"

I pointed to my knee while letting her know, "He made me fall! See!"

Mother simply shook her head, then left. I figured, she did not care, not even if I died! I felt so alone as I fell back on my bed with my hurt knee propped up.

I hated Frankie! I hated him so bad I wanted to do something bad to him. I pictured that mean kid in my head as I saw him one time at his grandmother's walking on the plank to the outhouse. Suddenly, a hidden memory spun out about a story of an outhouse and a teacher and I knew then what I could dream up to do to him! It went: *Julia and I had been skipping along on the path by the river minding our own business, as usual. Looking up the bank we saw the back of an outhouse, the one behind Frankie's grandmother's house. I whispered to Julia what we could do, and we did it. We drug a long skinny board up the bank then we stuck it in the vent hole at the bottom of the back of the outhouse. It was like a teeter-totter, with our end up. We laid on our bellies to wait. When we heard the squeak of the screen door of the house, then footsteps on the plank, we knew this was it! With Frankie inside the outhouse, Julia became scared and slid down the bank. It was up to me to do it all by myself! When I knew that mean Frankie had sat down I leaped high in the air coming down with my feet planted on that board!*

Thoughts of yecchy stuff on Frankie made me roll about with laughter. I imagined Julia on my bed with me as we both sang out, *We did it! We did it! We did it! We got even with mean Frankie!*

Then a twist of something was felt, like a power within me, as though fear had been a chunk of ice that had just melted away. Instead of hate for Frankie, I felt bad and guilty being more mean even in a dream than he ever was to Julia and me.

The next morning as Julia and I walked to school I told her, "I have a plan to stop Fwankie from scaring us." It was too shameful to talk about poop so I did not tell her my dreamt up story. I simply whispered to Julia my plan for after school. During morning recess, lunch time, and afternoon recess, we went over and over what we were going to do to Frankie.

When school was out Julia and I walked slow enough to give Frankie time to hide to wait for his moment to terrorize us. Walking down the alley we put on our planned act to look frightened like we were expecting him to scare us.

When we came to a cluster of garbage cans, it happened! Out he jumped! Instead of screaming and running, Julia and I did as we planned to do, we stuck out our tongues and sang, "Na-na-na-na-na!"

Frankie, with a goofy look on his face, did not know what to do! When he finally realized what had happened he broke out with a "Ho! Ho! Ho!" laugh, then said, "You guys have been pretty scared of me! I guess I better ease up on the two of you. Wanna be friends?"

Our plan had worked! We became friends with Frankie! He walked the rest of the way with us and many times more, even when going to school.

The Easter bunny left me with candied eggs and new anklets in my Easter basket and I got to wear my new pink birthday dress to Sunday School. Easter meant it was time to put our winter clothes away and I no longer had to wear my long stockings.

On warm spring days on the school grounds, marbles were won or lost and games such as pump, pump pull-away, tag, and mother-may-I were played. The tulips teacher had us plant in early fall were up and blooming. Mine was yellow; Julia's was red. One day in the classroom we had fun making May Day baskets. I made four!

On the first day of May, a school day, I left the house early to deliver a basket filled with candy to Howie and Lila's door. Neither one was fast enough to catch me and give me a kiss.

At school, Mrs. Welsh read a story from her book on how children long ago danced around a Maypole. That sounded like fun, but my thought was more on who Julia and I were going to deliver a May Day basket to: Frankie! After school, Julia and I were glad he did not walk home with us because we did not want to give away what we had planned to do.

At my house, we stopped long enough so I could fill my basket with candy for Frankie. After reaching Julia's house, she filled her basket with candy, then we snuck to the door of Frankie's grandmother's house. We set our baskets on the step, rapped on the door, then ran to beat sixty back to Julia's house. What we hadn't realized was that no one had ever given Frankie a May Day basket before and his reaction was slow. When he finally caught up to us, we had enough time to feel definitely safe from him trying to give us an ishy, ishy kiss.

We had fun with Frankie; he had lots of ideas on new places to explore. He joined us, too, when playing with our other friends.

One day when we were running across the open prairie playing cops and robbers, Frankie was a bad robber just like Bubber and Sonny. We girls were the good guys, the cops, after the bad robbers. Cracking our imaginary whips to get our imaginary horses to move faster, we'd all cry out, "Hi-Ho-Silver!" Like The Lone Ranger we'd seen at the picture show. The more we chased the more we cried, "Hi-Ho-Silver!" Frankie had surely become one of us, "Hi-Ho-Silver!"

After school was out for the summer, I played every day from early morning until the sun went down. Then two weeks of Bible school took away my mornings to do what I wanted to do. The last day, in the classroom in the basement of the church, I sat coloring and thinking of Frankie. He had to go live with his Mother someplace far, far away for the summer. I had never been far, far away and wondered, How far is far, far away? It seemed so sad to be far, far away. After coloring Jesus in many colors, I did like I had done before to the sheep. I painted one lamb pink, one blue, one yellow.

Saturday morning the window shades in the house had to be taken down. Before Mother left for work she left

Patty and Bobby with that chore to do. I wanted to help, even though Bobby, with a poky attitude, kept sending me mad looks as though it was my fault he was not allowed to sleep in.

His laziness got him into trouble with Patty. He didn't roll one shade all the way up before taking it down and then, throwing it to the floor created a lot of dust that made all three of us sneeze and sneeze. I thought it was funny, Patty didn't. After her burst of temper, Bobby responded by saying, "Why do we hafta do this? This dumb air-raid business is nuts!"

I did not know what Bobby was talking about, nor that it had anything to do with window shades. I asked, "What's an air-waid business?"

Bobby snapped at me, "Geeze! It's not a business!"

Patty then explained to me, "An air-raid is a siren that blows to alert everyone that the enemy is coming, like playing a game of war. When we hear the air raid siren we have to turn off all the lights and pull down all the new, dark shades that Mother will be putting up and keeping them down until the siren stops. It will be fun!" Bobby found a spider on its web at a window and he chased after me with it, out the back door and around the house. I ran in the front door locking it behind me, but Patty was right there unlocking the door. Bobby had to drop the spider in the peony bush before going back to his job of taking down the window shades. Then Patty suggested that I go find Lila to play with.

Julia and I, on our way to the city swimming pool Monday morning to begin a week of lessons, skipped along while chanting a song, "We git to go swimmin' with bowlegged women and dive between their legs. We git to go swimmin' with bowlegged women and dive between their legs." When close enough to smell the chlorinated water, we raced the rest of the way.

After we wiggled into our swimming suits, we joined other boys and girls in line at the pool. Our instructor said to watch her to know what we were to do in case we were drowning and needed to be saved! She dove into the deep end, and when her head popped up she was splashing wildly about like most drowning victims do, but then she stopped and shouted, "Do not do that! Panicking makes it hard for anyone to help you." Upending herself in the water she came up, putting on a milder splash act, waving and calling for help. When no one came to save her, she stopped splashing, rolled over on her back and floated with ease until she reached the edge of the pool. We then followed her to the shallow end to learn our first lesson, how to float on our backs.

I was quick to learn to be a good floater. I liked floating and did so with ease, just floated and floated until loud voices coming from the dressing rooms let us know, it was time for open swimming and we beginners had to get out. Entering the girl's dressing room, the girls flitting about were of the size that could make all those blotchy lipstick prints all over the concrete wall at the sinks.

When Julia and I were dressed, and leaving our stall we saw an older girl in her open stall, naked. We were embarrassed to see and dropped our sight to the floor when walking out of the dressing room. It was nasty to talk about being naked so I did not share my thought about the subject, but had another. I asked Julia, "Why do girls wanna kiss an icky cement wall?"

Julia paused in thought, then said, "I'll ask my mom."

After we two parted at my gate, when entering my house it was so quiet, I knew I was home alone. Just then a flood of thought filled me with wonder, could I make myself look like an older girl? Maybe, when wondering about what Patty had in her dresser drawer she would wear sometimes. Once in the kitchen to go upstairs, two steps up I stopped, to ponder my thought about what Mother had at the kitchen sink, her black, curly chore girl she used to scrub pots and pans. I dared myself, then sure did it, grabbed the thing and stuffed it into the pocket of my pants. I darted up the stairs and into Patty's bedroom.

Afraid of being seen I pulled the new dark green window shade down, and turned on a light. A sneaky, hush-hush thing to do had my heart thumping pretty fast when opening Patty's dresser drawer. I saw what I needed and pulled two bumps out, Patty's thick, shoulder pads.

The first shoulder pad I folded over to make a bigger bump. Then I shoved it under my t-shirt, pushing it up to where it was needed. Doing the same with the other, I shoved it up too hard and it popped out from the neck of my shirt! Once in place next to the other one, I had to squeeze my arms tight to my chest to hold them in place.

When eyeing my 'lady look' in Patty's mirror I did a fancy hoity-toity walk. Upon remembering another, I reached into my pocket, and pulled the crinkly chore girl out. As it was a wee bit greasy, it slipped out of my grip to the floor. To pick it up meant having to relax my arms and as soon as I did my 'lady bumps' dropped to the floor too.

I heard a noise. Downstairs! I panicked, afraid of getting caught, I quickly stuffed the shoulder pads back into Patty's dresser drawer, zipped up the window shade, and snapped off Patty's light. I was just about to leave the room when I saw the chore girl on the floor! I dashed to it, picked it up and stuffed it back in my pocket.

Patty emerged at the top of the stairs just as I scooting out the door. She asked, "What were you doing in my room?"

My heart was all a flutter, yet I came up with a sensible answer, "I had to look out ya window to see if Lila was in her yawd." Then I made a quick escape, dashing down the stairs and out the back door of the house!

I forgot about my grown-up act while playing. When I had to go home, I happened to slip my hand in my pocket and felt, yet, the chore girl! I had forgotten all about it! A terrible fear had me worried someone might ask why I had it, so I found a hidden spot in the yard, dug a hole, and buried it.

After supper I saw Mother at the sink, looking around for "you know what." When she mumbled, "The darn old thing must have fallen in the garbage can," I let her believe it did. Then, as a little girl would do when feeling free from getting caught, I did a hop and a skip, and flew out the door to play with my friends.

Collecting empty bottles was still an exciting and rewarding change from our usual play. The old, gray hermit could not be expected to have empty bottles for us all the time, so to find more bottles, we needed a new place to search.

One day, Sonny, Bubber, Kathleen, Julia and I, followed the railroad tracks to the far other end of town. We discovered a new country we'd seen only in storybooks; a large green meadow surrounded by a forest of trees and we left the tracks to go exploring. Our investigative search, though exciting, did not yield a hidden treasure, only lots of fresh cow pies from the milk cows eating the lush green grass.

Coming back to the cinder strewn tracks we saw a vacant hobo's camp under a railroad bridge. There was a large oil drum used for a stove and it was full of ashes. Empty cans, an old shoe, empty bottles and what looked like rolled up bedding made the camp look like someone might be back soon. Kathleen, Julia and I became frightened and wanted to get out of there. We gathered what bottles could be found and headed back for town and to Stan's bar to trade them in for money.

Two new stuffed animals added to Stan's collection were interesting, yet the buffalo head still left me dumb with grief. As we left Stan's bar, we felt rich listening to the jingle of money in our pockets. We then made plans to go to the Saturday Matinee the next day.

Inside the theater waiting for the movie to start, Kathleen, Julia and I sat three rows back from the first row and Sonny and Bubber sat a few rows behind us. Betsy came with another friend. I don't know where she sat. The chatter, though very loud, was fun to hear and it was interesting watching other kids. Some shared popcorn and candy, some made trips to the bathroom and some traded seats to sit with another friend. The lights in the theater blinked and all chatter stopped as those in the aisles scrambled for their seats.

The roar of airplanes was heard as the massive red velvet curtains began to part. We were all expected to stand when we saw the bombers on the screen flying in a V shape formation across the blue sky with a chorus of male voices singing, "Off we go into the wild blue yonder climbing high into the sky..."

Standing, while feeling patriotic, honoring our brave soldiers having to fight in this great war, I remembered the last time at the theater when, instead of bombers, we'd seen a fleet of war ships sailing on the mighty blue ocean. At that time the chorus had sung, "Anchors aweigh, my boys, anchors aweigh…"

The News Reel came on, showing pictures of the war. In black and white I learned the ominous impact of what Mr. Newsman said was an "Air-raid." Sirens whirled and whirled as beams of lights criss-crossed the night sky searching for enemy bombers that were dropping bombs on the city. I felt doom and gloom when seeing the destruction caused from the bombs that fell. Rubble, fire, smoke, and terrified people scurrying about made for a terrible scene, and another scene the camera captured left me with a great measure of sorrow. Standing on a pile of rubble stood a little boy with black curly hair. He was crying, and alone, and I wanted to know, "Who would want to hut you, little boy? I couldn't. My mother and father wouldn't, nor my sister nor brother, nor my friends eitha."

The serial started from where it ended the week before. Watching it, the comedies, the previews and the movie could not erase the plight in my thoughts of the little boy with black curly hair. Only when we stumbled from the darkened theater out into blinding light from a hot sun, did I forget.

As we walked along the tracks, the hot sun caused waves, like smoke, rising from the cinder strewn ground. The heat made me feel heavy with sleep, making me want to stop and just stare at the ground. I remembered what Mrs. Oister said about Uncle Sam when he got killed by a train, "Must have been the heat from the hot sun that paralyzed the old man." I wondered then, "Could this be what is happening to me?" I kept in step with my friends until near my home. We then parted.

The house felt so comfortable, cooler than outside. I went right to my bed and lay down on the cool covers, not for a nap, just a rest, but I slept.

I was awakened by Mother, home from work. She came into my bedroom and asked, "Are you okay?"

I answered, "Yup." After she made me correct my, "Yup," with a "Yes," I asked, "Why is there war?" Mother paused, and before she could come up with an answer, I continued, "I saw awful pikchas of the war at the movie."

Mother, with a glassy stare, simply said, "I cannot tell you why there is a war, why people cannot get along. It is a mystery to me as well." By Mother saying we shared a mystery made me feel closer to her. As she left my room I followed into the kitchen to watch her put our supper together.

When Mother announced, "Soups on!" we gathered around the table. As I ate I became lost in thought over the war until I heard a ripple of laughter from Dad. Seeing his stomach wiggle as another ripple of laughter shook him, shocked me; my dad laughing at the table!

I glanced from Mother, to Patty, to Bobby, then the spell of wonder was broken when Mother asked, "What is so funny?"

As Dad was now bent over in laughter, he had to try hard to tell his story to Mother, "During the air-raid practice the town leaders are going to turn the lumber yard into a fort! To watch for enemy planes, for a possible war here!" Laughing so hard, he had to suck in a deep breath to continue, "To protect us in this no-man's land with their rifles!" Dad had to push away from the table in order to compose himself.

He settled down in his overstuffed chair, blotting his teary eyes with his handkerchief. All of life seemed bright and good when my dad laughed. There was more to come. After he stopped laughing, he slapped his cheek with his hand as though remembering something, then laughing again as he said, "By damn, they even got me to put these new shades up for this air-raid foolishness!"

As the next day and the one after were as hot as the one before, Julia and I went swimming in the cool, cool water of our city swimming pool. In the evenings, as long as daylight lasted, I played outdoors with my friends.

We stayed out just a little bit later than usual one night. It was plenty dark when I went in. Everyone was home but Dad, he had to see our pal Stan to find out how a boxing match was going someplace.

I was standing at the kitchen sink getting a drink of cold water when I heard the fire siren wind up. Bobby, from someplace, shouted, "Air-raid! Air-raid!" He was right! The siren did not wind down to wind up again as for a fire, it whirled and whirled like the air-raid siren on the News Reel!

Mother and Patty jumped into action, pulling down window shades, and snapping off the lights. Before our eyes could adjust to the darkness we were filled with laughter as we bumped and stumbled our way to my bedroom where we'd been instructed to go during an air-raid.

The door to my bedroom was closed, the window shade drawn, and a dimly lit lamp turned on. We sat side by side on the edge of my bed, waiting for the air-raid siren to stop.

This was something we'd never done before; it was different and fun. The glow from my little lamp cast our shadows on the wall across from us.

Bobby stood on my bed to make his shadow look like a giant over ours. The siren whirled and whirled and Bobby made his hand look like a rabbit on the wall, making us laugh. Mother made a butterfly flutter about. Patty made an elephant that chased Bobby's rabbit. Then I made a snake with my whole arm and chased everybody's shadow.

With the window and door closed my bedroom became stuffy and hot, and with the siren whirling and whirling, we were all becoming weary. I needed to feel comforted and lay my head against Mother's chest. My despairing mood began to make me fret over bombs, rubble, and for that little boy with black, curly hair. The whirling, whirling siren whirled and whirled, then stopped. With a great sigh of relief we sat silent as we built up our strength to open the window and the door to my room!

There never was another air-raid drill in our town. I do not know if our town leaders continued to protect us by taking turns at their posts in the lumber yard, watching for the enemy. What I now profess to know is that everyone must have thought like Dad—the air-raid business was pure foolishness.

I pretended to strike up the band by making the beating sound of a drum, "Badoom! Badoom! Badoom! Boom! Boom!" as I led an imaginary band around the house early Friday morning. When Bobby got in my way I said, "Badoom! Badoom! Get away, Boobie!" I had let a name he hated slip and my strutting turned into a dead run down the hall for the bathroom to get away from Bobby. I slammed the door shut and locked it in time.

Bobby pounded on the other side as he let me know, "When I catch you I'm going to shove my dirty sock down your throat!" I simply rested on the stool to wait for him to give up and leave.

I had been waiting for the right time to go to Sonny and Kathleen's. The three of us were to hike to Bloomer's farm to spend the night. A long time ago, way last summer when we were at Mrs. Gouge's, and Mrs. Bloomer came to pick up the eggs, she'd invited us to her farm someday. Sonny had gotten there once, but not Kathleen, or me! It was our very own idea to spend a day and night, and the thought hadn't occurred to let the Bloomer's know we were coming.

I hopped off the stool and pressed my ear against the door. When I could not hear Bobby breathing, I knew he was gone. I tippeetoed up the hall. Seeing it was ten o'clock, I shouted for Patty to hear, "I am going now!"

From somewhere Bobby's voice rang out, "Good riddance!"

I could not help myself, I sang out, "Pooie, pooie to you, Boo-Bee!"

As fast as you could say Flash Gordon, I was across the street and to the tracks before Bobby was at the front door shouting, "You just wait! I'll get you, you chicken liver!"

Sonny and Kathleen were helping with a chore when I got to their house. I helped to empty the wash tubs while their mother fixed us sack lunches.

At the start of our hike to Bloomer's farm, a rooster crowed from the yard of the last house we passed. Once beyond, we had to carefully sneak past the mess of buzzing bee hives and, scooting down a little hill, discovered a cave with a door and a window in it. We peeked in and saw buckets of honey stored inside. Sonny believed, too, this was where bad bank robbers hid their loot. We agreed to explore inside the honey cave another day and arrest the bad robbers hiding in there and take them off to jail!

The crows of the rooster faded as we hiked over rocky ground. We were headed towards Mrs. Gouge's farm, but with Sonny knowing the way to Mrs. Bloomer's, we could at some time change our route. A cry of a Killdeer bird was heard. We spotted it on the ground strutting crazy like.

I cried out for the poor thing, "It's hurt!"

Sonny said, "No, it's not! It's just actin' that way to git us away from her nest that must be close by."

To get out of the way of the Killdeer and her nest, Kathleen and I started skipping, and singing, "Hippety-hop to the barber shop to get a stick of candy. One for you, one me, and one for sister Annie..." The rustle of our lunch sacks against our pant legs made a gopher, curious to know what the strange noise was, stick its head up out of a hole.

A jack rabbit a good distance away stood on its hind legs to watch us skip away. We came upon an ant hill and to prevent ants in our pants, strutted around it. Hearing the flutter of a pheasant's wings, we watched it glide close to the ground then lift up and up and fly away. On the shady side of a hill, the dry ground was brightened by a scattering of yellow dandelions. Kathleen and I picked a fistful to give to Mrs. Bloomer.

At the top of the next hill we could see the big, mean bull grazing in his pasture. Sonny had told us we wouldn't have to cross the bull's pasture this time, and I was glad! All we had to do was walk along the fence line, then cross the highway to get to Mrs. Bloomers.

Our bouquets of dandelions began to droop badly, so Kathleen and I let them drop to the ground and they landed near a pile of bones and bits of fur. We sat on our haunches to inspect the interesting find. Sonny explained to Kathleen and me, "These are bones of an antelope."

Kathleen whined, "What happened to the poor antewope?"

Sonny said solumnly, "He died." We had to keep shooing away flies so we left the bones for them and hiked a bit further.

We'd reached the end of the first half of our hike and looked out over the highway below and across to where we had yet to go. Beyond the highway we could see vast fields of flowing golden grain and too, a field of corn. Between the two fields was a straight stretch of dirt road, broken only by a wooden bridge in the middle.

Sonny began rubbing his stomach. "I'm hungry!" We sat on the ground and dumped our lunches out on our laps. As we ate, Sonny had a vision, then he took Kathleen and me on a flight of fantasy, "This hill we're on is a big mountain and this castle we are living in has water around it, oh yah, a moat, that's what it is called, and it has large alligators in it to protect us."

He stopped talking to take a bite of his sandwich, then made a swooping wave with his arm as his imagination grew. "That out there is all my land, 'cuz I am the king!" He looked at Kathleen and me. "And you two are my slaves."

Kathleen shouted, "No sir! Swaves are never girrs they hafta be boys! I am a princess."

Sonny said to her, "Here, take my sack." When she had the crumpled sack in her hand, he said, "Gotcha! That makes you my slave."

She argued as she ate her boiled egg, "I'm not either!"

I chipped away the shell from my egg then ate it. We shared the little jug of water Sonny had carried in his sack, then descended to lower ground to cross the highway.

We tramped through knee high weeds in a ditch until reaching the straight stretch of dirt road. By the time we walked and walked to get to the wooden bridge, it was time for a rest. We sat on the edge of the bridge looking down to a dry and cracked creek bed. There was a frog somewhere; we heard it croaking.

Sonny nudged Kathleen in her ribs to get her attention. "If ya find that frog and he gives you a kiss, then you'll turn into a princess!"

Kathleen peered over the rim of her glasses, giving Sonny a disgusted look. "If you kissed that frog you woud git warts!"

Sonny would not give up. "You don't believe, why, why, why—that same frog kissed a cow and the cow turned into a milkweed."

In unison, Kathleen and I shouted, "Milkweed?!" I had had enough of Sonny's baloney and exclaimed, "A milkweed was neva a cow!"

Sonny uttered, "Um . . . well you guys, tell me then why that weed gives milk."

Kathleen, not believing, looked out at all the milkweeds. "There's ots and ots of miwkweeds out there!"

Sonny's tone grew low and serious. "Those weeds could've been a whole herd of cows. Ya, coulda been!"

Kathleen, sighed and jumped up, acting exasperated. Sonny and I noticed up ahead a cloud of dust rising up from the dirt road.

Everyone yelled, "Jump!" We skidded down the bank to the dry creek bed then had to quickly shield our faces from the cloud of dirt that engulfed us as the farm vehicle zoomed by. Our mouths were full of grit and we had to keep spitting to get it all out!

Standing near the dry creek bed, Sonny spotted something of interest under the bridge. He walked to it, then hollered for us to come and help. He was tugging at an old car bumper stuck in the almost dried mud. We grabbed a hold and together we tugged and tugged to free it.

Kathleen wiggled her nose to move her glasses up as she asked, "Watcha want that for?"

First, Sonny said, "Don't let me forget it tomorrow," then explained why. "Becuz it's scrap metal and worth some money."

I thought this was another pipe dream of his and shrieked, "Sonny! Stop fooling us!"

Then he said something that made sense. "The army buys junk like this to melt down to make guns and things." The subject was dropped and we left the bumper to be picked up on our way back the next day.

Back on the dirt road, with "army" on the brain, Sonny started strutting like a soldier. Kathleen and I joined in, repeating, "Hut, two, three, four, hut, two, three, four..."

Sonny ran ahead, stopped, turned and drew his imaginary pistols from his hips. He aimed his pointer fingers at us and yelled, "Bang! Bang!"

Kathleen and I clutched our hands over our hearts, slumped to our knees and played dead for a couple of seconds. Then we ran to catch up, and like Sonny, we got in the action of whipping our imaginary horses to a gallop.

Sonny made an abrupt stop that caused Kathleen and me to plow into him! While pushing us away he grumbled, "Girls sure make dumb cowboys."

Sonny then directed us through a corn field as a shortcut. "Shhhhh, don't tell the enemy."

Kathleen screamed, "Enemy!"

Sonny said, "Yah! Doncha see them back there on the road?" We then had to play a game weaving between rows of tall corn stalks that hid us from the enemy Sonny'd conjured up. When he made us drop to our knees to crawl along I could not hold back my sudden thought of how funny we were acting and rolled over in laughter. This made Sonny mad and he said, in a huffy tone, "It's time for us soldiers to rest!"

The fields of tall, waving grain created a whispering sound on the prairie, but when resting among the tall corn stalks, the stalks created a barrier to that sound and we noticed how quiet it was.

The silence was nice, making me feel drowsy, until Sonny filled us full of his jungle talk. He tried to convince us the corn on the stalks were bananas. "You peel the husk away just like ya peel a banana!" That made Kathleen and me want to get out of there, away from Sonny's war talk and his jungle full of bananas.

Sonny pointed, "There's the Bloomers farm."

It was about a half a mile ahead and the closer we got the more it looked as though the farm did not farm anything at all. No tractor, no cows, no pigs, nothing but chickens and two buildings, the house and a barn.

We raced to be first over the broken down fence, then hopped up on the open porch of the house to knock on the door. No one came. We figured Mr. and Mrs. Bloomer must be someplace else on the farm. We could not believe they might not be home. We listened for them in the barn and out in the garden, but there was not a sound to give us a clue, so Sonny opened the door and we walked into the kitchen.

We searched all three rooms thinking they just hadn't heard us knock. We wondered why no one was home? Farmers were always at home, except on Saturdays when they went to town. With no telephone to call our parents, we went back outside to play and wait for Mr. and Mrs. Bloomers to come home.

After a brief stop at their one hole outhouse for each of us, Sonny ran to chase a chicken hawk. He saw it swoop down to snatch up a chickie and in helping him chase it away, we wound up hopping over potato plants in the garden. A funny scarecrow gave us the idea to imitate it and we waddled as we thought a scarecrow would and waddled our way out of the garden and into the barn.

Inside the barn, we interrupted the resting chickens and they flew out, scolding us with awful cackling sounds. On the earthen floor lay a dusty horse collar. Two wooden car wheels hung from big hooks and wagon parts, too. A lantern and garden tools hung from nails. In one far corner was a tool sharpener, it still worked! It had a big stone wheel and peddles to the treadle to make the stone go around and round to sharpen tools. Kathleen hopped on the seat to be first to peddle the treadle. With the stone spinning, I put my finger on it and was surprised by the hot burning sensation!

Kathleen and I saw Sonny disappear beyond a door in the barn. We caught up to him inside a small room with a raised floor. It smelled of a musty odor and had a look of mystery about it. A rocker sat tipped with one rocker missing and a dress form with no arms, legs or head seemed to be guarding the room.

Books that had once been neatly stacked had fallen from rot and mice eating the pages. A long barreled gun on the wall intrigued Sonny and a large trunk with a hump for a lid was of interest to Kathleen and me.

I blew the dust away from the lid and it flew up into our faces! The lid was stuck and in using a lot of strength to give it a heave-ho to lift it up, it lifted and dropped back with a loud thud: The leather straps had torn away from the trunk.

The inside of the lid had a colorful picture of a fine lady wearing a big hat with a feather in it, but the trunk stunk! It had a strong odor of mothballs and moldy clothing, but the dresses we found were very fancy, like what ladies wore in the cowboy days. Kathleen pulled out a black dress with velvet trim, and she put it on. It was much too big for her even after slipping into the high buttoned shoes.

I yanked at a green dress and the sleeve tore away from the dress! I smashed it back in. After that I was very careful lifting out a beige, satin dress and slipped it on. It, too, was too long for me. Kathleen, in her high buttoned shoes and me on my tippytoes play-acting uppity, while sipping our tea. Kathleen then tripped on her bunched up dress and knocked the old gun from Sonny's grip.

When Sonny realized the gun lay broken on the floor, he became so mad he called Kathleen names like, "Clumsy, ninny, nincompoop and poopey drawers." Sonny tried to patch the gun by hanging it back on the hooks; it worked, it no longer looked broken. Kathleen and I put the dresses neatly away in the trunk. We ran out of that room and out of the barn.

The three of us stood at the broken fence and stared down the dirt road hoping to see a farm truck. When not seeing a cloud of dust as far as the eyes could see, it was then we noticed a hazy glow settle on the land and a lonesome feeling settled in on us.

We were hungry and went into the house to find something to eat. Sonny shoved a bench to the cupboard and climbed up to search the shelves. He found a can of soda crackers, grabbed it and while hopping down gave the word of command, "Com'on!" And we followed him back outside.

We sat on the very edge of the wooden porch as Sonny divvied up the same amount of soda crackers for each of us. We knew what to do; we knew this game, so when Sonny said, "Go!" We crammed a fistful of crackers into our mouths and the race began.

We looked like funny clowns with full blown cheeks and laughing caused pain in my cheeks. As saliva flowed to soften the mass, excitement filled us as we chewed, swallowed, and tried to whistle, again, and again, and again until Sonny wheezed a squeak of a whistle. "I won! I won!" he shouted as he jumped about doing a victory dance.

Kathleen and I simply ignored him.

Our throats felt dry and parched after our game and in need of water, we ran to the pump. Sonny was first with his gaping mouth under the spout. Kathleen pumped until a thirst quenching dribble of water came out for him. Then

I was next waiting to catch a dribble of cool water, but Sonny pumped-de-pump too much and drenched my whole head with a big swoosh of water! That made me so mad!

Kathleen pushed him away so I could pump a dribble of a drink out for her. Then Kathleen and I ganged up together to fill our cupped hands with water to throw at Sonny. Screaming, while chasing, our echoes bounced back from the buildings. This caused us to stop and being very quiet, we listened, but heard nothing. It was ghostly quiet about the farm. Not a chicken clucked or got in the way; they were on their roosts. It may have seemed early to us, but it was their bedtime and that was our signal to go in.

We sat at the kitchen table eating crackers and honey as flies stuck to the flypaper overhead bizzed and bizzed. There were no lights to turn on and with it almost dark in the kitchen, a melancholy feeling troubled us and we retired to the parlor.

The parlor had a big window and the sun sinking over the horizon gave us some light yet to see by. Our view out the window was of the potato plants in the garden and the scarecrow with a frown on its face looking directly at us. We needed something to do and spotted what it could be: playing the organ that sat in the corner of the parlor.

Kathleen got to the stool first, but when she pressed down on the keys not a sound came out.

Sonny did an experiment; he pressed down on a pedal near the floor and it filled the organ with enough air to make a slight "hym" and a "hum."

Now that we knew what had to be done and finding it fun to pump the pedal, we filled the organ with lots and lots of air so we could make the organ play a loud "hym" and a "hum."

When there was no longer light from a setting sun to see by, we wound down our fun at the organ. We thought that at any moment Mr. and Mrs. Bloomer would be home, so we sat on the davenport to wait. We were adjusting to the darkness quite well, not realizing a soft glow from a rising moon was helping us to see.

In the midst of where we knew the garden was, was the scarecrow made of yellow straw and looking now awfully mean. Although I tried my best not to look in the direction of the garden, I had to, to make sure the scarecrow was still there.

We could see a wedge of the moon as it began to appear in a small odd shaped window at the other end of the parlor. It grew larger until a bright full moon was in full view in the odd shaped window. My fear exploded! I knew that a full moon meant the Werewolf would be out! It attacked the Bloomers and now they're dead! Now the Werewolf is coming after us!

My fit of horror lasted a spell until broken by Kathleen when she whined to her brother, "Sonny, that awfoo scarecrow is scaring me, and I'm so seepy."

Sonny tried to ease the fear of his little sister by speaking in a soft voice, "Don't be afraid of that dumb ol' scarecrow, ffffor sure there's nothing to be afraid of. We can go to bed, com'on."

Sonny took a hold of one of Kathleen's hands and I took her other hand and Sonny pulled us into the dark, dark kitchen. He felt of the wall until he came to the door jam of the bedroom and pulled us into the pitch black room. Each of us inched forward until our hands touched the softness of the bed and we crawled up on it. Once my head felt the softness of a pillow, I felt peaceful and ready for sleep. I was then rudely disturbed when hearing a sound of a "hum."

I sat up! Then I leaned across Kathleen to poke Sonny to make him get the message to stop trying to scare us!

A split second separated Sonny's stuttering words, "Wwwasn't mmme!" and another droning sound of a "Hummmmmm" from the organ caused a stampede of thoughts, dumping us in a state of frozen fear as we believed something was out there!

With a whimpering cry, Kathleen spoke of her fear, "It is the scarecrow."

Sonny stuttered an answer back, "It's nnnothing, no, no, no, nothing." I imagined, the werewolf!

The organ did not hum again. That was when, and in our wretched fright in the dark, we knew it was because the monster was coming to get us! I could hear its heavy feet; the monster was really coming! When a strike of a match lit up a dark, powerful figure in the doorway of the bedroom, we screamed! And screamed! The monster grunted and fell backwards.

When our eyes adjusted to the light of the match, we saw Mr. Bloomer! The Bloomers were finally home!

We hopped off the bed and ran into his comforting arms, and once calm, we told of our fright over someone playing the organ. Mr. Bloomer, after a boisterous laugh, explained how pumping too much air into the organ made it play back on its own. Sonny nodded with a sigh, "I figured it was somethin' like that."

I knew Sonny was trying to sound brave, that was okay, all that mattered now was the warm glow from a lantern that lifted our spirits. We sat around the table with Mr. and

Mrs. Bloomer and we ate food they brought home from the grange picnic where they'd been all day long.

Terror, then comfort and food fixed our mood for sleep. Most definitely! Two kitchen benches shoved together and padded with a blanket made a bed for Sonny. Kathleen and I shared the long davenport in the parlor. I said to my friend whose feet my feet touched, "Goodnight." She did not respond; she was sound asleep.

Saturday morning was bright and beautiful as we sat at the breakfast table. Mr. Bloomer, dressed in blue bibbed overalls, sipped strong smelling coffee as Mrs. Bloomer flipped a steaming pancake on my plate. Kathleen already had her pancake and Sonny was waiting for his. I drenched mine with syrup, then ate while listening to the crow of a rooster, cock-a-doodle-doo, cock-a-doodle-doo as the flies overhead bizzed, bizzed.

Mrs. Bloomer, at ease while busy in her kitchen, looked like a farm lady. Her hair was twisted in a bun, she wore a blue paisley dress stained gray in front and her stockings were rolled down to her brown shoes. While I watched her, my thoughts strayed out to the barn. Who wore the fancy ladies dwesses in the trunk? With a simple flip-flop of time back to the olden days when those dresses were worn, I figured it out. Shah! Those dwesses belonged to a lady who lived here before Mrs. Blooma. I bet so.

Mr. Bloomer, after finishing his second cup of coffee, rose from his chair and said to Sonny, "Got your muscles in shape, son? Potatoes have to be dug." Mr. Bloomer grabbed his greasy hat from its hook, placed it on his head and went out the door with Sonny, his strong farm hand trailing behind.

After the tea kettle on the stove whistled, Mrs. Bloomer poured the hot water over the washed dishes to rinse them. Kathleen and I dried what she had rinsed. When done, she asked us to please take out the slop and for one more chore, asked us to gather the eggs. We carried the bucket of slop out to feed the chickens and while the chickens were pecking at the slop, Kathleen and I gathered the eggs from their vacant nests.

We scooted to the farm truck and set the bucket full of eggs next to a bulging gunny sack of potatoes to be taken to market. Then we took off for the garden to wait for the last sack to be filled with potatoes. Although the garden scarecrow looked harmless in the light of day, we approached with caution. Once we were nose to nose with the funny straw man, we felt brave enough to imitate it, as we'd done the day before, waddling about while the last potato sack was being filled.

When ready to go to town, Mr. Bloomer crawled into the cab of the truck and Sonny, Kathleen and I crawled up and onto the bed of the truck with the potatoes and eggs. Sonny sat below the window of the cab and Kathleen and I near the tailgate.

We waited for Mrs. Bloomer. We waited and waited. When hearing the ooga, ooga of the horn we knew Mr. Bloomer was becoming a bit agitated. Then, Mrs. Bloomer came out of the house and we could tell, she was not quite ready. She set her purse down on the porch and while leaning over to realign her stockings from her ankles to her knees, her hat fell off. When she had her hat on again she secured it to her hair with a large hat pin. We were now ready to go.

As the farm truck motored to town on the dirt road, it kicked up a big cloud of dust and the cloud blocked our view of everything. There were many potholes in the road and Kathleen and I clung tightly to the side while getting a bumpy ride.

When approaching the wooden bridge, Sonny tapped softly on the window of the cab to remind Mr. Bloomer to stop. As the farm truck slowed, then stopped, the dust cloud engulfed us! We had to spit out the grit in our mouths, spit and spit as we tripped down the bank to get underneath the bridge. The three of us pulled the old car bumper up the bank and with a great heave-ho we got it up on the bed of the truck, just missing the bucket of eggs.

The smooth pavement of the highway was a welcome relief after such a bumpy, dusty ride. I felt great joy feeling the warm wind as the farm truck whizzed us back to town. From hiking the day before, it again was like magic to experience how fast we could get back in a motoring vehicle. I got off at Sonny and Kathleen's house and we played until noon when it was time for me to go home.

The next day, I had a great story to tell about the scare we got when the organ at Bloomers farm "hummed" on its own. I joined Julia at her house to tell her all about it. After I had finished my story, while sitting on the porch, we heard, "Hey, hayseeds, what are ya doin'?" It was Frankie! He was back from visiting his mother! After our initial jumping about with glee, we settled down to thinking of what to do on such an August "dog day." While thinking, we took to walking in the middle of the street in the direction of town.

I hadn't known anyone who had to go far away to see their mother. I asked Frankie, "What's your motha like?"

Frankie answered, "She's so pretty and very busy being as important as she is."

I never knew an important Mother and imagined she must look like a president.

Julia asked, "Do you miss her?"

Frankie scraped the tip of his shoe on the pavement before answering, "Oh, sure, but doncha know I'm sure glad to get back into these clothes."

I looked at his faded shirt and pants patched at the knees and wondered, what other clothes would a body wear when playing? After Frankie explained the kinds of clothes he had to wear all the time, it sounded like he went to a party every day.

We heard the sound of a vehicle behind us and moved to the side of the street to allow it to pass. It was a farm truck with a cow in the back. When the truck passed us, it swooped so far around as to lean in the dip at the side of the street and that cow leaped right out over the trucks railing! On a farm, a cow can be nice, but in town, this cow, with terror in its eyes, frightened us! We did a jig jag jog, not knowing what direction to run, but when the cow hoofed it towards us we dodged around it and it kept on going. We bragged about being so smart as to have outwitted the dumb cow—until the sound of its hooves alerted our senses. The cow had turned and was coming after us!

We raced pell-mell, Frankie in the lead, Julia and I neck 'n' neck, and the cow getting closer. Louder, louder, grew the clobber, clobber of hooves. When Frankie took to the track side of the street running between the warehouse buildings, Julia and I followed. We quickly scooted under a wooden walkway to a warehouse along the tracks. As the clobber of hooves faded away, Frankie pounded on his chest as Tarzan would have done. We had a good laugh over us city kids being chased in town by a silly farm cow.

Sitting under the walkway with just the tracks to look at, we chose to stay. The shade and it being so quiet, set the mood for Frankie to tell Julia and me about this place where his mother lived. He'd spent much of his time at a park with a big pond that had swans and ducks to feed that were tame. He liked the zoo the best. He saw an ape, a giraffe, elephants, "hippopotumses," lions and tigers, too! He even got to ride a camel and saw a snake so big it could eat a pig.

I stopped Frankie right there. "Fwankie, you fib, snakes jus' eat bugs, not pigs!"

He puffed up his chest. "It's true! These snakes are bigger than any you've ever seen. Hey! Lookey over there!" He was pointing and I figured he meant to scare us over a big pig eating snake coming our way, but when we looked across the tracks we saw a hobo running through the tall weeds. Thinking the cow was chasing the hobo we looked, but instead of a cow we saw a flicker of orange—a fire!

Suddenly the voice of someone alerting others was hollering, "Fire! Fire! Fire!" The first volunteer firefighters who got to the spot were there before the fire truck. They came running from a warehouse with gunny sacks and started beating the flames that kept spreading through the weeds.

Not much else around the tracks seemed very important, except maybe the tall silver tanks that read FARMER'S UNION. We heard the loud fire alarm and knew help would be coming. The fire station was winding up its siren. A signal for the real firemen to stop working and beat it to the station to man the fire truck. When the siren hit its highest note it died down, started up again, then down, up and down, up and down and continued as people congregated in front of us to watch.

Soon too many people were blocking our view so we scrambled up the steps to sit on the walkway and look out over their heads. I wanted so badly for all of my other friends to be with us. I searched, looking amongst the crowd for them. Not spotting even one, I felt sad thinking they were missing out.

The fire siren was louder than the clang, clang of the fire truck and we did not hear it until it was at the train crossing. It made a sharp turn, zoomed down the tracks, and stopped near the flickering flames. There was a great burst of energy as firemen unwrapped the hose and others hooked it to a hydrant. A powerful gush of water then shot way out from the hose causing the flames to smoke and sizzle until the flames died down to nothing in the weeds. The firemen paused, thinking they had the fire under control, but it whipped up stronger than before!

Frankie, Julia and I got wise to the fact that the fire was becoming alarming when a man in front of us shouted, "By damn, that tank may blow!"

I looked at the flames whipping around the base of one of the tall silver tanks and if it could blow up, I knew it would be important to keep the fire away from that tank. With the flames becoming hotter and hotter one observer bellowed out, "Holy mackerel!"

I became so swept up in the frenzy, I rocked and rocked from the intense excitement shown by everyone all around.

So did Frankie and Julia! When the firemen could no longer stop what they expected to happen, they shouted to those standing nearby, "Move back! Move back! Move back!"

We had the wall of the warehouse at our backs so we could not move further away. To make sure we were safe I looked at the adults standing on the ground in front of us, and they were staying where they were, watching those closer to the scene running! I had never seen anything so exciting and I rocked and rocked as orders again and again rang out, "Move back! Move back! It's going to blow!" Then it did! BOOM!!!

There was a deafening sound and I threw an arm up to protect my head. Then, out of the roaring smoke and flames from the burning fuel sailed the top of the huge tank. All attention was on the flying disk as it flew in the direction of the railroad crossing and came down on an empty parked car, smashing it to the ground!

The super heat from the fiery inferno was felt for a long time, and all spectators, including us, were so caught up in the excitement we dared not leave. There was still one more tank to save.

When the last flicker of flame was stamped out, with no more explosions to worry about, a loud cheer rang out from the crowd. As people began to leave, an elderly gentleman in front of us said, "This has been one hell of a lot of excitement for one day!" I looked at Frankie and Julia, each of us agreeing wholeheartedly!

We knew, having been the very first on the scene, we had to be the very last to leave. We remained on our perch until the clean-up was over and the fire truck was gone.

**Fire of 1942, the Farmer's Union Station
Glasgow, Montana**

With no one left, we scrambled down to the ground. We had a very exciting, mighty big story to tell any friend we could find, and could not delay, for the end of the day was near.

Chapter 6

My second grade teacher, Miss Porter, was old, and bony. She wore a wig; Carla said she did. Miss Porter did not like me. One day she scolded someone else really bad which made me very nervous, so when she called on me to read out loud from a book, my speech training ran out of my head and I read, "Wed Widing Hood." She said in scolding words that I had a bad speech problem and made me repeat the "r" sound over and over. Emily was next to read out loud and that was when I felt a sudden urge to go to the bathroom!

To be excused to go to the bathroom, students had to hold up one finger if we had to just tinkle, two fingers meant we had to do number two. I held up one finger and waited to be excused. Teacher glared at me and shook her head. I did not know why; I wasn't fibbing. I sat very still hoping the urge would pass, but the urge turned into an ache. I really had to go. I tried once more, raising one finger higher. Miss Porter frowned and shook her head again, a definite, "No!"

I could not help it, I let go and the flow created a relief that made the terrible ache go away. The warm sensation, however, felt like a horrifying run of shame. My dress was sopping wet and there was a little puddle on the floor under my desk.

Once, when another girl had wet her pants, kids teased her by singing, "Baby needs a diaper, baby needs a diaper."

I fretted in fear, sitting very still until school let out. It was not long before the bell rang and I took my time putting my school supplies away in my desk so I would be the last to get up. Keeping my wet backside averted away from everyone, I slipped unnoticed into the cloakroom, snatched my sweater from its hook and quickly tied its sleeves around my waist so my sweater hung down to hide my embarrassment!

Outdoors in the chilly air, with my skin wet from my soaked clothes, I was tormented "there" by a miserable, prickly itch! If I scratched, I might give my secret away to Julia and Frankie! A hop and skip helped to ease the itch, and too, twitching my muscles helped to get some relief. When I got home and was alone in my room, I kicked my wet clothes off and smiled. The itch was gone. I shoved those wet clothes under my bed and no one ever knew I had wet my pants in school, except maybe the janitor.

Miss Porter had taught us "Rules of Conduct" that would be expected of us in her class. By using a hanky, we could catch the germs if we coughed or sneezed, and by washing our hands and brushing our teeth, we were washing bad germs away. Every morning as Miss Porter called out a name from her roll call book the person called had to stand up and wave a hanky as proof they had one, then show their hands to make sure they had washed them, and grin to show they had brushed their teeth.

We tried our best to not disappoint our teacher. We learned how to make it through roll call with good "social graces" so we would not have to hear another lecture about bad germs. If someone forgot their hanky, it was easy to sneak one to that person before their name was called. For dirty hands, a little spit and a wipe on a dress or pants cleaned them and swishing the tongue across the teeth many times did a good job of making them look white.

Miss Porter had her favorites amongst the girls; They were Sharon and Ruthie. Neither liked being called "Teacher's Pet" so we never teased them. All the boys seemed to be in trouble with Miss Porter much of the time. She often screamed at them for being too restless, or for doing mean things like pulling a girl's pigtail. There was one boy in particular our teacher did not think well of, that was Eddy. Oftentimes she'd shame Eddy for having crust behind his ears, dirty fingernails and uncombed hair, but what she mostly disliked was his bad habit of snorting snot from his nose when on the playground.

Eddy liked to imitate Popeye, the Sailor Man. He was really entertaining, especially when making a ridiculous Popeye face at our teacher when she wasn't looking. We liked Eddy.

One day when quietly practicing our penmanship, we were distracted by our teacher looking for something. She was rummaging through her desk drawers rattling papers, going through this and that, behaving in a manner that made the rest of us feel something bad was about to happen. When whatever it was she'd been looking for could not be found, she looked at each of us with a mean frown, then fixed her gaze on Eddy.

After a moment of silence, our teacher asked, "Who stole my money? Eddy! Was it you?" Miss Porter tapped her fingers on her desk while waiting for his response.

When Eddy hung his head, he looked guilty to me, yet shook his head to say, "No."

Miss Porter belted out an order. "Eddy! You come here this very minute!"

Eddy pushed up from his seat at his desk and he shuffled along, making Miss Porter very mad! When he finally got within arms reach at her desk, Miss Porter grabbed at his shirt and pulled so hard she made all the buttons pop off! With a grip still on his shirt she demanded of him, "What did you do with my money?"

Eddy simply hung his head again and this time said nothing.

Miss Porter then pulled Eddy into the cloakroom out of our sight. When we heard a thud, thud sound we knew that was his head being knocked against the wall. Those of us who sat at our desks felt a great deal of pity for Eddy. I kept thinking, "Eddy must have needed the money awfully bad to be so bwave." As punishment, he was then sent out into the hall to spend the rest of the day.

Our teacher was so very upset she'd forgotten what our next assignment was. She then picked up her story book to read to us. When opening her book to a certain page, two one dollar bills floated out and down to the floor. The very money Eddy had been accused of stealing, surprising everyone!

After Miss Porter led Eddy back into the classroom, she apologized in a curt tone as though believing it could've been Eddy if the money had never been found. Eddy now had a smug look, like Popeye would after he had eaten his spinach, ready to chuckle and go 'poop-poop' with his pipe. During recess we patted his back, focusing great attention on him. Being so brave, he'd truly been a super strong Popeye.

The next day during spelling the classroom door burst open, startling the whole class. It was Eddy's mother, a large woman, marching down the aisle to teacher's desk.'

With a heavy voice she scolded Miss Porter for having ripped the buttons from Eddy's shirt! Then she took the shirt out of a sack and handed it with needle, thread and buttons to Miss Porter, ordering her to sew every button back on! Seeing a big lady give orders to our old, bony teacher was bewildering. For the first time, I saw how frail and gentle our teacher looked, accepting her punishment, sewing every button back on that shirt. Miss Porter never scolded Eddy after that day, yet sometimes, to make him behave, she wore a mean frown as she glared at him.

In school, all sixth grades were assembled in the great auditorium waiting for a marionette show to begin. The very loud chatter from the older kids was interesting to listen to as I studied the gaily painted puppet stage up on the big stage. Suddenly they appeared; the gay dancing puppets! I slipped into the world of fun they created, forgetting there were strings controlling them. I jumped when the puppets jumped, ducked when one clobbered another with a stick or missed, groaned sad when they made me feel so, swayed as they danced, and laughed and clapped when the good won over the bad. Up popped a sign that read, "The End" and I moaned as loud as the others around me did. The puppets disappeared without bowing or waving goodbye and we chanted, "Come back! Come back!"

A burst of marching music, rat-a-tat-tat announced their return! Two puppets marched across their little stage. One was dressed like a soldier and the other like us, a pupil. When the music stopped the two came to a halt! The soldier turned to the pupil puppet and said, "I am proud to be a soldier in the United States Army, ready to fight to preserve our freedom and democracy. Do you want to help our country win this war?"

When the pupil puppet answered, "Yes," we, too, all yelled, "Yes!" The proud soldier puppet turned and told the audience, "You can collect scrap metal to give to our United States Government to be melted down to make guns and tanks needed to win this war."

I immediately remembered last summer when I helped Sonny get the old metal car bumper out of the mud. I wanted to shout, "I did that already!" The 'rat-a-tat-tat' marching music played again and the two puppets strutted back and forth waving puppet-sized American flags in the air.

When the music stopped, they bowed and waved their goodbyes. Like my classmates, I jumped up and down while waving fondly to the puppets.

Frankie had become really good at hunting for scrap metal. Of those of us on the south side of the tracks, he was better than Julia, Lila or I, and even Howie! Nearly every school day, Frankie had some kind of scrap metal to donate to the heap of metal piled high on one corner of the school grounds.

As Frankie, Julia and I walked to school one morning, a wintery storm began to whirl about. The icy flakes were hitting us in our faces causing us to have to walk backwards. That was when I took notice of the fancy metal junk Frankie was carrying. I asked what it was and learned that it was a "door knocker."

Frankie shouted, "Hey! I got an idea! If you two take turns carrying this then it will be like you gave it, too!"

Frankie was such a good friend to want to share, I was first to shout, "Me first!" I took the fancy door knocker in my hand, but without mittens on it was not long before it felt mighty cold in my grip. I passed it off to Julia.

When Frankie got it back, he tossed it from one hand to the other until we reached the school grounds. Frankie threw his piece of metal very high to hear it go plunk, plunk when coming down on the snow covered junk. I could see yet, the tip of an old tailpipe dad had let me drag from the garage one day to add to the heap.

Outside the schoolhouse, Julia and I huddled together with other classmates to keep warm while waiting for the janitor to let us in. Once inside, out of the icy wind, the warmth was a great relief.

An important looking lady was standing at teacher's desk. This stranger said, "Good morning! I am   Mrs. Hollander, the county health nurse, here to talk to you about smallpox and smallpox shots." Some of the boys uttered painful sounds while slumping in their seats. Miss Porter clapped her hands to restore order, but Mrs. Hollander grinned as though she'd expected this kind of reaction.

After Mrs. Hollander explained about the dangers of smallpox and, "How important it is to be inoculated against the disease," she unrolled a very large sheet that read, "Educational information on the kind of reaction to expect from a smallpox vaccination." The shiny, colorful pictures of the upper part of the arm showed "how the shot will cause a pink spot that will change to a very red spot, then an ugly scab, and the very last, a scar. The scar will be our proof we will be forever protected from smallpox." I, too, groaned in fun with my classmates.

When the colorful sheet was in a roll once more, Mrs. Hollander dug into her bag and she pulled out a pile of pink slips. She explained what they were for, "You must take the pink slip home to have a parent read it, then sign it to be returned the next morning so you can get your shot later in the day, downstairs." I then caught her smiling at each pupil and the twinkle in her eyes made me feel glad to want this shot. She thanked us for allowing her to come into our classroom to speak to us and as she walked to the door to leave she reminded us, "Please, it is important to not forget your pink slip tomorrow."

Miss Porter followed Mrs. Hollander out into the hall and as the door clicked shut, David and Freddy, while moaning, slipped from their seats to the floor. Tom jumped up, grabbed his upper arm and with a twisted look of pain, described how that long, long needle would pop through the skin and go in and in and in until sissy Suzi screamed, "Stop it! Stop it!" Miss Porter walked in, shut the door behind her, and clapped her hands to establish order again. The morning had been eventful, full of stimulating entertainment.

As Miss Porter thumbed through her book to read a story to fill in the little time left before recess, I glanced down at my pink slip, thinking, "I will take my important pink slip to mother at work, right after school, and have her sign it right away!"

At the end of the school day, Julia and I headed for Yondell's Grocery Store. Once in the store, Julia and I stood over the floor furnace to get warm while I waited for a break between customers to bother mother.

When I thought mother was free to sign my slip, I saw another lady with an armful of groceries headed for the counter. I darted ahead of her. At the same time mother saw me, she had to reach out to catch the groceries falling onto the counter from the arms of the lady. Without delay, I held my important pink slip up high enough for Mother to read. After she did, her eyebrows shrunk to a frown as she snapped out her answer, "No!" Then she suggested, "Get on home."

I had been blown out of my snow boots! I had not expected Mother to say, "No." That meant to me, "Mother wants me to git smallpox and die! And be scawed for life from the pox!"

As I rejoined Julia I decided, "I will somehow save myself. I will git that important shot!" Not knowing how I was going to do it, I started by telling Julia, "Mother said she will sign my slip when she gits home." Julia and I buttoned our coats up and we went out into the cold air to head for home.

My emotions were in a tumble having been denied my shot, and having lied gave my nerves a heavy jolt causing my stomach to ache. I knew, too, I had to be careful with Julia because if she found out I already lied she might tell Mother, probably she would. By the time we got to the gate of my house I was freezing cold, yet I stayed, and I waved a happy goodbye to my very good friend as she continued walking up the street.

As the first one home, I flicked on a light and dashed to the floor furnace to give the key a turn to light it. As I stood waiting to get warm, my mind was full of befuddled thoughts on how I could get my important smallpox shot. I then figured, "If I ask Mother again to read my pink slip and the numba two ansa is 'no' again, for sure I dare not git the shot! But, if I don't ask again, I can sneak awound one 'no' as though I did not heaw it." I pulled the pink slip out of my coat pocket and I ran to my bedroom and threw it on my dark closet floor. With the tip of my shoe I shoved it way, way back out of sight.

Later, when Mother was home, I stayed out of her way for fear my very presence could remind her of the pink slip. I was afraid she might say no again, and luckily, nothing had been said by the time I went to bed.

The next morning on my way to school, I had Howie, Lila, Frankie and Julia to walk with. That was good. While they talked amongst themselves, I could think of the very words I needed to tell Miss Porter. "Mother said, 'Yes,' but I lost my slip of paper on the way to school." I repeated what I planned to say over and over all the way until there.

After hanging my coat in the cloakroom, I stood at the doorway where I could see Miss Porter at her desk. She was looking far more crotchety than ever before, making me feel very nervous, yet I was determined. I sucked in a breath of courage, darted to her desk, and said with a rush of words, "Mother said 'Yes' but I lost my papa!"

Miss Porter, sounding impatient, barked at me, "Paper!" I thought she was demanding my paper slip and I was sick with fright and became speechless, but when she said again, "Paper! Not Papa!" I knew she had been correcting my bad speech. I felt hot and sweaty, but greatly relieved when Miss Porter said, "Very well; now take your seat." I sat down ready for class to begin, feeling happy and lucky Miss Porter believed me.

In the afternoon, in the middle of our spelling class, we heard a knock at the door. which meant it was time to line up for our smallpox shot. I had to stay on the good side of Miss Porter so she wouldn't change her mind for not handing in my pink slip. I was very good and very quiet and she never looked at me.

As my classmates and I paraded down the stairs to the basement, we met the first graders coming up from getting their shots. Some were still crying. The basement smelled like a doctor's office and in one corner of the lunch room we could see Mrs. Hollander with a nurse's uniform on. Tommy and Sherman at the back of the line groaned in pain when the first, Joan, got her shot.

When it came my turn, I stepped forward fully ready for my shot. I watched every move by Mrs. Hollander. She tipped a bottle to soak a wad of cotton with the smell of alcohol to dab on my arm. Then she gently held my arm with her one hand and aimed the needle at the wet spot. I felt a prick that stung just a teeny bit, then it was over. Before Mrs. Hollander let go of my arm, I looked up at her and she smiled at me with that twinkle in her eyes, and I smiled at her.

I skipped past my other classmates in line, darted up the stairs, and popped into my classroom to join Joan, Bob, Gary, and JoAnn. As we waited we giggled over who would end up being the biggest chicken downstairs. I shouted, "Suzi!" Bob said, "No, sir, bet it's Ruthie."

Janice started giggling. "Wouldn't it be funny if Tommy fainted?!" We all giggled, forming our own picture of Tommy spread out on the floor from getting his shot. Freddy shuffled through the door; he did not look like any fraidy cat. He was just wiping his mouth dry from getting a cool drink at the fountain. Sharon, Jennie and Annie then came in acting very calm, as did Carla, Jack, Rita and Kay. Then Suzi walked in and she had no tears in her eyes. Eddy popped in singing, "I'm Popeye the Sailor Man, I ate my spinach and made it to the finish, I'm Popeye the Sailor Man." We knew Tommy would be next and with the wait kind of long, the first of us snickered thinking something went wrong. But then he sauntered in with Donna, Sherman, Gail, Wayne, and David. Tommy hadn't been a chicken after all and our fun was over. We did not pay attention to Paige, Darlene, nor Emily or Ruthie who entered the room last. Then Miss Porter came in and our next class began.

Two days had passed from when we got our smallpox shots. I stood at my classroom window gazing outside before class. The bright sun on the carpet of snow did not help to brighten my persistent thoughts over why my arm was not sore yet. Others were already suffering from their shots.

Class began and I took my seat. Seeing Kay's arm in front of me looking so sore made me worry more when wondering, "What will I do if my arm gits sore and mother sees it?" Miss Porter had to clap her hands to get my attention and in turning my head I caught the spectacle of brilliant colors of the rainbow reflecting from a bottle on the window sill. It was roll call and I answered, "Here," then stood to show my hands, teeth and my hanky I had taken from my desk.

One day in the week was craft time and not having had my chance at the giant easel painting with watercolors, I hoped this was the day Miss Porter would pick me. Since the school year began, I had made clay animals and carved an elephant from soap. The elephant was hard; I carved too much and I had a lot of soap chips and not much of an elephant left. Miss Porter gave me a jar to take the chips home so mother could use them in her washing machine.

After penmanship, and before craft time, Miss Porter read a poem fitting the month we were in, December. "*And now December's snows are here, the light flakes flutter down, and hoarfrost glitters white and fair upon the branches brown.*" She turned a few pages until finding more poems to read, but I was thinking only about what I could paint during craft time.

Then craft time came and I sat very tall at my desk hoping teacher would pick me to paint at the giant easel. Rita was picked instead! Rita whined over her arm hurting too much so teacher had to pick another, and this time it was me! I grabbed my tin of watercolors from my desk, filled a little jug with water, and I was ready to begin. I brushed on white for snow on the bottom half of the off white sheet of paper tacked to the easel, and I learned when a little blue and pink from my tin washed into my white that made the snow look more like real snow. I then painted an igloo. I built it block by block outlining each block with black paint. I had to paint an eskimo to go with the igloo and I painted him wearing lots of brown fur on his coat, hat and boots. I painted a black and white doggy just like

Julia's dog she called Spotty. Far away from the dog and the Eskimo, I painted a polar bear. Then I painted a blue sky and across the sky I painted the Northern Lights with colors of the rainbow.

When I was done, I stood back to get a good look. It was a beautiful painting! I was very pleased, especially when a few of my classmates praised my art work. Miss Porter overheard the praises and she said in a harsh tone, "Boys and girls! We must not praise anyone's work; all of you do as well as you can." I knew I did well and what teacher said did not bother me. I cleaned up my mess and then I took my seat to wait for my painting to dry.

I normally would be distracted by others still working with clay, or by those complaining over a sore arm, but I wasn't. All I wanted to do was look at my painting. The clock on the wall clicked close to the last minute of the school day when Miss Porter walked to the easel. With my painting now dry, she took it down, rolled it up and shoved it into a shelf with other rolls of paintings by my classmates. I thought it sad that I may never see it again; it was so beautiful.

When putting our coats on in the cloakroom, Julia expressed her puzzled thought when she asked me, "How come your arm is not red like mine?" I looked at her red blotch from the shot, then at my arm that wasn't sore looking and I quickly answered to shut her up, "It's beginning to feel sore, doncha know!" I had lied, again, and I began to understand how one lie could cause another lie to be told.

I now gave thought to what more I had to fear that could cause mother to find out I had lied; I feared Julia telling mother, for I knew, "If mother sees a red sore on my awm I will be in twouble, and if I don't git the red sore then Julia could keep asking why, awound mother." Then more came to mind, "If mother sees Julia's red sore, mother will say something about it and that could make Julia say something about me getting my shot!" With my head so full of worries, it became perfectly clear I would have to keep Julia away from my mother!

The next morning my arm was still not red, even a little bit. I did not want to give a reason for anyone at school to ask questions, so I wore a long sleeved dress. When I saw how much my classmates were suffering from such awful red and itching scabs, I thought that not suffering the same was my punishment for having lied, and I still had Julia to worry about spilling the beans to my mother.

It was a gamble, but I thought, in talking to Julia about our shots now might shut her up for good about it. On our way home from school, just Julia and me, I said to her, "I didn't git a scar from my shot." This was shocking news to Julia and she said, "That's bad luck! Now you can never, ever prove you got a smallpox shot." Because I had already had enough bad luck from my shot, I became very angry over being told about more bad luck! I then reminded her, "I did git it! You saw!" This had not been a contest with Julia to see who would win. She simply gave her shoulders an "I don't care shrug" and I hoped my worries were over for good!

Early in the morning the next day, after decorating our classroom for the Christmas season, our teacher told us,

"In the afternoon there will be practice in the auditorium for the Christmas program." Although this put a very merry feeling in me, it also caused me to remember a lot about our last year's program when I was in the first grade. I was given a hard part to say. The reason it was hard was because during practice when others had their parts to say I remembered their parts for them. Then, when it came my turn, it mixed me up and made it hard to say my part. I was such a silly girl, then! The very night of our program I said my part so very good and I can still remember it: "And hear the angels sing."

This year I wanted to be an angel and stand behind Joseph, Mary, and baby Jesus. I remembered last year when six girls were picked to be angels, three from the second grade and three from the third grade. I visualized myself wearing a pretty white gown with big sleeves and wearing big shiny silver wings and over my head having a sparkling golden halo. I will look so pretty! I will be an angel, I will, I will.

In the afternoon when the first and third graders entered the auditorium with us second graders, the older grades were already seated in their chairs. The same fifth grade boy, who'd called us babies once before, hollered very, very loud, "Here come the babies!" Mrs. Funk, the music teacher, punished him for us by bopping him on his head with her rolled up sheets of music.

After Miss Porter directed us to two rows of metal chairs to file in and fill, she took her place against the wall, standing with the other teachers who were looking so bossy with their arms crossed across their chests. Miss Rule blew her whistle to quiet the older kids who were clanging their metal chairs and talking loudly. It became so quiet, not a peep could be heard.

Miss Coffin, in charge of the program, stepped forward to explain it, telling it the same as I remembered the year before. "Listen carefully to my instructions. The first graders will have their parts to say. Those in the manger scene will be chosen from the second and third graders, and the ones left over will make up the chorus with the fourth graders. The fifth and sixth graders will be dressed like clowns and they will end the program doing a tumbling act."

Those in the tumbling act were then instructed to file to the back of the room to be fitted with their clown costumes. The first graders, with Miss Cleppen's help, were directed to go to another corner of the room to be given their parts to practice.

Miss Coffin was now ready to pick those in the manger scene, the angels first. As I sat on my chair I stretched my back, shoulders and neck so she could see me. Then I smiled like an angel would, ever so sweetly. Miss Coffin, though, seemed to be having a difficult time picking girls to be angels. After searching the rows, she started over, again! To have to hold my sweet smile for so long was becoming very difficult. I then raised my eyebrows and that helped to lock my smile in place. When Miss Coffin lifted her pointer finger she was ready to pick three angels from our class. The finger began its course along the first row and it stopped at Sharon, then it moved a little slower as though ho-humming who to pick next when it backed up to choose Suzi. The finger then picked up speed and zoomed by me to pick JoAnn! My shock over not being picked made me sink in despair and feel so brokenhearted!

I hung my head, pouting while three angels were picked from the third graders.

The lucky angels, full of excitement, scrambled up onto the stage to be fitted with their pretty angel costumes. Miss Coffin began picking boys to be the three kings, the shepherd boy, and Joseph. I thought, "I can be Mary!" To be seen, I stretched my body again and smiled with a kind look, but quick as a wink Miss Coffin picked the girl sitting next to me, Julia!

Julia acted like such a smarty pants, fluffing her long shiny black curls about and blinking her long black eyelashes! I hated my best friend as I watched her join the others on the stage to be fitted with her costume.

Mrs. Funk, the music teacher, made those of us stuck in the chorus move to fill the chairs in front of her, then handed out the music sheets with the Christmas songs. A big box full of maroon colored capes was opened by Miss Rule. A heavy smell of mothballs wafted out, causing us to choke and we choked and laughed while being fitted with a cape. Miss Rule instructed us to keep our capes to take home to be ironed. Mrs. Funk tapped her stick on the wooden stand and once she had everyone's attention told us, "By following the words on your song sheets, practicing here and at home, you will learn each song so on the night of the program you will sing from your hearts."

I was not interested in the first song, The First Noel. Instead, I wanted to watch those on the stage have their fun. The shepherd boy was wiggling into his gunny sack costume as the three kings were putting on their colorful robes. The next song, It Came Upon the Midnight Clear was sung as I watched the six angels being placed from the tallest to the shortest. All were dressed in their pretty white gowns, fluffy silver wings, and golden halos over their golden hair. Suddenly I realized, they all did have golden hair! It was clear now, with my hair brown, I would have made the angels look funny being the only one with brown hair.

I knew the words to Silent Night and could sing while watching what was going on up on the stage. Julia came from behind the curtain to take her place at the cradle and I saw she was dressed to look like the Mary I had seen in pictures. Julia, with her black hair, too, made her a good pick to be Mary. This helped to make me feel better; with brown hair I could never make a good Mary. Understanding why I was not picked to be an angel, or Mary, I sang the other songs as loud as anyone else to the very last: Joy to the World.

When school let out that day, Julia was behaving rather uppity. I was grateful to have Frankie and Lila walking home with us. I talked nearly nonstop to ignore the high-falutin' "Miss Mary." I said to Frankie first, "We're so very lucky to be in the special, wonderful chorus, aren't we Fwankie?"

I told Lila, "I can help you learn your fun, fun first gwade pawt, weally, weally I can." My attempt to "cold shoulder" Julia did not stop her; she kept acting like a high and mighty queeny for being picked to be Mary! By the time we got to my house I was so jealous of Julia I don't recall saying goodbye.

Once alone in my house, though, my jealousy changed to regret when I realized, "I will hafta pwactice my songs all by myself." Even the soothing warmth from the floor furnace did not help; I was just too saddened not having Julia practicing with me. But I certainly knew "with my best fwiend acting so happy cuz she gits to be Mawy," I could never let her know I missed her!

The next few days, in the house and practicing my Christmas songs, Bobby teased me by telling me I sang like a frog. Then he would imitate a frog by making a croaking sound, making me so mad!

On Saturday, Bobby was out of the house most of the day and I could sing in any room I wanted to. Sunday too, but he caught me singing as he came in at supper time and as we gathered around the table to eat, he made a low croaking sound without looking at me. I scowled, waiting for him to look at me and when he did I gave him a mean look and stuck my tongue out.

Patty, fearing trouble if Dad noticed us, said to Mother with soft words, "Did you know, Mom, that Mannings had a quarantine sign posted on their door? Now Lois is stuck inside even though she's not sick." A quarantine sign meant everyone had to stay inside until the sign was taken down, and this made me feel very sad for Patty that she could not be with her best friend, Lois.

Mother said, "No, I did not know. I am sorry to hear this. Do they have measles or smallpox?"

My eyes grew wide and my stomach churned—Mother had mentioned the word that I had forgotten about, "Smallpox"! The bite of food I swallowed went down like a lump of hard coal. I was still very fearful of my mother's anger over my having lied, and that made me feel very sorry that I had wanted the shot so bad I lied to get it.

My feeling of regret also made me think about what I never understood: why my Mother did not know that a shot would protect me from the smallpox? Or, did she know? I did a little thinking and figured out that I could ask mother if smallpox can be bad to get and her answer would then let me know if she knew.

To make sure it would be safe talking at the table, I first looked at Dad. He seemed at ease. Then, in a very calm manner, I asked, "Mother, is smallpox bad to git?"

Bobby poked his nose in by speaking first, "Doncha know, froggy, you can die from smallpox?"

To keep Dad calm over Bobby's snipe at me, Mother quickly answered, "Yes, smallpox can be very bad to get."

I felt stunned over Mother's answer. She did know! I could no longer hold back my sharp words. "Well, how come you wanted me to git the smallpox? And die!"

Mother's head snapped back as she stiffened in her chair. "What an awful thing for you to say!"

I froze. Everyone, including Dad, was staring so strangely at me. I knew at that moment they all hated me! I struck back, expressing my suppressed feelings, "Ya, but, you wouldn't let me git the shot! And I could have died from gitting the smallpox!"

Sternly, Dad spoke one word to settle me down. "Tootse!" At Dad's command, I sat back to try to settle down and in doing so hadn't noticed that Mother was deep in thought.

It was after a quiet moment when Mother said to me, "I see now. You did not need that shot because you were born with smallpox and that means you will never get smallpox again."

I was totally dumbstruck to be told that I, as a tiny baby, had had smallpox. Having lied to get something I did not need, but wanted anyway, and having been so scared, made me unable to put any meaning to the distress I had caused myself. I could not hold it back and blurted out, "I got the shot anyway!" I jerked back in my chair, free at last of the heavy burden I had carried for so long. I was ready to accept my great and enormous punishment.

Mother dropped her spoon and cried, "Uff-da! Uff-da!"

Bobby said, "You're nuts!"

Patty said, "You got a shot when you didn't need one? How silly!"

Dad, rolling a toothpick from one side of his mouth to the other, simply said, "That's my Tootse."

When we left the table, I sauntered to my bedroom, closed my door tight and sat on my bed to brood over my mixed emotions. I had made a mountain out of a molehill over having lied to get my shot and as it turned out, it did not matter to anyone!

Bobby, thinking I had been quietly practicing my Christmas songs, made a croaking frog sound through the keyhole. I darted out of my bedroom to get him, forgetting that Dad was still home. As I chased to try and reach my mean brother, I awakened Dad from a snooze in his chair. The two of us, fearing Dad's wrath, scrambled up the stairs far out of his sight. When a moment had passed and we hadn't heard Dad's voice raised at us, we guessed it had been his time to wake up anyway to go out for the night.

Out of school or in school, I was a good friend to Julia, except during practice for our Christmas program. That was when I felt a fit of jealousy because she would act so special! It was not until our Christmas program was over that my jealousy and naughty thoughts ended for my best friend.

On the very first night of our two week Christmas vacation from school, we had Toyland to go to. I dressed warm, then ran out the door of our house to meet Frankie and Julia. Before I could get to the gate, Frankie was already beyond it, motioning with his arm and calling out to Julia and me, "Com' on, catch up, let's git to Toyland!"

As we rounded the corner of Front Street to reach Second Street, it was like a Halloween night with kids everywhere, all going to Toyland. When we reached the furniture store a long line had already formed in front of the locked door. Frankie saw one of his buddies way up front who'd give him cuts and left us. Julia and I took our places at the end of the line.

With many kids in line, out of line, and coming, I gave my undivided attention to anyone who shared fun stories about someone, or a happening. Their laughter added a bright feeling to the dark night and made me think of that jolly fat man who tells us we better be good! I knew what Bobby had told me and what kids at school had been saying, but with everyone acting so gay, I did so want to believe in a Santa Claus.

A car's headlights down the street shined on Sonny, Bubber and Betsy coming. Poor Kathleen, I thought, I knew she was home with the mumps. Betsy dropped away from Sonny and Bubber to join a girlfriend at the very end of the line. Betsy and I weren't special friends like we once were. I knew I was the same, but she seemed older and more grownup. Sonny and Bubber were very, very loud while working up the line, mooching cuts. When they got to us, Sonny slugged my arm with his fist hard enough to feel through my coat sleeve, yet I knew it was a good jest from a friend greeting a friend. I yanked Julia forward to make room in the line and the two jumped in behind us.

Both boys were so full of spunk they became the only ones entertaining the kids near us.

When the door of the furniture store opened, a string of loud, "Hurrays!" erupted from the head of the line. Julia and I followed those marching in and the heavy stomping of our overshoes along the rope draped aisle sounded like many horses clopping in beat to the jingle of bells in the Christmas music.

Reaching the top of the stairs, Julia and I stepped into a wonderland of Christmas in Toyland. Seeing each toy on the other side of the white picket fence we marveled, laughed, and found much to wish for. All too quickly we were at the end of the white picket fence. It was sad to have to leave such gaiety, but our turn was over.

As Julia and I tripped down the stairs with our big treats, I spotted Frankie in line going up, again! When he saw us he put his finger to his lips to signal us to be quiet as he patted a bulge in his pocket.

We stood waiting outside the door for Frankie, our mittens dangling from pins pinned to our sleeves, crunching the munchy, good caramelie taste of our popcorn balls. Soon Frankie bounded out, taking a first bite from his popcorn ball and snickering all the while. His pocket was still bulging—he had two!

We headed for home, walking slowly, sometimes stopping to watch other kids who were enjoying the gay night, too. By the time we reached Front Street our popcorn balls were devoured. Julia and I shamed Frankie for the spare one he had until he unwillingly said he'd share, and we stood underneath a street light to watch as he broke it evenly in three chunks.

When we reached Stan's Bar we were licking the last good caramelie taste from our fingers. The noise coming from inside the bar made our curiosity flare. We pushed our noses to the glass. Through the cloud of smoke I saw Stan behind the bar, then I focused on the big buffalo head behind him and wrestled with my feelings until something new caught my attention. On a shelf was a stuffed two headed goat! While staring at such a thing I sank deep in thought over what it would be like to have another head. Would I still be just me? Or could I be me, and the other head? If we did not like each other, what would we do? And what if I wanted to go someplace and the other head didn't!?

Frankie yelled, "Ah, they're not pulling the wool over my eyes! You guys see that two headed goat up there? They glued another head on, that's what they did!" My spell of very unusual thought had been broken by Frankie and, like him, felt smart because old Stan could not fool us!

Since my eyes had adjusted to the light in the bar, the night seemed much darker which made the white blanket of snow covering the ground even more noticeable. I began to feel the cold from the snow and pulled my coat collar up around my neck. I put my mittens on.

The corner drug store was closed. Frankie, with his hands in his pockets, nudged his shoulder against Julia, then me to signal us to stop. Standing at the glass door we looked in. Unlike the light in Stan's Bar, the only light in this store was a dim yellow glow coming from a showcase that gave all else in the store a ghostly appearance. The phantom of the mind tricked me into hearing sounds; the whirl of the milkshake maker, the squeak of a stool at the soda fountain, a murmur of voices from the booths in the back, and I could sense someone sitting on the funny book rack. To break the nighttime spooky spell I pushed away. The other two followed.

The red brick shoe repair shop had a big window for such a small shop. By simply walking by, we could see all the stuff inside. The rows and rows of shoes and cowboy boots reminded me of chickens on their roosts for the night. This made me think of my comfy warm bed.

A need for warmth and sleep let me almost forget Frankie and Julia were with me. Then I heard a loud "Eeeeeeeeeeeeeeee!!!" screech that came from Frankie! He'd dashed and slid on a slick tire track in the street. Julia and I perked up to join him. We filled our lungs with cold invigorating air and after a good run slid and screeched "Eeeeeeeeeeeeeeeee!!!" down the road. When we reached my house I dropped out and had little time to yell, "Goodbye!" before the other two were out of sight.

I kicked my boots off and left them in the vestibule, darted through the front room door, and ran for the floor furnace. I could not see Mother, but from the clattering sounds of pots and pans from the kitchen I knew she was there. I shouted for her to hear me. "I'm home!" I figured I had better let her know what I saw at Toyland that I wanted. I wasn't sure Santa would have room in his toy sack for a dollhouse for me so I added, "I liked the dollhouse best!" I knew she heard me because I heard back, "Hang up your coat!" How was it she'd known I had thrown it over a chair?

When I was about ready to step off the floor furnace and head for my room and to bed, Bobby burst in. I then held my ground on the floor furnace knowing he would want to hog it. Bobby knew I had been to Toyland and poked me with his finger while chanting, "Ha, ha, ha, ha, there's no Santa Claus, ha, ha, ha, ha." Then with his rump he bumped me off the furnace!

This so enraged me I could not hold back my sharp words. I shouted, "You poopey shitty doo-doo!"

We heard, "Bobby! Stop your teasing!" Then Mother's face appeared in the kitchen doorway and with her finger shaking at me scolded, "And you stop talking with a dirty mouth!"

I was so mad I stomped off to my bedroom and slammed the door shut so hard I scared myself when the walls rattled. I sucked in a breath and waited for another scolding from Mother. When it did not come, I let my breath go with a big sigh. I brushed my teeth, put my flannel pajamas on, and crawled into bed.

With my head under the cold covers, my breath warming them, the far away sound of a train rumbling into town with its, "Whoooooah" followed by its strong "Chug-choo, chug-choo," I was lulled to sleep before the last whistle blew.

As Christmas vacation went on, the snow became a strong force that worked its wonder to renew a special bond between old friends. Julia and I, with Frankie along, joined our friends on Beaner Hill to go sledding, something he'd never done. Betsy was my big surprise. She was fun like she'd always been; not so grown-up after all. Kathleen was the only one not playing; she still had the mumps.

When I got tired of sledding I wanted to show off to Frankie more things we old friends knew about, so I took a "take charge" attitude and suggested, "Let's go to the cemetery! We can show Frankie Mista Rip!"

Sonny, Bubber, Betsy, Julia, Frankie and I, pulling our sleds, headed for the cemetery road. While trudging up the road in the snow I was quick to let Frankie know what I knew when pointing out to him, "That's where the hermit lives and he has lots of inventions!"

Frankie asked, "Like what?"

I had to think, then remembered one. "A mouse catcher! And just . . . lots more." I knew how much of a junk hunter Frankie had become and I let him know about a pile of junk I remembered in one messy yard up the road. Sonny and Bubber looked at me with queer expressions and I wondered why? Then I discovered when we reached the house, the junk in the yard had been cleaned up! I felt like a big, foolish fibber, but then Sonny saved me when he said, "We already got to that!"

Before entering the cemetery we propped our sleds against the fence and in my mind's eye, the sleds looked like horses tied to a hitching post, a fitting reminder of Sonny and his play horse riding. Heaps of snow acted as a buffer to any noise and with it so quiet in the cemetery, Sonny got the bug to conjure up a ghost story. I was not about to waste my time acting like a fraidy-cat, I wanted to show Frankie what I knew, so I told Sonny, "Oh, dry up!"

I sparked a race to Mr. Rip, the monument, and it took a great surge of energy from all to leap through the snow to reach it. With my friends beside me, I looked up at the stone cross while proudly showing Frankie, R.I.P., then telling Frankie, "He's our Mista Rip!"

Frankie said something then that greatly miffed me, "Wouldn't cha know it; it's a preacher who lies here."

Then Bubber, after he'd focused on a plaque that Frankie had seen, miffed me more when he said, "By jiminy you're right! Father Monahan is buried here."

Sonny asked, "When did he land here?"

Betsy said, "Maybe he has been here all along and they just now added the plaque."

I was saddened that an old part of our life had been wiped away by Frankie. Our stone cross was not for our fun "Mr. Rip" after all; it was a monument for a dumb "Monahan!"

Instead of Sonny neighing like a horse like he used to do to get us to gallop along, he said, "Let's go hunt up a ghost or two!"

I was certainly glad when Betsy, so smart like, said to Sonny, "Oh, rooty-toot-toot, keep your dumb old ghosts to yourself!"

Shuffling through the deep snow made it hard to see where the graves were at. This caused Julia to remind us of her bad luck story, "If you step on a grave someone in the family will die."

Frankie was ahead of us and spun around. "That's bunk! Where didja hear a story like that?" Julia ignored Frankie and did not reply, but I was grateful to Frankie for speaking up and making the bad luck story sound "hogwashy."

As we weaved about the cemetery, the warm rays from the sun directly overhead drained us of our energy. With our "ho-hum" attitude, we could think of nothing more to do there. Then the distant "Whoo-ooooah! Whoo-ooooah!" from the Noon Skiddoo was heard and Sonny complained, "I'm hungry!"

Bubber yelled, "Me too! Follow me."

We zipped down the slick snow covered road on our sleds, then pulled them to Bubber and Betsy's house. Bubber ran inside and returned carrying a soda cracker can and two already opened cans of deviled ham. We knew of one place no one would bother us and slogged off in the direction of the giant V shaped billboard.

As we neared the billboard, and passing the very house I lived in once, I got Frankie's attention by telling him, "I lived in that house a long time ago."

Frankie's excited reply surprised me as he said, "You did! Really?" This made me want to take Frankie inside the house, yet with strangers now living in the house I felt locked out. I could only imagine my family doing what my memory recalled, now seeming like ghosts in the house, and I said no more about where I once lived.

Inside the big V of the giant billboard, we sat down on the snow that had already been packed down by someone else. Bubber snapped off the lid of the cracker can and we each grabbed a handful. By using our crackers we scooped out the deviled ham in the cans until it was all gone. A handful of clean wet snow took care of my thirst. When Bubber reached for a fistful of snow, he uncovered a big cigarette butt that was not very old.

With the butt between two fingers and speaking in a manly voice, Bubber told Sonny and Frankie he'd share. The three laid back on the snow for a casual rest, sharing the cold cigarette, acting like big men. Julia and I expressed our "blah" distaste over such nonsense. Smoking a hot cigarette had been a terrible experience we could never forget! After a lackadaisical rest, we left the cave like dwelling and pulled our sleds with a destination in mind—Beaner Hill, again! Then, as friends must do when dusk begins to settle in, we separated and headed to our homes.

Christmas Eve, the night all kids wait for, had come. After the fun of picking one present to open was over,

I retired to my bedroom down the hall. Feeling God's calming grace after my bedtime prayer, I pondered in wonder over a jolly fat man until Mr. Sandman came with grains of sand~~~~~~~My journey through sleep seized that time to dream of greens 'n' reds 'n' smell of pine and to see me by the adorned tree alone, wanting to know, had Santa come during the night?

In my dream, I looked out the window. On the new fallen snow, pretty 'n' white, were two very long ruts made by a sleigh~~~a sleigh~~~a sleigh~~~a sleigh~~~~~~~The sway of my dream caused me to awaken. It was morning bright and I ran from my bed to the tree to find a beautiful, two story dollhouse, all mine! I breathed a contented sigh. I "believed" and so Santa had come in his sleigh that Christmas Eve of nineteen hundred and forty three.

The first day back at school was so cold and blustery Miss Porter had to keep us in during recess. To pass the time away she'd planned an event for us girls to act out the story of Little Miss Muffet. The boys were told to file to the back of the classroom and to sit and be quiet while playing with clay. As instructed, we girls seated ourselves on the little wooden chairs in a half circle around our teacher at the front of the classroom.

A noise arose from the back of the room before we could begin our play. Teacher clapped her hands, a reminder to the boys to play with their clay quietly. That worked for just a little bit.

First, Miss Porter, alone, recited the Little Miss Muffet ditty, while interjecting, "Eddy, give back Freddy his clay this very minute!" Although it was funny with Eddy and Freddy in the ditty, we girls had to choke back our laughter so as not to make our teacher angrier. Then teacher, lifting her hands in the air signaled us girls to stand. With the swoop of her arm we walked in a circle like in musical chairs and upon hearing, "Little Miss Muffet sat on her tuffet," we sat down with Jo Ann plopping so hard on her chair she toppled over! With her now sitting on the floor, our teacher had to order the boys to, "Stop that snickering!"

When all the Miss Muffets were finally composed on their chairs, Miss Porter continued the ditty, "Eating her curds and whey." We mimicked by scooping up make-believe spoonfuls of curds and whey. "Along came a spider." Like teacher, we rolled our eyes upward and in my imagination I witnessed a fat, black, squishy spider hanging from a web. "And sat down beside her . . . " I squirmed on my chair imagining the spider beside me, too! "And frightened Miss Muffet away." We shrieked! Then we stood up making a motion to run.

"Girls, girls!" spoke Miss Porter to stop us from running away. Composed again on our chairs, and teacher, having our attention, asked, "Who can tell me what Miss Muffet said when she saw the spider?"

I did not understand, we had already responded with a shriek, but Janice understood and let out a loud squeal, "Eeeeeeekkk," that sounded pretty good to me. Our teacher didn't think so. "No, no! Someone else, please."

Annie stood up with the back of her hand to her forehead as though to faint as she whimpered, "Oh, dear."

A sigh came from our teacher, then she said, "That is not at all what Miss Muffet cried!"

Rita then gave it a try by jumping up while uttering, "Oh! Oh! Oh!" Surely, I thought, that was right, but our teacher said, "Girls, girls! Doesn't anyone know what Miss Muffet said when she saw the spider sit down beside her?"

I ask *you*, do you think you could sit still with a spider beside you? I think not, and neither could I!

Focusing for so long on that fat spider, I began to shutter and shake until I could no longer contain my anger! I leaped to my feet and shrieked, "Ishy! Ishy! Ishy!"

From the back of the classroom laughter drowned out , teacher's harsh, negative response to me!

After Miss Porter established order again, a quiet pause followed as our teacher composed and prepared herself to act out the correct response by Miss Muffet. The boys, too, were interested in hearing the finale.

Miss Porter became poised on her tuffet, and in a genteel way, she held a pretend spoon while eating her curds and whey. With agonizing slowness, she rolled her eyes upward to see that icky spider! With a "la-ti-da" attitude, she rolled her eyes away without shrieking a word until that wretched spider again sat down beside her. Her eyes widened, the back of her hand covered her mouth, her voice faint, she cried, "Oh-my, oh-my, oh-my."

The month of February's warm chinook winds blew and created a slushy mess from the melting snow. Valentine's Day had come and gone and there was still slush everywhere. I was in my bedroom when mother walked in and pleaded with me, "Please, remove your Valentine cards from your dresser so I can dust."

Being reminded of my cards by mother, renewed my interest in wanting to look at them again. The only one not standing up was the floppy, crocheted heart. Frankie's grandmother made it and one for Julia, too. Frankie had them crumpled in his pocket before giving them to us on the morning of Valentine's Day.

I picked up the floppy, crocheted heart and I laid it across my hand. I studied the fine work while I traced the outline of its shape with my finger. My thoughts then drifted back in time to the day I first met Frankie when he had peed on our mudpies! How foolish and sorry I felt for being so afraid of him then. We could have been friends all along.

Sadly, I reminded myself, "Frankie is gone now." He had to go to live with his mother at that place with a park and a zoo because his grandmother was not well.

I then recalled the night before Frankie went away. It was a school night and with a bright moon to see by, Frankie, Howie, Julia, Lila, and I played tag in the middle of the street; it was great fun for all. When Frankie was 'it', it seemed he chased Julia and me more than he chased Howie and Lila, but he had to tag Lila because she runs too slow. After Lila was called in and we stopped playing tag, Frankie wanted to stay and talk to Howie. Julia and I left them at the stairs to the apartment house and I walked Julia part way home.

Coming back alone, I spotted Frankie under the glow of the street light and he was alone. For a reason I do not know, I felt shy and I wanted to walk right on by, but I could not when he asked, "Whatcha doin'?"

I had to reply, "Going home."

He then moved to the fence and he rattled a few slats with the toe of his boot before he said, "I have something for you." He reached down and from under a dead looking shrub, he pulled out a car's hubcap. I stared at it as he directed me on what to do. "Would cha please take this piece of junk to school tomorrow cuz I won't be around to toss it onto that heap of scrap. And tell Julia tomorrow that the doorknob she finds on her doorstep is from me."

Taking the hubcap was my answer that I would do it and I shuffled through the slush on the sidewalk, away from him. I remember that funny feeling I felt in my stomach when I got to my gate, I paused then to look back and I saw Frankie just a dark figure up the street. That feeling panicked me and I shouted, "Bye, Frankie! Bye!" I am so glad now he heard me, he turned and he waved and I waved back.

While placing my Valentine cards in a shoebox, I wondered, *What is Frankie doing now? Has he forgotten Julia and me?* The floppy, crocheted heart was the only Valentine I did not put in the shoebox. As soon as mother had my dresser dusted, I placed the one heart back there. I then left my thoughts behind as I skipped out of my bedroom and out the door of the house to play.

That day, Frankie's grandmother died. The next day the warm chinook winds changed direction and new snow fell and fell to cover the dirty slush the warm winds left. Winter stayed to the time in March when seven was no longer my age. I had turned eight.

April came and gave me the seven year itch which lasted seven days. Mother had to wash my bed sheets everyday and rub my body with pink lotion to relieve my dry and itchy skin. It smelled like rotten eggs!

The fourth day of April, and fourth day of my itch I was sell enough to go to school. Walking into my classroom, I immediately sniffed a heavy smell of rotten eggs. And knew, some classmates had the pink lotion on their bodies, as I.

After settling down on my wooden desk seat, I soon had a rude memory come back of the day I wet my pants. The same kind of prickly itch on my bottom, with no pink lotion there, hit like lightening! When having to lift to scratch, my desk seat squeaked! Tommy had a squeak in his desk seat, Paige too! Kay, in front of me jumped! Startling me so bad!

During penmanship, with a volley of squeaks rippling around the classroom, our teacher became pretty crabby.

To get our attention, Miss Porter tapped her ruler on her desk, then ordered us to put our tablets away!

After picking up her poetry book, she took a moment in thought, to then, with a calming whisper, explain, "When reading or listening to poetry, there is a rhythm you feel, like little calming waves in water."

I remembered first grade and marching in "whythm," but did not understand how "whythm" could be in a poem. And there were never wee-wee "waves" in my bath water!

The book flopped open to the page Miss Porter had marked and as she read the poem "My Shadow" we guessed she thought by reading it to us, it would ease our itching! A little bit it did.

The next poem, of her reading of "The Wind" a magic spell of "rhythm" was felt, and the soothing "calm" in her voice, a magic spell of floating happened, like in a dream.-

"*Who has seen the wind?*
Neither I nor you.
But when the leaves hang trembling,
the wind is passing through.
Who has seen the wind?
Neither you nor I.
But when the trees bow down their heads,
the wind is passing by."

I peered out the windows to see if I could see the wind and there was not even a breeze passing by; the branches of the trees, without leaves yet, appeared not to move at all.

The title of the next poem was, Jump-jump-jump-jump away. Teacher added action with a slight jump of her shoulders with each, "jump" in the title, and we found it smart to mimic teacher. By raising up our whole body before the prickly itch hit kept it from happening. The poem, we discovered, was loaded with jumps,

"*Jump-jump-jump-jump*
from this town to the next.
Jump - jump - jump - jump over the moon;
Jump all the morning and jump all the noon —
Jump-jump all night.
Won't our mothers be a fright?
Jump jump-jump-jump over to the sea;
what wonderful wonders we shall see.
Jump-jump-jump-jump far away;
and all come back home some other day."

Teacher then said, rather angrily, "Children, you must go out for recess, *now!*" We leaped up without making one itty bitty squeaking noise.

After school, on Tuesdays, I had my job to do at the garage picking up messy papers from the floor in the office. I did not always buy a stamp for my war bond book with the dime I earned; sometimes I wanted a funny book instead. I got another job too, Kathleen and I together, on Thursdays after school, sold the weekly paper in her neighborhood. Each of us earned enough money for a sunday at the corner drug store. My favorite was chocolate ice cream with marshmallow topping and lots of crushed nuts.

On the sunny side of the schoolhouse, the red and yellow tulips planted by the first grade kids were all blooming. Also on the sunny side, where the ground was dry, marbles were played. I had my own pouch of pretty marbles and I had to learn how to shoot with them in order to compete with the boys. Then the page of the calendar turned over to the month of June and we had just two days left of school. The tulips were all dead and my pouch with marbles in it was not as heavy as it had been; I was still learning how to shoot.

On the first day of June, we prepared our classroom for a visit by our parents the next afternoon. We cleaned the room, our desks, and we taped our papers of some school work to the walls, except for the best, our watercolors. The art work had to stay in rolls on the shelf. The showing of those, as teacher explained, would be the very last for our mothers and fathers to see. Miss Porter gave us specific instructions on how to properly present ourselves for the showing of the watercolors.

That night my thoughts were filled with such stuff summer vacations are full of: to run, to discover, to play, to feel the warm sun all day and feel no more the fear of being marked tardy and ruin a perfect record.

On that very last day of school, we had to fill the morning with something to do. We told stories, with also Miss Porter telling about a happening when she was a little girl. I tried very hard, but I could not pull into my thoughts our old and bony teacher ever being a little girl. "Our teacher and her friend had been swimming in a river. Her friend got a cramp and was drowning, but our teacher saved her because our teacher knew how, she had taken life saving lessons." That was the end of her story, yet she continued with a lesson, telling us, "How important it was for us to learn how to swim. To never swim alone and if someone is drowning and we do not know how to save them we must get help." I figured that was good advice from our teacher and I knew then that maybe she cared about us after all.

A murmur of adult voices were heard outside the classroom door. Because it was teacher's wish for us children to learn good manners, we were taught how to introduce our parents to our teacher when they entered. I became very nervous over the possibility of making a mistake so I practiced, to myself, the very way teacher taught us. Miss Porter, I would like for you to meet my mother, then I say my mother's name only, my dad wasn't expected to attend.

When the clock told the time we had waited for, we lined up in front of the closed door. Miss Porter opened the door and the mothers and two fathers began walking in. I was second in line to give a proper introduction, yet my mind suddenly could not assemble the correct words, and I said, "Miss Porter would you, I, I mean! I wish for you to meet my mother, Mrs. Baker!" My teacher, who knew my mother all year long said, in a very proper manner, "I am delighted to meet you Mrs. Baker." My mother then said, "I am pleased to meet you, too, Miss Porter." I felt proud over such fine talk from my mother. She was a very proper lady.

My classmates were all as pleased as I was when showing our parents our good work taped to the walls. I was excited, too, overseeing my beautiful painting again and to show it off to all the parents. Then, by Miss Porter's announcement, the exciting time was to begin.

As our parents started seating themselves, we lined up, shoulder to shoulder. Lalon at the end of the line fell sideways against the one next to him, and so on like dominos for good fun for the last time with classmates in the second grade. Miss Porter, to stop our play in a lady like way, clapped with a soft patty-cake. We respected her kind reaction to our bad behavior by standing like well behaved pupils, ready for our showing to begin.

I glowed within, knowing I would feel the glory of pride, again, in the showing of my beautiful painting. Yet the way Miss Porter was handing out the rolls I had to wonder, how did she know we were getting our own? It all seemed very strange to me. I unrolled the one given to me and I discovered my suspicion was correct! I had someone else's painting and it was ugly! Feeling broken, hopeless, very sad over being cheated of my glory, I dipped forward to look down the line and I saw it was Eddy holding mine! He looked like Popeye ready to poop-poop his pipe and I knew why; my painting of an igloo, eskimo, polar bear, and a dog, all on snow, and the colorful northern lights all over the sky was still as beautiful as I remembered.

At the end of the showing, teacher instructed us to roll the paintings up. I felt such terrible anger I responded by saying to myself, "I know enough on my own to roll it up!

Then find who to give it to. And get mine!"

Miss Porter gathered the rolls and with a coolness about her, placed them back on the shelf! I had felt her sting once more! By not letting me keep it, she was crushing what she did not like, pride in one's own work. I was afraid then to ask for it out of fear she would want to shame me in front of everyone for wanting to get credit for my beautiful painting.

I could not honor my teacher with good etiquette by smiling and saying goodbye to her like my classmates were doing. Instead, I tugged at Mother's hand to pull her away from Miss Porter towards the classroom door. Mother stopped me and with a bewildering look on her face, asked, "Aren't you going to say goodbye to your teacher?"

I answered, "No! I already did!" My statement confused Mother; she shrugged her shoulders as if wondering, when? I did not care that I had fibbed, and pulled Mother out of that classroom!

Once in the great hall, my spirits were lifted by older kids acting in a slap-happy way when rushing for the out of doors. Most were shouting, "Hurray, it's the end of our captivity!" I, too, needed to feel the end in such an ecstatic way to help me forget what caused my shattered pride.

I did not know on that day that second grade with Miss Porter would be remembered more than any other grade in all my years in school.

To run, to discover, to play on a sunny summer day time was forgotten. Julia and I, when we realized we had spent too much time doing all with Kathleen, Sonny, and Bubber, we hurriedly skipped hie-d-hie all the way until we crossed over the many iron rails. Slipping down the cinder strewn ground from the tracks to the street, Lila came running to meet us.

The three of us made plans to meet after supper, then Julia cried, "I gotta git!" While I was backing up to my gate away from Lila I said to her, "Git Howie to play with us for a change."

Lila said, "No! He won't unless other boys are there to play."

In disgust I spat out my words, "Howie stinks! We don't play silly girls games!"

Dashing for the door of the house, I smelled a spray of lilacs from the few still in bloom and the sweet aroma made me think of my grandmother who died.

Once indoors and relieved to see I wasn't late, I noticed Bobby looking at me as though he'd suddenly realized he had someone to say something to. He said, "Hey, peabrain! We're moving!"

I said, "Huh ah!" My big brother, I knew, was full of wind just trying to tease me. I called him a liar.

Then Patty, who'd been setting the table, spoke up. "It's true."

"Huh ah!" I said again. Thinking they were both full of wind, I knew Mother would tell me it wasn't true.

The smell and noise coming from the kitchen made it easy finding Mother. I went in there to tell her, "Patty and Bobby said we're moving!" Because I had stated a fact known to Mother, she figured there was no need to respond. That was the way my mother saved her energy when she was busy. I knew her lack of reaction made it true, and asked, "But where to?"

After a frown and a long sigh that caused her lips to sputter, she answered, "Oh, ah, to a white house with green trim!"

I had to ask. "But when?"

She snapped, "Someday!" That had to satisfy me for I had to get down the hall to the bathroom in a hurry!

While sitting on the toilet thinking, I thought about the "someday" for the move. That meant not today, nor tomorrow, nor any day soon, and I was glad of that. A house painted white with green trim was okay. I knew there were many houses painted the same close by, even Kathleen's house and Mrs. Gouge's in the country were painted white with green trim.

After I hopped off the toilet to reach for the door knob, I saw what I hadn't noticed when entering. In place of the milk-glass window in the bathroom door, hung a dishtowel! As Dad passed by me in the hallway, wanting in the bathroom, he asked, "Feel better now Tootse?"

I was in a hurry with a flurry of questions in my head over that dish towel, and not knowing why I should feel better, I answered, "Um, guess so."

I ran to Mother in the kitchen. "How come that dishtowel is on the bathroom door?"

Patty and Bobby overheard me asking. Looking fearful, both said to me, "Shut up!"

Mother, in a weary tone, hushed the two. Then she said to me, "After I tell you, I do not want you to bring the subject up again." What happened sounded serious and I nodded to let Mother know I could be trusted. "What happened, happened," Mother said. "Patty and Bobby were arguing today. One chased the other down the hall and when the bathroom door closed the hands of the other went through the glass, breaking it. That's why the dish towel hangs there."

Bobby poked me to get my attention. "So don't blab!"

I could tell by the way Patty and Bobby were behaving, they feared big trouble from Dad when he came out of the bathroom. Dad would surely want to know why that dish towel hangs on that door! I felt Patty and Bobby's anxiety and that made me fear I could get into trouble, too. The tension was great when dad was heard coming up the hallway, but he said nothing! Yet we knew he would ask about it later.

After the call, "Soups on!" We gathered around the table to eat. Patty and Bobby, showing very good manners, ate with good grace. Bobby, however, not trusting me to not blab about the dish towel, kept giving me sly mean looks to remind me to keep quiet! We had made it to the last of our meal and we were about to push away from the table when dad cleared his throat like one does when ready to say something. I stared at my plate not wanting to see the expected consequences of Patty and Bobby's fighting. A surprise then happened when Dad said, "Must have been a strong wind that blew through the house today that slammed the bathroom door shut so hard it broke the glass."

As Dad retired to his favorite chair, I felt great relief, feeling so lucky for that strong wind that day. I let Mother know, "I'm goin' out to play!"

Outdoors, waiting for Lila to join me, I giggled over my funny thought of Patty and Bobby being the wind blowing down the hallway. Yet I had to think much of hiking on the prairie that day; a strong wind did not blow that I could remember. My deep thinking about a wind finally blew away when Lila joined me. The two of us skipped up the street to Julia's house. From there the three of us stomped through the weeds to reach the bank to slip down to the riverside.

As we strolled quietly along amongst the trees and weedy shrubs, the evening air was made very pleasant with a fresh smell from the river. A splash was heard in the water and ripples were floating outward from a jumping fish. No-see-ums flitted about, here, there, everywhere, and crickets and frogs were harmonizing with a bird adding its nightly song.

We came upon a section of a big pipe that had rolled down the bank and we sat side by side on that pipe to become more mesmerized by the sounds by the riverside. On the ground I saw a dead little lizard and at the same time I heard a weak voice say, "I have a secret."

The whisper had come from Julia. This sparked an interest in Lila to want to drop to the ground to sit at Julia's feet, so she could look up at Julia when she told us of her secret. I scooted in closer on the pipe.

We saw Julia's face drawn to a frown in a fearful way as she whined, "But I don't think I better tell."

That made me want to hear the secret all the more! I urged, "Com'on! You hafta tell." Lila urged her as well, tugging on Julia's leg as though trying to pull the secret from her. What I said finally worked, "We're friends and you hafta tell friends your secwets."

Julia, with a finger to her tightly closed lips, signaled us to keep her secret. She also made us cross our hearts, many times, which was our special promise not to tell. Lila gave Julia's leg another tug and with difficulty Julia whispered, "My dad, he, ah, talked to one of those, ah, up there. Today. And that one, ah, gave my dad a letter to mail."

I gasped in shock as Lila yelped, "You guys! We're not suppose to talk about them!" That was very, very true, no one was suppose to talk about them, children especially! We knew "up there" was the airport on the hill and "those" kept up there on the other side of a fence were prisoners to be very afraid of; worse than the kind that just rob people or banks, they were dangerous prisoners, captured in the war! Julia's secret, at that moment, did not cause further conversation over "those up there."

The secret we could not talk about, but tried to, made us feel closer to each other and we took a hold of each others hand as we strolled along. I, however, was not one to drop a subject so easily and knowing Julia's dad was working up there building something for them, I wondered about that letter. I created an interesting plot by mentioning, "You suppose that one was sending a message to the enemy?" Lila still would not talk about them, but Julia said, "My dad would know about it, don't you think?" I was able to figure out how, and I said, "Ya but, how wouldja dad know if it was written in a secwet code? I mean like, love, could mean, attack!" My eyes grew big and I screamed, "Then an air-waid would be for real!"

Lila knew that an air-raid would be the dropping of bombs on us, and the fear she felt made her shout, "Shut up! Shut up!" Ahead of us loomed a mountain of dirt that formed the beginning of the dike and we dropped each others hand to climb up the dike. Once we were standing on the high ground, I liked the refreshing, velvety feeling of the evening breeze that then was caressing my face. To enjoy the good feeling, we shuffled along on the high ground until we dared not go further. We squatted Indian style on the dirt dike.

Julia let herself roll back to stare up into the sky as Lila sat braiding tall weeds she had picked. I was watching the braid form while listening to a dull sound of a pump from the pumphouse below the dike. I looked at that pump house and I recalled the time when a bunch of us kids snuck into that place. That was scary! There was a big black hole down, down from the stairs we climbed to reach a higher floor and when looking down that hole to see where the powerful noise was coming from, I had a great fear of falling into that hole and being ground to bits by the powerful pump going up and down. There was a strong smell, too. The smell was coming from sacks of lime and the floor had lime all over it that had spilled out of the sacks. We were lucky no one got sick from the lime or got killed falling into that deep, scary hole.

A distance in front of the pump house was the large plot of bare ground that was our ice skating rink in the winter time. In my sight further away, was the first street of houses. There were two houses painted white with green trim and they jogged my thoughts to remember I had a secret, too! Yet I held back my secret because I believed if I did not talk about it, it wouldn't happen. To shake the urge to share a secret I did not want to share, I scooted down the dike while bellowing a loud squeal, then I headed in the direction of the icehouse with the other two catching up.

At the icehouse, we scraped the sawdust around and around in search of chunks of ice. I found one too big to suck on so I slipped it down the back of Julia's blouse and she shrieked! We all giggled while she did a silly, wiggly jig to shake the cold ice down and out. Then we dog trotted through the weeds next to the icehouse and, once in the alleyway, raced to the old hulk of a car. Julia won and got to sit behind the steering wheel. I crawled in to sit in the middle and Lila sat on the outside.

It was fun to hear ourselves talking in the car because our voices had a hollow sound, like when in a cave. Suddenly a heavy clopping of shoes interrupted our talk and we saw Howie coming down the stairs of the apartment house. After his feet hit the ground, he dashed for the other side of the old car to duck out of sight. We quickly ducked, knowing Howie had gotten himself into trouble with Mrs. Oister!

When Howie had waited long enough, he said through the opening where a window had been, "She can't run fast cuz she has the gout."

When Howie realized he was safe, he yanked open the driver's door and demanded, "Give me a turn at the wheel!" Julia and I scrambled over the seat to sit in the back, leaving Lila in the front. Howie, with the wheel, twisted it left, right, back and forth, then screamed, "Let's go to Tim-buk-tu!" He did his usual; he drove and he drove and he drove with his motormouth revved to a loud roar. Far, far and further we rode with many twists and turns of the steering wheel until I became tired of trying to get to this "Tim-buk-tu."

I yelled, "Let's go see Fwankie!" Howie agreed and reduced his twisting and turning, slowing the car to a purr. He listened to Julia and me speaking of the zoo we would see, and see

Frankie dressed in fancy clothes and to get to meet his mother who Frankie had said was so important. Yet, like Tim-buk-tu, we never got to where Frankie lived. Howie tired from so much driving, and when he became quiet, we girls did too.

The warm breeze and a yellow glow from the rising moon brought back a carnival Julia and I had been to at nighttime. My memory first was of the smell of spun sugar, then of calliope music, then the laughter and chorus of screams coming from people on the rides. Then! Like the bright colorful lights of the carnival, I lit up, full of life, remembering one ride that made me want to share with Howie and Lila what Julia and I saw!

I poked Julia. "Rememba that carnival night and that lady puked?"

Julia bent forward and screamed, "Yah!" She laughed, starting the story over like a slap happy clown. "Remember that old lady who was going around and round so high in that swing?" Julia and I screamed, "She puked!" our words jumbling together. "And puke splashed all over the faces of those guys on the ground!"

After Howie made a barfy, choking sound, I added, "She pwo'bly puked up eggs and ham!" I was laughing so hard I had to grab at my aching side.

Howie yelled, "What makes ya think it was eggs and ham the old lady threw up?"

I shouted, "Cuz! I got sick on eggs and ham once. I threw up chunks of yellow eggs and red ham!" I stopped laughing. That had been too vivid a reminder of when I had really been sick. With my mouth suddenly full of a bitter taste, I scrambled out of that old car to gulp fresh air.

Howie, Lila and Julia hopped out and we spent the rest of the night just walking around our neighborhood.

Two days later when Julia, Lila and I were romping about in my yard, I saw Dad coming in a pickup loaded with empty boxes. I could no longer keep our move a secret from my friends. I told them.

Julia asked, "To where?"

Lila asked, "Will you forget us?" Those were thoughts I had kept bottled up and I grew sad. I did not have the answers.

Rather than talk more about it, I told my friends, "I have to git in now!"

Inside the house, I had to step around boxes dumped haphazardly on the floor. After Dad left to go back to work, I thought of a new game and quickly built a fort in the room with a few of the empty boxes. Then I hid, waiting for Bobby to come by so I could scare him, but Mother and Patty were first to walk by and I scared them real bad! The two did not appreciate being scared by me and their screams let Bobby know where I was hiding.

Mother, having the three of us kids together, took the opportunity to tell each of us to take a box to our room to fill with whatever we wanted to take with us.

"And please," Mother pleaded, "Throw away what you can."

Seeing Bobby make a grab for the biggest box, I grabbed for it, too, and a tug of war developed. When the box began tearing, I let go of it first causing Bobby to fall backwards and land on top of another box, crushing it. Bobby was mad!

Mother laughed as hard as Patty and I until she realized two boxes had been ruined. She gave me a nasty sneer along with a snap of her fingers to get me going to do the job she'd asked me to do.

Except for my skates and sled that hung on the back porch, all my other play things were on my closet floor. With a box and a waste paper basket by my side, I fell on my knees at my bedroom closet and pulled out a shoe box filled with my valentine cards. I thumbed through them, picking one out to read again, the nasty one from Tommy, "RoSes ar Red ViletS ar blu skunkS Stink and So du yu." I placed it and all the others in the box to save.

I found a paper sack filled with brand new packs of cigarette rolling papers that I had forgotten about. They'd come from my grandpa's store and I could not throw them away. My Old Maid playing cards, a box of crayons, and a coloring book. I definitely wanted to save those. The game of Monopoly that I did not like but decided to save. My dolly, with stubble for hair that I hadn't played with for a long time. I propped her up by my side so she could watch as I reached for more.

My jacks were scattered about, but I found five, plus the crumpled wad of pink paper that was supposed to be for my smallpox shot. I threw it into the waste paper basket. I did not know what to do with my paper doll book. I had cut around the clothes, forgot and cut the tabs off, then nothing was left to help make the clothes stay on the dolls.

My dolly's bottle had fuzz stuck to its nipple that I had to swish across my sleeve to rub off. My jump rope was curled up on the dark closet floor and reminded me of my pet snake. Feeling sad, then angry over the killing of my pet I snatched up the box of bottle caps Mr. Gruder had given me, causing some to spill out.

Dropping the bottle caps, one by one, and hearing the plink, plink as they landed in the box, set my mood to think of a forgotten blink, blink of lit up bottle caps in a dream. By concentrating, bits of that dream came back. About an angel, my guawdian angel! I remember! She took me to see my pet snake all well again, and my baby mice, too! A loud thump, like a shoe hitting the wall, broke my concentration. Probably, I thought, Bobby was mad over something.

I found the lost mate to the lone sock in my dresser

drawer. Three story books and another game almost filled the box. A pair of shoes were too big for the box. I set them aside, but could fit in the hairpins, a button and the ball to my jacks.

Dust balls were all that were left on my closet floor. I picked up the waste paper basket with its pink slip, an old candy egg, and my paper doll book. To move the heavy box, I had to push it with the toe of my shoe to slide it up the hallway and into the front room.

The full boxes stacked on top of one another created a fun maze for Bobby and me to crawl around in, chasing each other. Finally, I was closing in on Bobby to give him a good pinch on the rear, when he made a vulgar sound that spewed a foul smell right in my face!

Bobby acted mortified at first, but seeing me bolt in reverse made him laugh! I called out, "You nasty pig!" Once the air had cleared and I was no longer mad, I asked him, "Where are we moving to?"

Bobby snapped me on the forehead with his finger as though waking me up. "You don't know yet? Well, geeze, to the far other end of town on Second Avenue."

That evening, it seemed I was making a nuisance of myself by feeling angry over having to move "to the far other end of town!" The next morning, Mother told me I would be staying with Julia all that day and night.

I stuffed my pajamas into a sack and hightailed it up the street to Julia's house. Then the two of us hightailed it across the tracks to be with our best friends for a whole, big day.

I knew I had to tell my other best friends that I was moving, but they already knew. Their mother had told them. Sonny did not think "the far other end of town" was so very far away. Nor did Bubber or Betsy. Bubber reminded me that we'd gone there when we followed the tracks out to the hobos camp. I recalled that day, too, which had been an exciting adventure, exploring new ground, and felt better about moving in that direction. Our talk about me moving petered out.

The last time we'd gone for a walk in the country, Bubber and Sonny had wanted to hike to the airport to see what we weren't supposed to talk about: the prisoner of war camp. But we girls had been too scared to go.

Again, with us all together, Bubber announced, "Me and Sonny are hiking to the airport and if you girls don't want to go, you can just stay behind."

Julia reminded us, "We could get into trouble if we get caught! You know that!"

The idea meant another fun hike in the country, and at that moment, getting into trouble did not scare me. With Kathleen willing, we talked Julia into saying she thought it would be okay.

Betsy was the killjoy, she let us all know, "Going there is very idiotic!"

As she was sashaying away to go back home Bubber called out, "Adios!"

Our course took us beyond the cemetery. With still a stretch to go, Sonny asked, "Has anyone heard of the javuh stone?"

Julia asked, "The what?" Bubber was laughing, giving it away that Sonny was about to tell another goofy story of his.

Sonny picked up a small stone, placed it in his pocket, and did a hop, a skip, then began, "Mighty Bernard Chinard, the King—silver were his guns and spurs as he rode his black steed in the cavalry. He rode the Dakota territory with the Indians!"

Julia was smart and piped up, "You said he was in the cavalry!"

Sonny said, "At first, true! That was when Bernard Chinard was scouting for the cavalry and came upon a grizzly bear and an Indian brave. Mighty Bernard Chinard knew it was sure death for the Indian and he jumped off his steed, picked up a stone and threw it at the bear hitting it smack in the middle of its eyes—killing it dead!"

Julia interrupted again, questioning Sonny, "Why didn't he use his silver guns to kill the bear?"

Sonny's answer was, "Becuz he forgot them at the fort! Don't you want to hear the end?" And so the end was heard. "The Indian brave afterwards was so happy he made Bernard Chinard his blood brother and the stone that killed the bear was called a javuh stone, Indian talk. And from that time on, mighty Bernard Chinard, the King, road his black steed with the Indians." Sonny took the stone from his pocket, took aim at a post, then threw it hitting the mark.

Sonny said, "See! I killed it with my javuh stone." I giggled over Sonny imagining the post to be a grizzly bear.

The ground around the post was where a farm had been at one time; the post was what was left of the clothesline. The farm, bare of all but wild grain, had become part of the airport. When alerted to the sound of an army truck approaching on a network of runways, we knew we were in the thick of the "secret operation." Paralyzed with fear, we hid low to prevent being seen by what Sonny called, "A full force of the military, with guns!"

When the coast was clear, we had to continue our mission to spy on the enemy. By darting a distance, lying low then darting again a distance and lying low, we came to a small hill. To take the hill we used strategy so as not to be seen, crawling up on all fours.

Bubber was the first to reach the top and scared the rest of us by whispering, "Great guns! Look at that!"

Our mouths dropped open as we peered up at the high barbed wire fence surrounding the prisoners camp. A very scary warning that gave me an eerie feeling.

From our ground surveillance on our bellies, we could not spot one prisoner on the other side of the barbed wire. Nor was there a guard to be seen. The stillness was spooky and it caused fear to grip me when thinking, The war prisoners have killed the guawds and they have all escaped, pwo'bly in those army trucks that passed us way back aways. I believed at any moment they could sneak back around and come up from behind us and capture us!

Then, in the camp, a door opened. A man walked out. Somebody was really alive! The man walked across the grounds and entered another building.

Sonny, with a scary thought, whispered, "That door could lead to the torture chamber." Aghast over a place of horror so near gave cause for us to start an exchange of questions and answers on the morbid subject of torture.

Bubber started by whispering to Sonny, "Would you talk if you were tortured?"

Sonny answered, "Heck no, mate! Would you?"

Kathleen whispered to her brother, "If we git caught wi' we be tortured?"

Sonny whispered back, "I guess so; the enemy is in that camp."

Then, I whispered, "How would they torture us?"

Bubber described, "They will yank out your fingernails. Or tie you to a chair and let drops of water drip, drip, drip on your head. Drives ya crazy."

I felt great agony over anyone yanking out my fingernails, but the other caused me to raise my head up to whisper to Bubber, "A wee little drip, drip could not cause me to go cwazy."

Bubber raised up to whisper to me, "Oh, ya. Try a little drip, drip, drip for a week on your head, that means lots of drips, and see how crazy you git!"

Julia, feeling perplexed, whispered, "I'm confused. Who would torture us?"

Bubber, thinking Julia had not been listening, whispered, "Torture us? They would!"

Julia, with her finger pointing at us, whispered to him, "We're not the prisoners!" Then pointing her finger at the camp, said, "They are."

Bubber wore a stupefied look before setting Julia straight. "Yah, I know that, but if we were the prisoners they could torture us, doncha know!"

Sonny interrupted all our thoughts by whispering an alarm, "Get ready! Zero hour is here!" Sonny had spotted an army truck on a runway and informed us, "The prisoners are in that truck, I bet. We can watch as they are unloaded."

The truck rolled up to the gate, the driver got out and he thrust up the handle of the gate to open it. He got back in the truck, drove in and pulled up to a door. We expected the shackled war prisoners to fall out of the back of the truck, but instead, a crew of men came out of a building to help unload heavy boxes from the truck.

The crew spoke with harsh words that were hard for Kathleen, Julia, Sonny and me to hear and to understand. Bubber became the informative one as he whispered his discovery, "They are the ones, the prisoners, unloading those boxes!"

Our expressions of surprise prompted Bubber to explain, "Ya, becuz they're talking German like my gran'pa talks."

Learning that those men were the enemy was a real stunner to me! I had believed the prisoners were evil, meanie swines, and my jolt of disappointment over seeing normal looking men caused me to yelp, "You lie!" The others hushed me while eyeing all around to be sure I had not been heard. Then we watched until the crew of prisoners had moved the last of the boxes inside the building and we saw no more of them.

Another door opened and one man came out. Julia gasped, "That's my dad!" I recognized Julia's dad, too, carrying a tool box while walking to his pickup outside the gate. He got in and he drove away down the runway. Seeing Julia's Dad was a reminder of terrible trouble for her if we got caught. With fear in Julia's voice she whispered, "Com'on, guys, we gotta get away from here!"

We slipped down the hill on our bellies and crept silently away. When we were finally out of hearing range of anyone at the secret operation, Sonny said to Bubber, "Now that we've had a dry run, just you and me can come back tomorrow. I'll sneak my dad's binoculars so we can see better." I wanted so badly to come back with them, but I said nothing; I knew I would be busy moving.

The next morning as I walked home from Julia's, I felt a sad ache, like I had felt when seeing Frankie for the last time before he'd moved away. I fixed my gaze on all that was familiar to me. I just wanted to.

When approaching my house, I saw the pickup parked at the curb with Dad ready to pull away with Bobby riding in back with the load of full boxes. When Dad saw me running to catch up he stopped the motor and said, "Tootse, you better hop aboard to help hold the boxes on." With his toothpick waving about in his mouth, he laughed as he added, "If we lost a box, your mother would not know what the hell it was we lost!"

After letting Mother know where I was going, I climbed in back and was on my way to see this white house with green trim for my very first time.

The ride was smooth up Front Street, but turning at the bank building to reach Second Avenue the boxes shifted a little bit, then again when the pickup turned on Second Avenue. Dad drove four more blocks until coming to a stop in the middle of the street at the last house. Dad turned the pickup around and backed it up onto the lawn, then to the porch of the house. The house wasn't white with green trim. It was the color of a peach!

Bobby wanted to show me all that he knew about this house and I followed him up the stairs to where there were two empty bedrooms. The one he picked for himself had a built-in shelf, just right to hold a chemistry set Bobby was saving his money to buy.

The other bedroom Patty and I would have to share. I thought it looked big enough to divide, knowing that was most important to Patty! Stomping back down the stairs, the echoes of our steps reverberated in the empty house. After a showing of the downstairs by Bobby, he opened another door at the kitchen doorway and we went down to the basement.

The basement was very big and dark and I imagined it to have secrets yet to be found. I searched and found more steps, wide concrete ones leading up to two trap doors. Bobby whispered to me what was beyond those doors, "A secret room." I became all excited then to see this mystery and when Bobby pushed the trap doors up, he laughed! The secret room was the back yard! Bobby left me to go help Dad while I ran from corner to corner in the back yard to view all that I could see. When I went back indoors, I found the house looking like our other house: a mess with lots of boxes. Dad said, "Let's go back for another load!"

After the next load was ready to go, we took a break to eat lunch. Then Dad said to me, in a serious tone, "Tootse, you will be doing your mother a great big favor if you stay and help her." Mother's reply was a sigh. When I looked at her and saw her sneer, I figured she was expressing how really tired she was. I stayed to help, but sometimes

I tried too hard to help and got into trouble, like when I accidentally tipped a box of Patty's pretties, spilling the contents all over. That was when Mother sagged down in a chair and let Patty get mad at me. I ran away outside to find Lila to play with.

Back at our old house, Dad and Bobby had taken off with many more boxes and furniture. Lila left and I went indoors. I could hear how the empty rooms talked back to me with echoes. I noticed the marks on the walls where our pictures had hung. It came to me what I remembered of our other house after we'd moved away from it; how my memories of my family made me feel we were ghosts still living there. I pondered feeling the same with this house and as I did, felt a crazy spin of split second thoughts. This second house was like a cuddly, lovable pet we were leaving behind; a very protective house that had kept us warm and safe; and the fun of scary places, and with a ghost, too! Then I felt pulled, as if Dad had said, "Time to go."

With a dresser, box, floor lamp and Dad's favorite chair all loaded, our busy time was over in the house we were leaving behind. Mom and Patty crawled into the cab with Dad, and Bobby climbed up in back with me. Bobby braced himself against the dresser to keep the floor lamp steady as I sat smartly on the comfy chair like a queen on her throne, but facing backwards.

From my bird's eye view I saw all moving away from us, including the tracks, I remembered the 12 o'clock Skiddoo! What then whizzed through my thoughts were memories of the many times my friends and I had greeted our train as it whistled its way into town. Feeling down, I drooped in sadness, and cried on my queeny throne, "Oh, no! Mista Engineer will wonda where I went when he never sees me again with my fwiends."

By the time we got to Gruder's garage I had lost sight of our yellow stucco house. The glistening red pop machine caught my eye, then we passed the row of little houses, the red brick shoe repair shop, and all the taverns and stores on Front Street.

As the pickup motored up Second Avenue and we were passing the lumber yard that was built like a fort with high walls, I hatched up an exploring game. Another building of interest was an old, gray garage-like building with wide doors that went all the way up to its roof. Stretching my imagination, I freaked out over a stagecoach from cowboy days hidden inside and could hardly wait until my friends and I could sneak inside to see it, and the fort too! We drove past more houses for two blocks, then the pickup stopped and we all got out at the peach colored house.

Mother became mean in the next two days; she growled like a bear with too few rooms to put away what we'd brought with us. Patty wasn't nice either; she wanted my side of the bedroom for her things. When I was tired of being stubborn I gave in, and then she was nice to me. On the third day, like magic, the house became orderly with a place for everything and Mother was happy again.

Bobby had a friend, Glenn, he knew from school who lived close by. Patty was silly over a boyfriend named Guy. He was very nice; he would laugh when I said, "You have cully haih," which he did! I did not have a friend; mine all lived far, far at the other end of town. Feeling alone and sorry for myself, I poked around out in the front yard.

On the boulevard I picked up a long twig and I drew a sun, tree, hills and a house in the dirt while thinking of my friends. It was a good day for a hike. I bet Kathleen and Sonny are heading out for Mrs. Gouge's farm, or they are with Betsy and Bubber collecting empty bottles, and I bet Julia and Lila are playing together. All, I knew was, they were having fun, and without me. Feeling downhearted, I took the twig and I wiped the sun, tree, hills and house all away.

While hanging my head and pouting, I left the boulevard to stroll along on the sidewalk, dragging the long twig behind me. I had reached the third house from mine when I heard a girl's voice say, "Hi." I looked up to see, on the other side of a gate, a girl my size! She had fat braids and some freckles.

"My name is Virginia," she said, "Want to try my stilts?"

A BREEZE

It is a day that puts my spirit in a long ago time,
do not know when, as a little girl maybe or later in my
teens or later to add to a memory. As I sip coffee, yes,
with my mother at her table, a smile across her face
is the love she shared. It is summer and would be hot
if not for a rain just yesterday to create today a breeze
soft and fresh flowing in through the screen and across
my face. The flutter of leaves, the whisper of their song
stirs, too, my memory of past times making me feel light
in my mind . . . Grand'ma, this could be a day spent with
you on the prairie of flowing golden grain. Yes, it is you,
full of peace not in words as you sit under the light from
a lantern to crochet. Love for the art you passed on to me,
and with each hook of thread I feel your peace. I am alone
yet not, thoughts now in my memory makes me feel any
moment three little girls will come in from play, all gay,
sensing the good in the air as I, today. One of the three
added two, and one of the two added one, with, I am sure,
more to come completing the family tree. With my heart
so full by a winsome, passing breeze, I am reminded of
the parable of the "Mustard Seed."

LAEL MARIE

AND

ANNA MARIE

1941

ABOUT THE AUTHOR

L. Marie Baker was born and raised in a charming and small railroad town called Glasgow, Montana, during the 1930s and 40s. As the youngest of three, she knew great amounts of freedom amidst a close-knit community of family and friends. After graduation she married George, the love of her life. They became lifelong residents of Oregon and raised three daughters. In no time at all the girls were grown. She and George shared an interest in reading about ancient history, and, with more time on her hands, she took up the hobby of researching her *own* ancient history. Muddling through the past stirred up scores of memories, like time travel. Soon she was tapping out true-life stories from her own childhood adventures by the pageful.

Her late George used to say, "Write what you want to—write what you feel." His matter-of-fact statement still resonates and encourages the author as she strives to bring her stories to life on the page.

The riverside snapshot above was taken many years ago. L. Marie Baker is now 86 and hopes you've found 12 O'Clock Skiddoo to be a fun read.